The Last Days Of Black Beard The Pirate

"You cannot destroy a popular belief merely by proving it to be false."

The Last Days Of BLACK BEARD The Pirate

Within Every Legend Lies a Grain of Truth

Kevin P. Duffus

Looking Glass Productions, Inc.
Raleigh

> ALL THAT HAD
> HAPPENED WAS
> STILL THERE,
> JUST BEYOND THE
> THIN CURTAIN
> OF TIME.
>
> HOWARD BAHR
> *THE JUDAS FIELD*

Kevin Duffus photo.

Springer's Point and Teaches Hole Channel
Ocracoke, North Carolina

THE LAST DAYS OF BLACK BEARD THE PIRATE

©2008 by Kevin P. Duffus

Looking Glass Productions

Published by:
Looking Glass Productions, Inc.
Raleigh, North Carolina, USA.
www.thelostlight.com

All Rights Reserved under International and Pan American Copyright Conventions.

Except for the use of brief quotations embodied in critical articles and reviews, no part of this book may be reproduced or transmitted in any form by any means, electronic or mechanical, including photocopying, recording, or scanning, or by any information storage or retrieval system, except as may be expressly permitted by the 1976 Copyright Act or by the publisher. Requests for permission should be made in writing to Looking Glass Productions, Inc., P.O. Box 98985, Raleigh, North Carolina, 27624-8985, USA.

To contact the publisher for comments, customer service and orders, E-mail: looking_glass@earthlink.net

All photography by Kevin P. Duffus unless otherwise noted.

Book design and cartography by Looking Glass Productions, Inc.

Library of Congress Control Number: 2008922924

ISBN 1888285230

Printed in China
First Edition/First Printing

Dedicated to John Oden, Jane Bailey and Allen Norris, and researchers like them, who have the courage to peer into the darkness of the past with open minds.

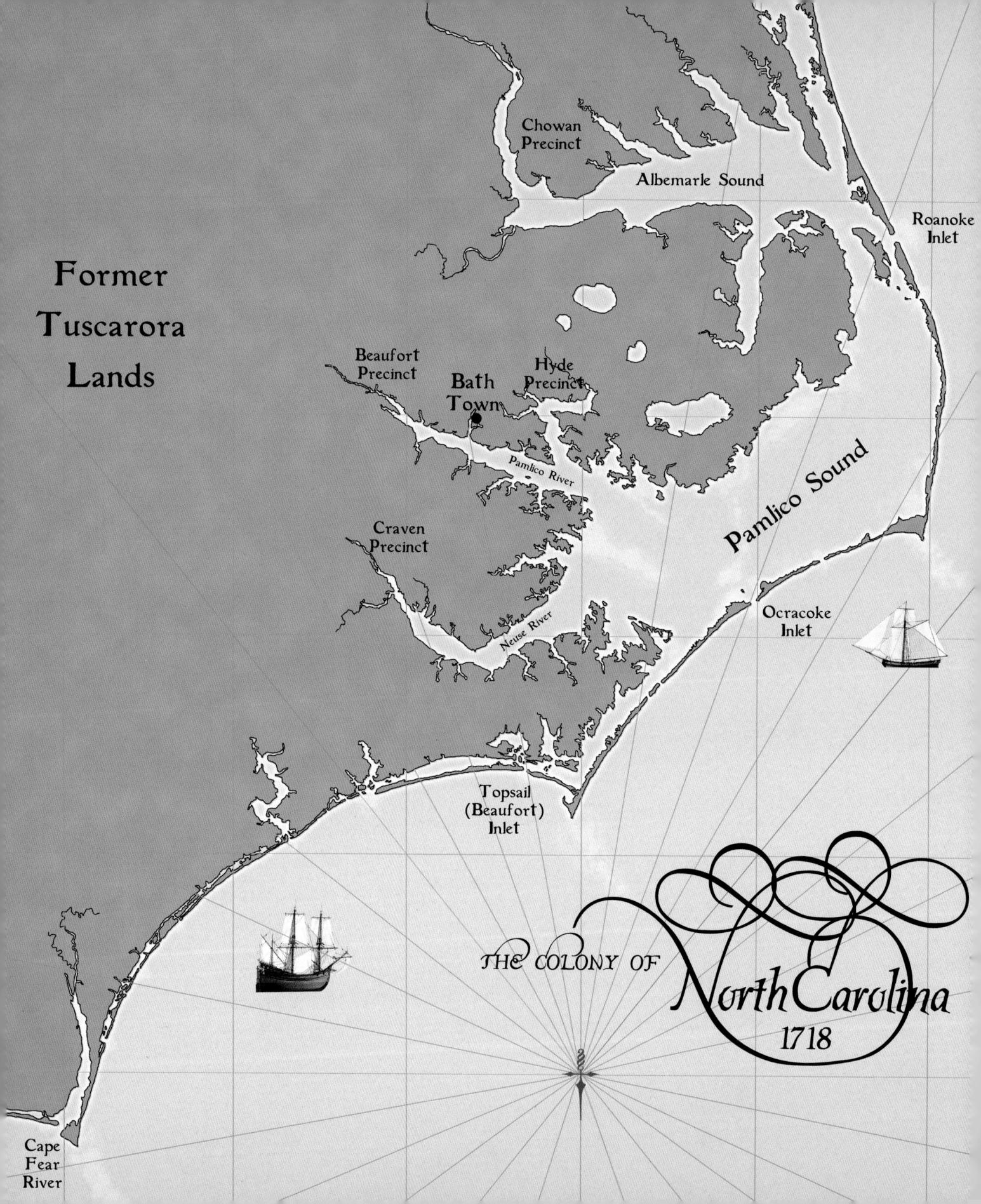

Contents

A Note From the Author.....11

Prologue—Sister Susie.....13

One—The Man We Made Him to Be.....21

Two—The Historiography of Blackbeard.....27

Three—A Bristol Man Born?.....33

Four—Two Years a Pyrat.....41

Five—Near the Old Watering Hole.....51

Six—Ragged Remnants of History.....57

Seven—Subtle Whispers of the Past.....67

Eight—Business in Bath Town.....77

Nine—A Fruitless Vineyard.....87

Ten—Lurking About High Street.....93

Eleven—"A Sail! A Sail!".....101

Twelve—Midnight Run to Bath Town.....111

Thirteen—The Ides of September.....119

Fourteen—Colonial Chessboard.....131

Fifteen—Mysterious Tides of History.....143

Sixteen—Such a Day.....157

Seventeen—The Bath County Pirates.....163

Eighteen—Black Beard's Blood.....179

Nineteen—His Story.....189

Twenty—Treasure Islands, Skulduggery and Other Tall Tales.....195

Twenty-one—A Link In the Chain.....211

Epilogue—Sister Susannah.....223

Appendix One—Family Connections.....226

Acknowledgments.....228

Bibliography.....229

Notes.....230

Index.....234

A Note From the Author

In 1968, the Walt Disney Company released the movie, *Blackbeard's Ghost*, starring Dean Jones, Suzanne Pleshette, and Peter Ustinov playing the spirit of Capt. "Teach." On the day the film opened in my hometown, I was one of the first kids scrambling through the doors of the theater. I don't think I was aware that the movie was a comedy, not that it would have mattered—I was there to learn about Blackbeard and his history.

In the film, Blackbeard haunts his former inn, which he built of salvaged timbers from the wrecked ships of his victims. Early on, we are told that the pirate captain had been killed in a battle in the bay, near the rocky, ragged, cliff-lined shore, atop of which stood his enormous hotel. Upon the arrival of Dean Jones—the newly-hired track coach for the local college—it is revealed that nefarious casino developers, led by "Silky Seymour," are scheming to take Blackbeard's ancestral home away from the sweet old ladies who run the place. The ladies, who call themselves "The Daughters of the Buccaneers" because they are the descendants of Blackbeard's crew, inform Jones upon his arrival, "We accommodate the living, but who should accommodate the dead?"

By chanting "Kruh Vergo Gebba Kalto Kree," Jones inadvertently conjures up the ghost of the pirate captain (I tried it—it doesn't work). The ghost of Blackbeard tells Jones that he must do a good deed to atone for his transgressions and thereby release his soul from purgatory. Of course, the track coach is the only one among the living who can see Blackbeard. As the movie goes on, Ustinov's portly and meddling Blackbeard steals a policeman's motorcycle. He helps to "coach" Jones's pathetic track team to a victory over the perennial favorites. And he turns the tables on the crime boss Silky Seymour and saves the Blackbeard Inn for the sweet old ladies.

Being young and naïve, I hadn't questioned the historical basis for the movie. A few years later, when I was able to travel to Ocracoke, North Carolina, and visit the site of Blackbeard's demise, I realized that I hadn't learned anything factual about Blackbeard's history from the Disney movie. (I was also shocked there were no rocky, ragged cliffs on Ocracoke.) Many years later, I decided to write this book in an attempt to atone for the transgressions of Hollywood and for all of the others who have taken liberties with Blackbeard's story since his death 290 years ago.

If a writer were to faithfully tell the story of Blackbeard the pirate based entirely on the extant records relating to the pirate's brief appearance in history, the result would probably be a fairly thin volume. The fact is, the amount of primary source material about him is relatively sparse. As readers will learn, most of what the public knows about Blackbeard comes from a 1724 book by an author whose identity, and sources of information, remain a mystery.

This book is an attempt to divine the true story of Blackbeard by looking in places overlooked in the past, and by scrutinizing the available records more closely. Nevertheless, there are moments in Blackbeard's last days that are not remembered by history—gaps in his narrative that would not ordinarily be considered in a conventional historical account. In order to provide greater continuity to the story, I have composed passages that hypothetically describe what may have happened during these undocumented days. So that there should be no confusion that these passages are fictionalized, I have set them in an italicized typeface. The italicized narrative is not intended to be read as factual material, but is a thoroughly-researched version of what I believe took place.

There are a few other things about which the reader should be aware. I have intentionally preserved the spelling and punctuation of the original sources, unless, by doing so, it would confuse the meaning of the sentence. Also, most writers of historical events during the first half of the 18th century have to face the question of how to represent dates, since Britain and its colonies continued use of the Julian (Old Style) calendar, while most of Europe had converted to the more accurate Gregorian (New Style) calendar. As a result of the difference between the first days of the respective years—January 1 for Gregorian, and March 25 for Julian, many writers identify events occurring between the two dates as 1718/19, in order to reduce confusion. For simplicity's sake, throughout this book, all dates between January 1 and March 24 are based on the Gregorian calendar, unless the date appears within a document. Finally, astute readers may notice the variability in the treatment of the name, Blackbeard or Black Beard. The reason I have done this will become evident in the pages to come.

Kevin Duffus
Raleigh, North Carolina

Kevin Duffus photo.

Prologue—
Sister Susie

Sometimes, our thoughts of the departed will draw them near to us. Out of the long passageway of time they may come, longing to tell us something, even though we may be a stranger. They are anxious for us to know the truth—the truth of their history, as faithfully as the living are able to remember it.

Often I am reminded of the preceding conviction, but particularly when I recall a mid-autumn's day in my youth when I searched for the final resting place of the so-called sister of the notorious pirate, Blackbeard. The eastern North Carolina fable of "Sister Susie White" had been a time-worn tale handed down the generations by honest, God-fearing people. The legend was alluring, but I knew that if I were to become a believer, too, I would have to see her gravestone for myself.

I remember it being a peculiar day when I searched for her gravesite along the banks of the historic Tar River. A rare easterly breeze was pushing a parade of wavelets, leaves and the occasional fishermen's trash up the turbid, coffee-colored waterway. The river seemed to flow upstream, ambivalently, as if the detritus and memories of man had been rejected by the sea—an omen that things were not always how they appeared. And unseen, beyond the limits of my youthful vision, and beyond the restless, brooding surface, flowed the eternal currents of the ages—past, present and future intertwined—following their own mysterious, meandering paths—the secret river of Time.

As I looked around, the land appeared to have been bypassed by civilization—inhospitable, untamable, unlivable. Why would anyone have ever lived and died there? Masses of thorns, slithering cottonmouths, and unrelenting swarms of voracious deer flies seemed to be at every step—a land rightfully devoid of people, save for myself on that day. But time tricks the eyes of those who see only the present. Somewhere within the wilderness lay the grave and headstone of a soul, who, some historians claimed, was often visited by the greatest, richest and most ruthless pirate who ever lived. Blackbeard supposedly walked the same ground, and maybe left some of his treasure. With curiosity urging me forward, I stepped into the dark woods and began a great adventure.

Since that day I have often thought of how hard it is for us to preserve the truth of our own history—much less others'—as memories of our past inexorably wear away into diffused and dimly-lit images, like those on faded movie film. Time winnows our recollections, casts off what seems uninteresting, unremarkable or complicated, while it magnifies, dramatizes and refines that which fascinates us—much the same effect the passage of time has on written history. As such, perfecting the accuracy of our past is a solemn but seemingly impossible challenge—so much history is unknown, unrecorded or has evaporated with legions of dying breaths; human experience is buried or records are burned and lost to the ages. Secrets lay with the dead, but myths and falsehoods eagerly rise up to fill the gaps in their history, embraced by the credulous as the truth.

So it is now, on the scratched and flickering screen of my memory as I watch myself looking long and far in a malevolent, mysterious swamp along the Tar River in eastern North Carolina, amid ancient cypress laden with the gray beards of Spanish moss. I accept that my mental images of that day searching for Blackbeard's sister are not entirely unembellished—no more precise than my earliest memories of walks with my grandmother when I was 4 years old. Hand in hand, we followed a trail into a vast dark forest I now realize could have been no more than a small patch of undeveloped land surrounded by rows of post-World War II apartment buildings in suburban Alexandria, Virginia. It makes me smile when I think of it now; why it could not possibly have been the dangerous woods invented by my childhood imagination that my grandmother and I explored together. You see, even when our memories don't always survive the ages intact, the tiniest truths manage to hold fast. When I think back upon it, my elegant grandmother always wore high heels.

Years later, as I sought the grave of Susie White without the soft, reassuring hand of my grandmother, I was unaware that time and civilization had not bypassed that portion of the river. Nature, too, has a way of prevailing over the past. It was later that I was to learn that the land I was exploring had been home for generations of Tuscarora, cleared by anxious colonists, plowed by forlorn slaves and patrolled by pickets of the Union and Confederate armies. The ancient trees along the river banks witnessed the passage of innumerable watercraft—log-hewn canoes, pole-propelled periaugers, flats laden with casks of tar and bundles of tobacco, shoal-draft steamboats and military troop transports crowded with passengers. Even the intrepid John Lawson passed this way as he neared the end of his historic, 59-day exploratory sojourn through the Carolinas in 1701. Such places of our past are like a stage upon which we can walk, where myriad dramas of days gone by might still be performed—invisible, except to our imaginations. An unfamiliar and alien world.

I passed in the shadow of an enormous dead cypress standing in a black pool of water, noticeably taller than any of its neighboring trees despite its missing crown. How long had it stood there and who may have passed beneath its ancient boughs? I wondered, gazing skyward.

Turning south, the gentle lapping sounds of the river receded in the distance and I ascended a prominent bluff. On the left bank of a dry watercourse, my untrained eye initially missed the repetition of rectangular depressions in the ground that I later determined, with greater scrutiny, marked the graves of African slaves, their hand-carved cedar crosses long ago absorbed into the earth along with their remains and the bitter memories of their harsh lives. These days even the depressions have faded away and it is terrifying to think of sharing their fate, to be forgotten for all of eternity, as if we had never existed. What were their names? Records I possess suggest there could have been a Violet buried there, a Cimrick, a Toney, Priamus the shoemaker, and a young girl, Hannah.

I trudged upward, cresting a rise as I kept a watchful eye on the ground for snakes and poison ivy, unaware that I was just a few hundred steps into my own John Lawson-like journey of discovery, a formative chapter of my own history.

I tripped and fell to the ground.

Not ordinarily a clumsy person, I looked for what caused me to fall, an unseen vine or tree root, perhaps. But it was a hole in the ground, a deep hole. A rabbit hole maybe?

A vague thought flashed of Lewis Carroll's Alice:

"Oh, what a fall I've had down that hole, and yet I'm not in the least hurt. I wonder how many miles I fell?" Later, Alice meets the Cheshire cat who offers her a choice of two paths, one leads to the Hatter, the other to the March Hare, although both are mad.

>Alice: But I don't want to go among mad people.
>Cat: Oh, you can't help that; we're all mad here. I'm mad. You're mad.
>Alice: How do you know I'm mad?
>Cat: You must be, or you wouldn't have come here.

My rabbit hole turned out to be not a rabbit hole, or any kind of animal hole at all, for that matter, but what I did next might be considered by many as madness.

Inside the hole I noticed some very old bricks forming a 90-degree angle, a corner if you will. My initial reaction was that I had potentially discovered the foundation of a very old house, possibly from North Carolina's colonial era. My search for Susie White had momentarily taken a side trip.

I found a flashlight, and I began to carefully and methodically enlarge the opening, maybe not to the liking of a trained archeologist but with care and respect just the same. Illuminated by the flashlight, a sort of level floor appeared. My hypothesis was bearing-out. It was really beginning to look like part of a house. But without conducting an invasive excavation, there was only one way to investigate further. I reached through the hole and rested the flashlight on the dirt floor, its beam shining off into an unseen darkness. Quickly, so I didn't have time to imagine the possibe outcomes, I lowered my head into the hole.

It is curious how the human mind begrudgingly adapts to the unexpected—that nano-second-long process which ranges from expectation to disbelief, with waves of shock, bewilderment, uncertainty, realization, and panic. On my knees with my head in a hole in the ground, I was not looking into the long-lost remnant of a colonial dwelling; I was staring into the gaping, soulful eye-sockets of a rotting human skull. I had plunged my head into someone's grave. Evidently, it was a burial crypt of someone, someone important, or wealthy, and most likely both, as it was capped by a graceful arch of bricks. And it must have been very old since there was no headstone to identify the occupant.

My first reaction was that I felt regret for looking into the hole, not just that I had disturbed the resting place of the departed, but I had an odd sensation that I had taken a step onto a path in the woods from which there could be no return.

I caught my breath and shook from my head flecks of soil, twigs and a lingering sense of dread. I looked around and realized I was in an old burial ground and Susie White must have been nearby.

She was. Fewer than 25 yards or so, hidden beyond the trunk of a 200-year-old oak.

You should know how I came to search for "Sister Susie," the mythical sister of Blackbeard the pirate.

A year or two before, I had been randomly roaming the shelves of the county library where I happened upon a somewhat unremarkable charcoal gray, cloth-bound volume titled, *Sketches of Pitt County, A Brief History of the County, 1704-1910*, by journalist and amateur historian, Henry Thomas King. It's the kind of book that has been long-shunned by educators for its antiquated, prejudiced, unscholarly style. Many counties in America have similar early histories, and they should be required reading for all middle school students. King's book contains a treasure trove of vanishing history and lore. Like the legend of Susie White.

King summarizes the very early history of Pitt County—the years between 1681 and 1715—in three quick pages. Then he gets to the good stuff. He describes a time, a few years after the appalling Tuscarora war, when the pirate Teach, aka Blackbeard, was "a frequenter of Carolina waters." He shares, with a hint of relish, the traditionary tale of a pirate and his sister:

>"A sister, Susie White, lived near Boyd's Ferry, on the Grimes farm. Tradition says that Teach very often visited her. When he would return from a cruise and wanted to take a rest or vacation, he

would visit his sister. Not far away, in the low-grounds, stands a cypress, once famed as the lookout of Teach. It was known as 'tabletop,' being much taller than any of the surrounding trees and had a large flat top, very thick. Into its body were driven spikes, or were cut notches, so that it was not difficult to climb. From its top could be had a splendid view of the river to, and below Washington. There Teach resorted to see if the river was clear of a hostile boat, or to watch them, and then act according as circumstances demanded. A few years ago a storm broke off the top of this cypress, but the body is still standing."

King then adds an alluring anecdote: "Many and wonderful are the tales told of Teach's buried treasure in this section, and almost as many are the attempts that have been made to find it. In the lands on both sides of the river many a hole has been dug, but there is no record of the treasure being found. It has not been so very long ago that the grave of Susie White was disturbed by unknown midnight treasure seekers."

It was the legend of Teach's treasure and its nefarious midnight seekers that captured my youthful curiosity and led me to Susie White's grave. That, and an old map of the county confirming my intuition that Boyd's Ferry, long-discontinued even 35 years ago, was near the site of the modern-day Grimesland Bridge. It was an early lesson in my life-long avocation of historical riddles and unsolved mysteries—bridges were often built where ferries once operated because that was where the roads were.

As I neared Susie White's grave, I wasn't sure what to expect—an epitaph on her headstone announcing, "Here Lies Blackbeard's Sister," perhaps? A skull and crossbones? Craters in the ground courtesy of "midnight treasure seekers?" Blackbeard's surly ghost?

What I actually found was all-together unexpected, and disappointing. Had the treasure seekers bothered to study their history, they needn't have gone to the trouble of digging. The instant I read Susie White's—no, actually, Mrs. Susanna White's headstone, I knew she could not have been Blackbeard's sister. Susanna White was born 37 years after the famous pirate was killed near Ocracoke Island in 1718. She was not "Sister Susie." Mystery solved. Or was it?

It has been a question which has haunted me ever since: Why was Susanna White, in eastern North Carolina folklore and legend, purported to be Blackbeard's sister? No, it would not suffice to simply dismiss the connection between Susanna and the pirate.

I returned to Mrs. White's grave not long ago, decades after my first visit. The woods didn't seem so threatening. Development, although modest, had altered the landscape once again. A home or two now stood near the cemetery and the woods appeared to have been thinned. I knew as I approached the grounds that many more people had been buried there than I had first observed. A document I had recently come across indicated that, decades earlier, at least 18 graves could be identified at the site. All but two are unmarked and forgotten today. Instinctively, I said a little prayer in their memory.

Who were they, these forgotten souls who once lived along the banks of the Tar River?

On that recent peaceful spring afternoon as I stood before Susanna's headstone, I recalled the words of Edenton orator, James Hathaway, on the challenges of accurate historical research. He said, "We may repair to the cemeteries and pressing close to the portals of the tomb, ears acutely tuned to catch the faintest whisper that falls from human lips, ask the sleepers there, who they are? Whence they came? What they did? But, alas! the oppressive silence is broken only by the echo of our words, wafted back by the wind, as it sings through the waving grass and rustling leaves a requiem for the repose of those who sleep beneath."

I posed Mr. Hathaway's questions to Susanna but could hear nothing but a soft exhalation of a fragrant springtime breeze.

"Accuracy [is] the intrinsic value of history," Hathaway explained to the attendees of the 200-year anniversary of the establishment of St. Paul's Parish in Edenton, North Carolina, in 1901. Without the participants of history to interview, he said, we are left with only one choice: "We must turn to the dusty pages of the centuries; the faded ink and moth-eroded paper must, with microscopical examination, be carefully inspected and closely scruti-

The Grimesland, NC, bridge crosses the Tar River near the site of Boyd's Ferry of long ago.

nized that every fragment may be utilized in forging link by link the historic chain that binds together the events of the past."

There was a reason for the existence of the fable of "Sister Susie." So, what was it? Why was Susanna White connected to the pirate Blackbeard?

Standing before her canted, mottled, moss-covered marker, I tried to imagine the people who had gathered on that very spot two centuries before me, to grieve and weep for the loss of their beloved mother, sister and friend, Susanna, and those who returned, year after year, until there was no longer anyone who could remember her. *Who were they?* I wondered. Her kinsmen might be the key that could unlock the door to the secret of Susanna. And her secret—a treasure map leading to a lost chapter of history. A faint whisper seemed to reverberate in my mind, an old proverb: *within every legend lies a grain of truth, within every legend lies a grain of truth, within every legend...* And, I knew, I would have to turn to "the dusty pages of the centuries" in order to find the grain of truth.

And so I did. I found the grain of truth—the secret of Blackbeard's sister, Susanna, and the secret of Mrs. Susanna White.

And by finding the grain of truth, my circuitous path through the wilderness of legend, myth and fable may have provided me a revealing glimpse of the authentic Blackbeard, the real man behind the legend. He is restless for the truth to be known, the truth of his history.

And it will change everything, after all these years.

"We may repair to the cemeteries and pressing close to the portals of the tomb, ears acutely tuned to catch the faintest whisper that falls from human lips, ask the sleepers there, who they are? Whence they came? What they did?

But, alas! the oppressive silence is broken only by the echo of our words, wafted back by the wind, as it sings through the waving grass and rustling leaves a requiem for the repose of those who sleep beneath."

James R. B. Hathaway
Edenton, N. C.
1901

Kevin Duffus photo.

Who was Mrs. Susanna White and why was she believed to be Blackbeard's sister according to folklore?

One—
The Man We Made Him to Be

Delaware's tall ship, Kalmar Nyckel

WHAT IF THE STORIED HISTORICAL FIGURES OF the world were not who we think they were?

Blackbeard the pirate is one of the most widely-recognized, most popularly documented historical figures of early American history. Read a published litany of pirate names throughout history and his is almost always among the first names listed. Ask anyone to name a pirate and he or she will usually come up with Blackbeard.

Is there any wonder? For more than 280 years, his piratical adventures have been told and retold by dozens of writers, scholars, newspapermen, poets, jurists, dramatists, and folklorists. Even Benjamin Franklin was among those who helped to elevate the pirate to mythical status. By their words and imaginations, Blackbeard has become the quintessential pirate hero, a paragon of pirates, precariously straddling the middle ground of criminal folk heroes and outlaws with unforgettable names, such as Robin Hood and Baby Face Nelson. Today he towers above his cohorts as an amalgamation of pirates. "In the person of 'Blackbeard' has been concentrated the whole disreputable spirit of his age. In the popular mind he is practically a synonym for Bahamian piracy," wrote Professor Michael Caton, author of *History of the Bahamas*.

Despite his sinister reputation, the pirate's shaggy sobriquet, Blackbeard, and his supposed surname, Teach, have been co-opted by marinas, hotels, inns, retail stores, festivals, sailing clubs, amusement parks, restaurants, taverns, breweries, board games, weblogs, and rock bands. Businesses in geographic areas where Blackbeard never traveled such as Padre Island, Texas, and Bangor, Maine, and hundreds of miles inland, have adopted the great pirate personage and capitalized on his marketing allure. A business selling "boats and fun cycles" in the foothills of the Blue Ridge Mountains, 350 miles from the coast of North Carolina, is just one of "Blackbeard's" far-flung establishments.

Today, one can regale themselves with Blackbeard flags, plastic cutlasses, t-shirts, posters and action figures. Television networks, both commercial and public, cable channels specializing in history and new discoveries, and venerable geographic magazines have all cashed in on Blackbeard's visage. If no one has yet to find his fabled treasure of gold, silver and jewels, it seems everyone, at least, wants a piece of the pirate's mystique and popularity. Could anyone prove a lineage to the pirate, he or she would inherit his ultimate treasure—a fabulous king's ransom of royalty payments.

But just who was Blackbeard and what do we know about him, really?

To begin with, he must be one of the greatest contradictions of all time.

Blackbeard, also commonly known as Edward Teach, has been frequently described as one of the richest, most ruthless, and bloodthirsty pirates who ever lived. He has been called by various writers: "a knight of the black flag;" "lord of the Outer Banks;" and, "Commodore Teach—the boldest and most ruthless corsair of them all." Alternatively, he has been described as "the late and unfortunate Edward Teach, pirate, lover and benefactor of his neighbors."

Although he never sat for a painting and lived more than a century before the first photographs were taken, and not a single one of his many biographers had ever seen him in person, Blackbeard has been scrupulously described as "grotesquely conspicuous a villain as can be found in the annals of crime." He was "a figure to be gazed upon with fear and apprehension." And he was described as, "a picture sufficiently repulsive without calling in his dusky face and savage eyes with a supernatural glare." Illustrations of the bearded pirate, from the 18th century to modern day, consistently show him laden with weapons—slings of pistols, a knife in his teeth, cutlass poised to swing. But from there, the same illustrations feature a range of appearances from mature and well-groomed in knee-length coat and stockings, to young, wild-eyed and Rastafarian-like in dungarees. On stage and in film he has been portrayed by men often short and rotund—as amiable and jolly by Peter Ustinov to cartoonish and campy by Robert Newton.

"From the hairy mass hulking on his shoulders was a pair of bat-wing, mutilated ears, bulging red-veined eyes, a twisted, broken nose, and raw, curling lips that blubbered when he was in his usual state of drunkeness."
Addison Whipple, Pirate: Rascals of the Spanish Main

A popular pirate reenactor from North Carolina, who is of average height, plays Blackbeard as an impeccably dressed but bellowing and angry brute. The solitary eyewitness description of Blackbeard was that he was "a tall spare man with a very black beard which he wore very long." That's it—tall, thin and a long beard. There are no other legitimate sources that tell us more about the famous pirate's appearance.

In both history and legend, Blackbeard the pirate has shared the world stage of villainy and carnage with repugnant monsters like Attila the Hun, Ivan the Terrible, Jack the Ripper, the Boston Strangler (although no amusement parks have been named for Attila, Ivan, Jack, or the Strangler). Writers and historians in four different centuries have attributed to Blackbeard countless brutal but unsubstantiated murders. One such author described him as "the most notorious, despicable and ruthless pirate ever to slit a throat."

How many throats did he slit?

Writer Howard Pyle described Teach in contrast to

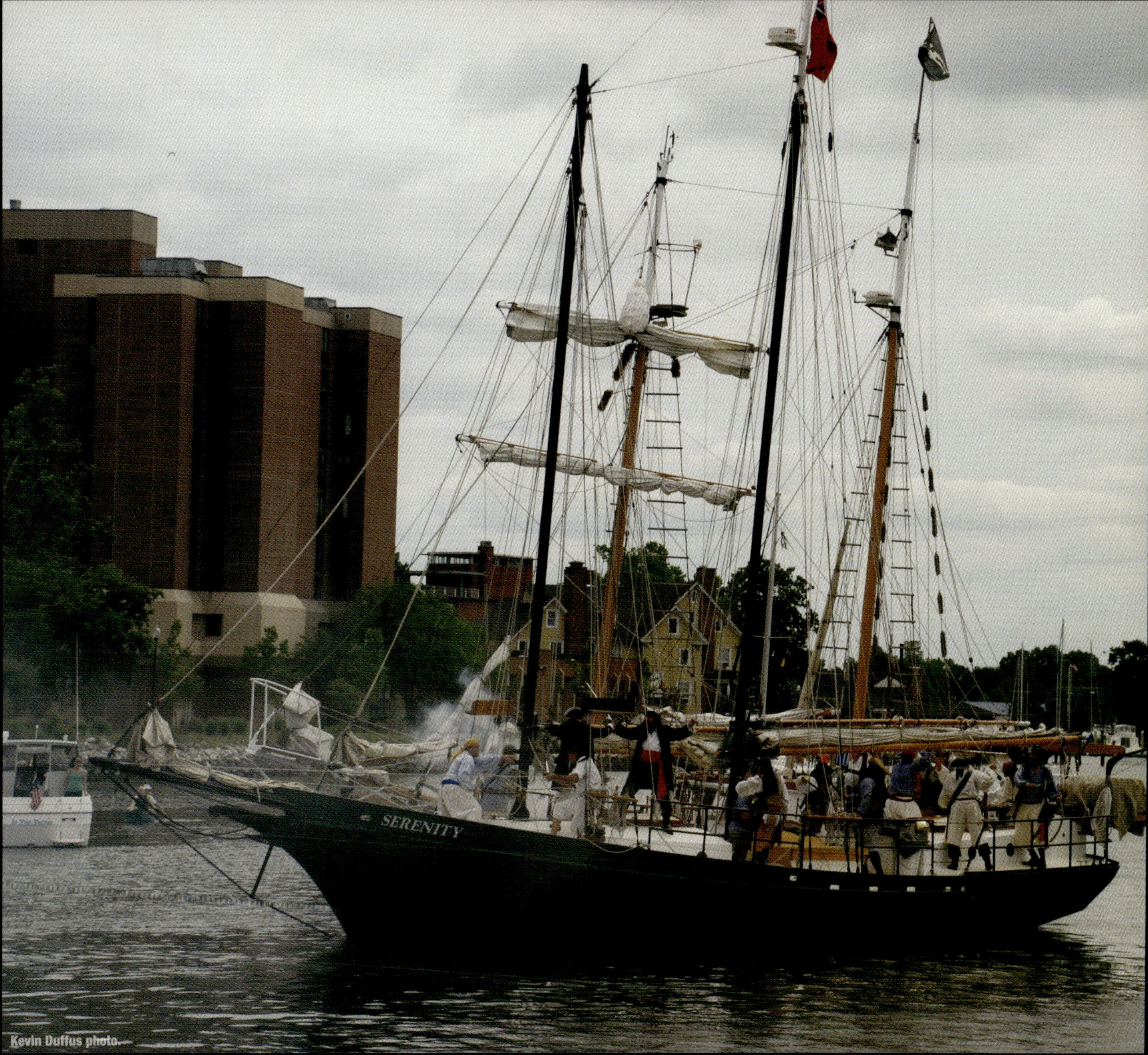

Kevin Duffus photo.

Kevin Duffus photo.

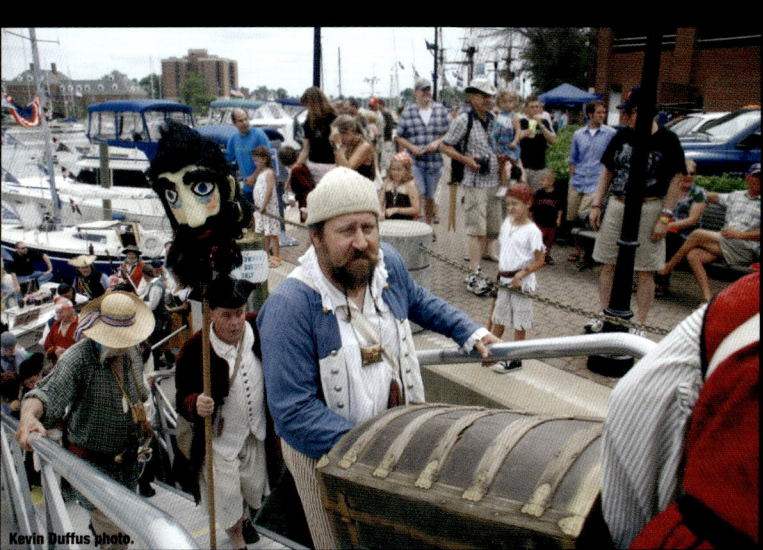

At Hampton, Virginia's annual Blackbeard Pirate Festival, pirate re-enactors portray the clash between Lt. Robert Maynard and the notoriuos pirate, Blackbeard, aboard the ironically named schooner, Serenity (above). After the famous battle is concluded, Blackbeard's head, purposely designed to not frighten children, is paraded before hundreds of spectators crowding the waterfront (left).

the ambiguous pirate exploits of the great Capt. William Kidd, whom Pyle said should be "relegated to the dull ranks of simply respectable people." But in the case of Blackbeard, Pyle wrote, "it is different, for in him we have a real, ranting, raging, roaring pirate per se—one who really did bury treasure, who made more than one captain walk the plank, and who committed more private murders than he could number on the fingers of both hands."

Where did he bury his treasure? What captains did Blackbeard make walk the plank? How many private murders did he commit?

Ill-informed, obstinate victims reluctant to surrender their precious rings to Blackbeard were liable to soon part with their fingers as well, according to a respected geographic organization. Another favorite author of pirate lore said that when Teach captured two French ships east of Bermuda near the end of his career, he "murdered everyone aboard both vessels." Yet, today, a few responsible historians suggest that there is absolutely no evidence Blackbeard ever killed or maimed anyone until the day he fought His Majesty's Navy in self-defense and was vanquished at Ocracoke Island in November, 1718.

Blackbeard's Castle, St. Thomas, USVI
Photo by Martin Lie, Wikimedia Commons

By reading best-selling histories we learn that Blackbeard didn't just frighten his human victims. An author once wrote that "dogs, cats, birds and other creatures credited with premonition fled the area a good hour or two before [Teach's ship] sailed into the harbor." One can only imagine what sea creatures did as his ship cut its dreadful wake, flying fish frantically skipping the wave tops to make way for the pirate captain.

Somewhat confusing for the novice Blackbeard fan is choosing between Blackbeard the lover or Blackbeard the serial rapist and killer. Depending on which scholarly historical account you read, Blackbeard either fell in love with every woman he met or he murdered them. On land, he was described as a "sensual polygamist," marrying as many as 14 women and over two short years fathering as many as 40 children in ports on both sides of the Atlantic Ocean. Alternately, the pirate captain treated his wives to "brutalities such as even his hardened crew could not witness unmoved with pity, and yet which no one dared to reprove." A recent pirate history recounts that when Blackbeard discovered women aboard his captured prizes at sea, he indiscriminately strangled them to death and threw their bodies overboard, with no exceptions. (The latter version of the pirate is probably not someone you would want to name a hotel or beer after.)

Oral traditions and written word have insisted that the pirate Blackbeard frequented settlements from New Hampshire to Georgia on the United States mainland and slept in nearly as many homes, ordinaries and inns as the beloved General George Washington. An inspired architect, Blackbeard is believed to have built retirement homes in Bath, Elizabeth City and Ocracoke, North Carolina. Local lore on more than one Caribbean island claims he constructed stone castles and lookout towers on rocky headlands high above the turquoise sea. One popular writer described Teach's edifice overlooking Nassau's harbor: "Atop the hill he built himself an impressive watchtower; the remains of it are there today. From it he could see out across the blue-green waters of the Bahamas. It was also an idyllic hideout from dunning tavern keepers and women." Then there are the many who assert with almost pious conviction that Blackbeard buried his treasure at secret locations in New Jersey, New Hampshire, Virginia, North Carolina, Georgia, and numerous islands of the West Indies. In many places the ground is pockmarked with the holes of the faithful although no one has yet to claim to have found the pirate's lost fortune—not that they would.

The infamous Blackbeard sailed the Caribbean Sea and the coast of colonial America commanding as many as six ships and hundreds of men in 1717-1718, and captured dozens upon dozens of prizes. History remembers him as the greatest, most successful pirate who ever lived. His exploits and "lawless depredations" have "placed him among the very greatest of marooning freebooters." No one, however, has ever described the dreaded Blackbeard as unlucky, wretched, and disillusioned. But when he was captured, killed and beheaded at Ocracoke Inlet, he was in the company of just 20 men and the only treasure found in his possession was some sugar, cocoa, cotton and a mysterious letter.

Who, truly, was Edward Teach, a.k.a. Blackbeard, and from whence did he come? What was his true name? What did he do? And where may he have hidden his treasure?

Howard Pyle wrote the following about Blackbeard: "Capt. Teach stands par excellent in an unique personality of his own. Perhaps there are few figures so picturesque as that suggested in the description of his get-up upon the occasions of public appearances—the plaited beard, the face smeared black with gunpowder, the lighted matches thrust under his hat brim, the burning sparks thereof hanging down his face. The fiendish grimness of that figure has made fully as much impression of the past as even that of Capt. Kidd, in spite of the celebrated song that emphasizes his fame."

Kevin Duffus photo.

Two
The Historiography of Blackbeard

WARNING: "YOU ARE ABOUT TO ENTER TREACHEROUS WATERS." WITH THOSE WORDS ADDISON BEECHER Colvin Whipple introduced readers to his swashbuckling 1957 book, *Pirate: Rascals of the Spanish Main*. No doubt Whipple had not realized the irony behind his light-hearted advice.

Indeed, for the unsuspecting reader and pirate enthusiast, the vast and varied ocean of three centuries of pirate literature and history, makes for navigating treacherous waters. The truth is, few topics or periods of world history have been documented with more errors, reported with more distortions, and publicized with more fictional fabrications than the general study of pirates. Whipple, himself, like many of his fellow writers, had no difficulty taking liberties with historical facts throughout his pirate book.

Traditional pirate literature began with Alexander Exquemelin's 1679 classic, *Bucaniers of America*. Then came Capt. Charles Johnson's more widely read, often-referenced two volumes, *A General History of the Robberies and Murders of the Most Notorious Pyrates*, and, *The History of the Pyrates*, published in 1724 and 1726 respectively. Since then, the popularity of pirate lore has never waned. By 1950, according to English author Patrick Pringle, hundreds of books had been written about pirates, and most were based on Exquemelin's and Johnson's time-worn standards.

The release of three successive Hollywood feature films between 2005 and 2007 based on a pirate-themed amusement park ride has sparked a resurgence of pirate interest. Scores of recent books, scholarly papers, magazine articles, travel narratives, television documentaries and docudramas, Internet Web sites and forums, have all become new places to plunder pirate treasure. Some have made their producers, publishers and distributors substantial sums of money. Unfortunately for posterity, printing deadlines and broadcast schedules have often taken on greater importance than historical accuracy.

Also igniting a renewed interest in the pirate Blackbeard, Florida-based treasure hunters discovered in 1996 what is believed to be the submerged remains of his famous, 40-gun flagship, *Queen Anne's Revenge*. The former French slave ship grounded and wrecked on the outer bar of Beaufort Inlet (formerly Old Topsail Inlet) in June, 1718. Ironically, it was not the silver-laden Spanish ship the salvors and their investors were looking for, but the discovery changed lives nonetheless. News of the find produced newspaper headlines, TV reports, and pseudo-documentaries. It tantalized history and pirate fans both young and old, and it put a fresh breeze in the sails of the becalmed careers of novelists and pirate re-enactors. When Blackbeard's crew first spied the ship off the Windward Islands in the fall of 1717, they looked upon her with lust and envy. Two-hundred eighty years later, people were seeing the ship with the same sense of desire—it could be said that their ship had come in.

The discovery also presented an exciting opportunity for underwater archeologists, conservators, and state administrators. Like an enormous mosaic with tens of thousands of pieces, the recovery and conservation of artifacts from the wreck most experts believe is the *Queen Anne's Revenge* has begun to tell a story of life on board a pirate ship. Since 1996, according to the official state reports, "over 2,000 artifacts have been recovered and conserved and thousands more await removal from concretion and treatment in the laboratory. The artifacts reflect many aspects of early eighteenth-century maritime culture." Raised from the sandy bottom and identified have been numerous cannon, a bilge strainer, fasteners, ballast stone, a bronze bell, a blunderbuss barrel, gunflints, lead shot, grenades, a whetstone, navigational instruments, medical instruments including a pewter syringe, a clay tobacco pipe, clothing accessories such as buttons and straight pins, bottles, ceramics, pewter plates, a pewter spoon, animal bones from shipboard livestock, and gold dust.

A cannon being raised from the shipwreck believed to be the Queen Anne's Revenge. Photo By: Karen Browning courtesy of NC Dept of Cultural Resources

If proven to be the *Queen Anne's Revenge*, the state of North Carolina could claim one of only a few 18th century pirate wrecks in the world. However, the ten-year-long archeological project has been thrown off course by the destructive winds of hurricanes and inexplicably slowed by the doldrums of funding shortfalls, political ambivalence and public apathy. State officials hoping to muster support have said "that by studying the artifacts, archaeologists have been able to gain valuable insight into the period's naval technology, colonial provisioning, the slave trade, shipboard life, and the material culture of piracy."

Unfortunately, neither the ocean's floor nor the word processors of pirate historians have yielded new, substantive information about the captain of the *Queen Anne's Revenge*—that "real, ranting, raging, roaring pirate," Blackbeard. It is not that the historians haven't tried.

Two new Blackbeard biographies were published in 2006, clearly timed by their publishers to capitalize with the fervor generated by the Hollywood films. The books joined just a few others written in the past 200 years dedicated solely to the history of the pirate commonly known as Edward Teach. Previous Blackbeard standards include Rev. Dr. Shirley Carter Hughson's, *Blackbeard & the Carolina Pirates*, first published in 1894, and *Blackbeard the Pirate—A Reappraisal of His Life and Times*, published in 1974 and written by the late Wake Forest University law professor, Robert E. Lee. Both Hughson's and Lee's books are still in print and offer a moderately accurate and thorough account of the pirate's brief appearance in history. But none of the recently published material on Blackbeard has been able to delve much beyond the basic story as told by his original biographer, Capt. Charles Johnson, in his *General History of Pirates*.

Most every writer who undertakes a retelling of the story of the pirate, Blackbeard, leans heavily upon the words of Capt. Johnson. Johnson is something of an enigma, and there has been a decades-long debate among scholars as to who he really was. There are many who subscribe to the theory that Johnson's style and familiarity with nautical issues suggests he could only be the celebrated Daniel

Defoe, author of *Robinson Crusoe*. Other experts disagree but offer no other evidence as to who Johnson really was. It is generally accepted that Johnson had more than an armchair familiarity with the workings of a ship, the principles of sail and navigation, and day-to-day life of men of the sea, but knowledge of sailing itself does not make one a sea captain.

Some writers have offered the possibility that Johnson was himself a pirate, although their reasoning may be a bit of a stretch. In the first edition of his *General History*, Johnson intimated, in the third person, that he was not *always* an eyewitness to the events which he described. His statement is a bit vague as we don't know what events he witnessed. Johnson simply may have been referring to pirate trials at Old Bailey Courthouse or pirate hangings at the Wapping Stairs on the River Thames for which there were thousands of eyewitnesses. Furthermore, it seems suspicious that he would not have claimed to have been a pirate, since it would have made his book all the more marketable.

The more interesting and more meaningful mystery, however, is not Johnson's identity, but what and who were his sources, from where did he get his information, how accurate were his facts? The author, who has been called "the famous historian of scoundreldom," wrote chapter-length biographies of 35 of the western hemisphere's best known "highwaymen" of the sea. Certainly, Johnson knew his featured pirates' sensational stories of villainy, debauchery, and general mayhem would sell books—lots of them. In less than a few months, Johnson turned out a second edition, and a couple of years later, another edition that included a second volume. More than 280 years later, new editions of his books are still being sold. As a result, much of what the public knows about pirates, such as Henry Every, William Kidd, Calico Jack Rackham, Anne Bonny, Sam Bellamy, Bartholomew Roberts, and Edward Teach, hinges on the veracity and scholarship of Charles Johnson.

The question of Johnson's accuracy is especially pertinent when considering the story of Blackbeard. Many of the enduring Blackbeard myths—his Bristol, England, birthplace; his 14 wives, including his last, whom Johnson claimed Teach shared with five or six of his brutal companions on his wedding night; the burning of fuses in his hair to frighten his victims; his hours-long and successful battle with a British warship; his personal diary containing the story of the troubling day when there was no rum for his crew; his covenant with the devil for possession of his buried treasure—all can be traced back to the pen of Johnson. These are the stories most people know, even if they have never read a book about Blackbeard.

Conservator Sarah Watkins-Kenney and QAR lab manager Wendy Welsh clean a cannon from the shipwreck believed to be the Queen Anne's Revenge. *Photo By: Wendy Welsh courtesy of NC Dept of Cultural Resources.*

What should readers believe?

The fact that Johnson was a contemporary of Blackbeard and his fellow pirates of the "Golden Age," provides sufficient credibility for some scholars to believe his information implicitly. For them, Johnson is the original, if not, definitive reference. Other respected pirate historians of late have recognized a number of Johnson's errors, but then are willing to accept his version of other important events as broadly accurate. Unfortunately, it is a trap that many have fallen into. Not among them is Patrick Pringle, author of *Jolly Roger—The Story of the Great Age of Piracy*, who casts a wary weather-eye toward Johnson's unintended reference book of pirates. Pringle wrote: "All written history is selective... these 'classics' [meaning both Johnson's and Exquemelin's book] were written for entertainment. They were not serious histories; they were written to be popular."

As for those who cherry-pick some of Johnson's information while spurning his obvious errors, Pringle quoted the words of English historian James Froude: "Historic facts are like a child's box of letters. You have only to pick out such letters as you want and spell any word you like... Select such facts as suit you, and leave alone those which do not suit you, and let your theory of history be what it may, you can find no difficulty in providing the facts to prove it."

Pringle's admonishment of those who depend on Johnson's pirate biographies is clear. "It is not the fault of Exquemelin and Johnson that their works have been credited with canonical authority for the last three centuries. [Other writers] deserve stronger censure for their blind faith in the magic label 'contemporary.' Even worse 'crimes' against the pirates were committed by those writers who exaggerated or distorted piratical characteristics and incidents found in Exquemelin and Johnson. Twentieth-century writers have drawn much less on their imaginations, although those who have not troubled to go back to primary sources have perpetuated many of the earlier embellishments."

Some authors not only perpetuated Johnson's embellishments, they compounded them, creating new, fantastic fables that have become absorbed and preserved in the public consciousness. The subject of piracy is unusual in historical writing. It attracts a broad range of expertise and talent, from the scholarly, traditional historian to the authors of melodrama, the mythical and supernatural. The latter group seems to be the more successful. Among the best-selling, most-popular books featuring Blackbeard are the ones that revel in the stories of his wandering headless ghost; his silver-plated skull being used as a drinking cup by a secret society; his lost treasure off the coast of New Hampshire; his king's ransom of gold, silver and jewels buried beneath an old oak tree.

It is left to the reader to know when the crystal-clear waters flowing from the primary sources of pirate history begin to become muddied by the imaginations of peddlers of lore. This brings to mind a popular book written by a former newspaperman about the people and events of four centuries of life on North Carolina's Hatteras and Ocracoke islands. "This is not a history. I am not a historian," the author begins with his fair warning to readers. And while there is some historical matter within its pages, the out-of-print book has nonetheless become a sort of cherished textbook on the islands' history. Our hero, Blackbeard, made its pages, of course, and was said to have buried some of his treasure under a gnarled holly tree behind the author's quarters near the point of Cape Hatteras. The author also claims that Blackbeard's quartermaster, William Howard (identified as Henry Howard in the book), escaped death when their sloop, *Adventure*, was attacked at Ocracoke. Purportedly, Howard slipped over the side, swam ashore holding a silver goblet, and lost himself among the native population. It makes for a good story but official records have no one on the pirate crew eluding capture. Furthermore, the real William Howard was bound in chains in the Williamsburg jail on the day the *Adventure* was attacked. Such are the myths that are often accepted as facts by secondary writers and,

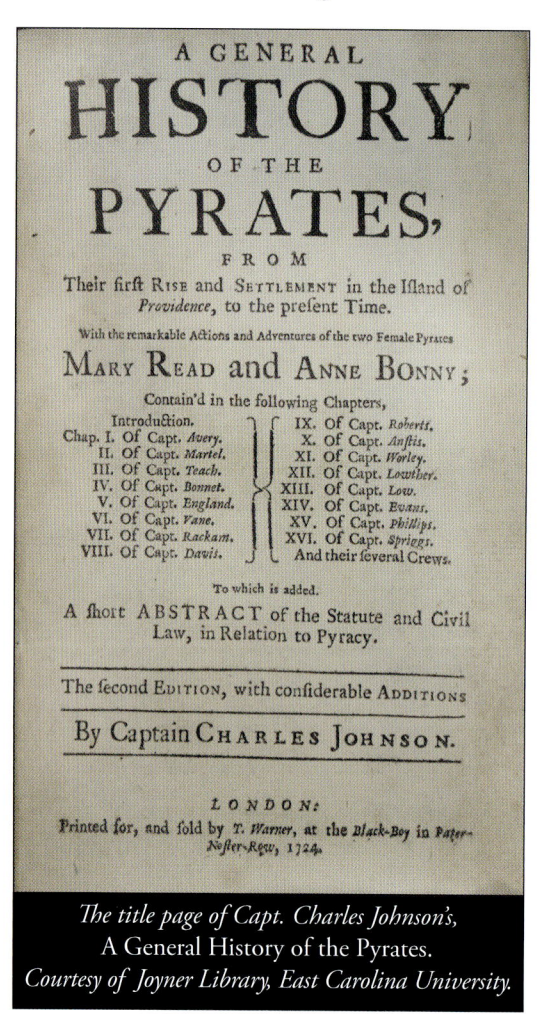

The title page of Capt. Charles Johnson's,
A General History of the Pyrates.
Courtesy of Joyner Library, East Carolina University.

The bible of pirate history: Capt. Charles Johnson's History of Pirates, *volumes I and II, at East Carolina University's Joyner Library Special Collection reading room.*

subsequently, by the public.

It is awfully tempting for writers to rely on their predecessors, to avoid the trouble, inconvenience and expense of spending long hours in crowded archives attempting to decipher faded and torn parchments, poor spelling, bad handwriting, and searching endless pages of documents that seemingly have nothing to do with the researcher's subject. Writers might think that if an event or fact has survived the ages and the scrutiny of generations of historians, it must be true. If they do, they are venturing into Addison Whipple's "treacherous waters."

It raises an interesting question: is it possible to go back to the trodden ground of original sources—trial depositions, minutes of colonial Councils, Governors' records, deed books, wills and inventories, and log books and letters of the British admiralty—and learn something new about a popular historical figure? After so long, is it possible to learn something new about the pirate known as Blackbeard? That's what I intended to find out.

The Historiography of Blackbeard

REDCLIFFE PARADE

Above a rocky cliff honeycombed with a maze of caves is Redcliffe Parade, a row of sea captain's townhouses overlooking one of the oldest quays in England dating to 989 A.D. According to Bristol pirate authority Peter Martin, the caves served as hideouts for smugglers, kings, and the notorious pirate, Blackbeard. On a street behind the townhouses is a basement flat where local lore says that Edward Teach, aka Blackbeard, lived as a young boy.

Across the harbor is the tavern known as the "Hole in the Wall." Legend remembers a time when Capt. King (who lived in the red townhouse seen behind the mast) would signal to the tavern to serve free drinks to the sailors there on Saturday nights. As a result, the sailors got drunk and were captured by press gangs the next morning and forced to fill vacant crew positions on soon-to-depart slavers. When the drunken sailors awakened from their stupor, they'd find themselves on board a ship bound for Guinea, or Madras, or the islands of the South Seas, never to be seen again.

It is estimated that ship owners and captains of Bristol, England conducted 2,108 slaving voyages and transported 2.6 million slaves from Africa to colonial America and the Caribbean between 1698 and 1807 when the trade was finally abolished in Great Britain. But Bristolians would rather their city be known as Blackbeard's birthplace.

Kevin Duffus photo.

Three— A Bristol Man Born?

Who was Blackbeard the pirate and from whence did he come? Thanks to an obscure 18th century author, most people believe the infamous pirate captain was a native of Bristol. England. Capt. Charles Johnson introduced his chapter on Blackbeard with these abiding words: "Edward Teach was a Bristol man born, but had sailed some time out of Jamaica in privateers, in the late French war." And with that single, tenuous statement and without any other evidence, history has been willing to accept Bristol as the birthplace of the man who became one of world's "best known" pirates. Imagine—not anywhere among the voluminous records, including a 1698 Bristol census, nor millions of words written about the infamous bearded pirate, is there a single, conclusive, definitive shred of evidence that Edward Thatch or Teach came from Bristol.

Blackbeard biographer Robert E. Lee contended that because of the overwhelming number of historical sources which identify Bristol as the pirate captain's home port, it must be the truth. In the endnotes of his book, Lee provided an impressive number of sources which state that Blackbeard was born in Bristol, including the *Encyclopedia Britannica*, the *Dictionary of National Biography*, and Philip Gosse's, *The Pirate's Who's Who*. What Lee doesn't share with his readers is that every single source he cites derived its Bristol reference from Capt. Johnson's 1724 history of pirates.

So, before I was willing to endorse Johnson's claim and Lee's endorsement, even halfheartedly, I decided to travel to the medieval port city of Bristol, on the river Avon, to learn more about why history is so set on Blackbeard's roots. I contacted the Bristol Visitor's Bureau and asked to be referred to a local historian or pirate scholar. They told me they knew just who I needed to see.

The train from Paddington Station rumbled over age-worn tracks and a maze of switches and slowly began to escape the run-down, graffiti-covered walls of London's amorphous western outskirts. Seated in a car nearly empty, I took advantage of the solitude and began to review my notes on Bristol, its history and the recently emerging Blackbeard legends that have helped to reinvigorate the city's tourism business.

At one time, prior to the scourge of Black Death in the 14th century, Bristol was England's third largest city; during Blackbeard's time, its volume of maritime traffic ranked second only to London. Like London, it was a bustling town on a navigable tidal river, and as the city grew, so did its influence on the maritime interests of the world. Unlike London with its eastward-flowing Thames, Bristol's River Avon flowed west, providing mariners a more expeditious route to the Atlantic shipping lanes, trade with Ireland and the rich fishing grounds of Newfoundland, for which it was said London was jealous. Many important voyages of exploration and discovery set sail from Bristol, including John Cabot's first European landing on the North American continent in 1497. Other Bristol natives of note included Sir John Yeamans, who was influential in the settlement of Barbados, the colony of Carolina, and the city of Charleston; and William Penn, founder of the colony of Pennsylvania. Shipbuilding became a major source of pride, as were the successful exploits of famous privateering captains such as William Dampier and Woodes Rogers. Bristolians today, however, may be less proud of the city's significant hand in the promotion and exploitation of the Atlantic slave trade, but they are quick to remind you that their city also played a supporting role in Britain's abolition of slavery.

Bristol's pervasive nautical atmosphere also became the backdrop for one of the most influential works of pirate literature: Robert Louis Stevenson's, *Treasure Island*.

As my train hurtled toward Bristol and as the green English countryside streaked past the window, I recalled Stevenson's description of the seaport through the eyes of Jim Hawkins, which had so captivated my imagination as a young reader:

> "...and on our way, to my great delight, lay along the quays and beside the great multitude of ships of all sizes and rigs and nations. In one, sailors were singing at their work, in another there were men aloft, high over my head, hanging to threads that seemed no thicker than a spider's... I saw the most wonderful figureheads, that had all been far over the ocean. I saw, besides, many old sailors, with rings in their ears, and whiskers curled in ringlets, and tarry pigtails, and their swaggering, clumsy seawalk; and if I had seen as many kings or archbishops I could not have been more delighted. And I was going to sea myself... to sea, bound for an unknown island, and to seek for buried treasures!"

I was as delighted to be going to Bristol as Jim Hawkins was to leave it. And I wondered, could a young Edward Thatch have been one of those sailors who joined the crew of a West Country ship, like young master Jim? The people of Bristol certainly think so.

In recent years, Bristol pirate enthusiasts and historians have nurtured and fed Capt. Johnson's unsupported claim of Blackbeard's West Country heritage. One account reads: "Born on the wrong, desperately poor, side of the River Avon, in Redcliffe, Teach was born a rebel and refused to obey orders. Teach, known as Blackbeard, was an exceptionally tall man with piercing eyes, cauliflower ears, a bashed-in nose, and a very loud voice." Another description says, "young Edward Thatch grew up in the streets around the river docks and the sea was in his blood. He probably lived in the congested Redcliffe area just a few yards from the working waterfront. The Thatch family was not poor; Edward received some education and he was later able to read and write. One legend has it that Edward Thatch's father died in Bristol in 1693 and his mother re-married soon after. The man she married hated his step-son and beat him unmercifully on numerous occasions. After one beating, at the age of 16, Edward turned the tables on his step-father and nearly beat him to death. He had no choice but to leave home, and he ran to the Bristol docks, where he signed on as a cabin boy on a ship bound for Jamaica."

As it happened, I was myself Bristol bound to meet the author of the preceding Blackbeard narrative, Peter Martin, who is somewhat of a pirate himself. Martin had offered to take me to Blackbeard's childhood home, and who would pass that up?

The train slowed as we approached the mid-way station at Swindon. There, two tattooed and heavily pierced British teens boarded my car and threw themselves loudly into the seats directly across the aisle. It didn't take long to size them up. Immediately, both pulled out cell phones and seemed to compete with each other as to how loud they could shout into their phones while their MP3 players blared rap music. Each of their sentences was laced with a limited repertoire of profanity—pretty much the same word, really.

I was annoyed by their presence. But then, I tried to imagine what kind of boy Blackbeard might have been. Would he have been much different from the two teens seated next to me? As a youth, was the future pirate boisterous, obnoxious, disrespectful, and angry? Did he despise authority? I hoped my contact in Bristol could tell me.

A well-dressed woman seated across my table peered over the top of her reading glasses and stopped the conductor as he passed through the car to see if anything could be done about the noise and profanity across the aisle. He seemed reluctant to get involved, as did many people annoyed by pirates during Blackbeard's time.

Soon enough, the train eased into Bristol's Temple Meads Station, and within an hour, I was walking the wharfs and cobblestone streets of Blackbeard's hometown with the colorful, knowledgeable, and engaging Peter Martin.

Pete the Pirate, as he is self-billed, is modern Bristol's undisputed pirate expert, and unofficial visitor guide to the haunts and hang-outs of Blackbeard, Woodes Rogers, Alexander Selkirk of Robinson Crusoe fame, and the true-life pubs and ordinaries adopted by Robert Louis Stevenson for his swashbuckling book. Martin promised to take me to *Treasure Island*'s Spy-glass Inn, today known as the Hole in the Wall Pub. In Blackbeard's day, the quayside drinking establishment was known as Coaches and Horses, and was an occasional target of the press gangs who rounded up drunken sailors to fill vacant crew positions on soon-to-depart slavers bound for the Ivory Coast. Teach drank there often, I was assured by my guide.

"We're at a fantastic place at the moment, one of the oldest quays in England dating to 989 A.D.," Martin says as we walk along a stone pier at the base of a cave-riddled cliff. Above the cliff is perched a row of colorful townhouses overlooking the harbor. Gesturing, Martin says: "Across there is the Hole in the Wall used in *Treasure Island*, directly opposite these houses of the 21 sea captains who ran all of the ships of Bristol. They all lived cheek by jowl and these houses are built over a network of honeycombed caves, and it was a great refuge for Bristol's pirates." I'm not sure how the pirates fit in to Martin's rambling story but his passion for the city's traditions is infectious.

Martin explains to me the Bristolian method of recruiting unwitting and unwilling sailors. "In the red house there, Capt. King, if he wanted men to go on his ship, he would signal across to the Hole in the Wall and they would serve free drinks on a Saturday night." Presumably on Capt. King's tab. "Now nobody could resist that could they?" asks Martin, jabbing me in the shoulder. And the next day, I am told, when the drunken sailors awaken from their stupor, they'd find themselves on board a ship bound for Guinea, or Madras, or the islands of the South Seas, never to be seen again. Or so the story goes. Surely, Blackbeard never fell for the free drinks ploy. Before I could ask Pirate Pete why the hung-over recruits didn't simply jump ship during the tediously slow, week-long journey down the narrow, twisting Avon River to the open sea, we were on to another historic destination.

Along the way, Martin wanted me to meet a pair of salty-looking dock workers who were eager to contribute a little extra color to our seemingly well-rehearsed pirate walk. "Yeah, there are still pirates around 'ere," one says, scratching his beard with all seriousness. I'm intrigued, or more like it, hooked. "Where would we find one?" I ask. "Yeah, just over there lives Long John Saliva, an' 'e's the spittin' image of his dad." I wasn't sure whether I was expected to tip the men or not.

Our tour soon took on a more reverent tone as we climbed a steep street that led to the childhood home of little Blackbeard. It is a peach-colored Queen Anne building on Guinea Street in Redcliffe which has somehow survived German bombs during World War II and the construction of adjacent concrete apartment towers. And in a basement flat, pointed out by Martin, young Edward Thatch lived with his mother, who worked as a cook for the sea captain upstairs. Martin believes that someone years ago remembered the story of the Thatch family and adorned the historic building with two conspicuous symbols—carved stone medallions set into the lintels of a pair of windows. Presumably, this would be among the most hallowed places in all of piratedom, but there were

Blackbeard lived here? A Queen Anne house in Bristol, England, believed by some to be the former home of the infamous pirate

no other historical markers or signs indicating this was the Redcliffe home of Blackbeard, one of the world's most famous pirates.

"Well, this house has a lot of history and somebody in the past has put it all together. And if you look at these gargoyles here, see the date—1718. And right at the top we've got Blackbeard's effigy," Martin says as he folds his arms and then nods, satisfied with the obvious proof of the pirate's former residency.

That's it? That's the proof that young Blackbeard lived here? I guess the face could be Blackbeard's, or plenty of other bearded men with big eyes for that matter. Although now I think I know where the idea of Blackbeard's cauliflower ears and bashed-in nose came from.

The date of Blackbeard's death is thought to prove that he once lived here.

I'm not sure why my imaginative guide failed to point out that Edward Thatch was raised in a Queen Anne house, and he later named his flagship, *Queen Anne's Revenge*—now there is compelling evidence. Only, when Queen Anne took the throne Edward Thatch had to be about 22-years-old, according to the theories of most historians, and long-gone from the streets of Bristol.

"What else do we know about their time here?" I ask, as I try to picture young Thatch playing in the street.

"Yes, well let's look at Blackbeard himself. He was a big lad, and a bit of a rascal. He had bulging eyes, a big temper and one day he had a big fight, a bit of a punch-up in the Golden Guinea Pub here, and the mother had a problem. His mother was a widow, his father had been lost at sea at Jamaica aboard the *Berkeley Galley*. So she hid him in the cave below the Ostrich Inn."

Blackbeard's effigy?

With that, we immediately set out to see the Ostrich Inn. At such a hurried pace, I failed to ask Martin about the alternative story he features on his Web site about Thatch's father dying in 1693 in Bristol and Thatch later being raised by an abusive stepfather.

On the way to the Ostrich, I did ask Pete the Pirate why Blackbeard never returned to Bristol after becoming a pirate. "Well, Blackbeard, as we know, had his head chopped off, now didn't he?" Martin says with a chastising tone. "Oh, right," I answered, "that would have been a problem."

His story didn't end there, however. Martin tells me that Blackbeard, before he died, had entrusted his lieutenant, Israel Hands, with his plunder of diamonds to be passed on to his mother (despite the fact that Hands had been recently shot in the knee by Blackbeard). Hands was pardoned and returned to England and Bristol. But before he could fulfill his mission and give the diamonds to Blackbeard's mother, local merchants spotted Hands and "nicked" the diamonds off of him. "And that was the start of a famous bank in England, now the NatWest Bank, and the diamonds were the collateral that started it," Martin tells me without even the hint of a smile. I suppose it could be true. I have read that the College of William and Mary in Virginia was begun with a similar line of capital.

At the Ostrich Inn, I see the famous tunnel where young Blackbeard was spirited away after his punch-up. I tried to imagine him being pursued by bullies, his tall body crouching and crawling into the darkness on his escape to a waiting vessel and his storied life on the sea. While we were in the pub, Pirate Pete gave me a lesson in pirate comportment, and it conjured up another vision of Blackbeard and his propensity to fall in love when he was in port. There was a young couple quietly enjoying a pint or two at a table near the window. Martin gives me a wink and says, "Aye, there's a pretty one." He brushes by the gentleman and charmingly greets his buxom, blonde companion.

Pete the Pirate: 'Allo there. You're lovely. Can you cook?
Woman: I can cook. I'm a brilliant cook.
Pete the Pirate: Would you like to join my crew?
Woman: Why, I would love to join your crew, any day. Ha, ha!

It must have been how all of Blackbeard's romances began. I should add, the gentleman looked on disapprovingly but reasonably crestfallen at the sudden abandonment of his mate.

After we left the Ostrich, Martin and I retraced our steps up the street in front of the stately row of captains' houses. We passed a parked car which not 30 minutes earlier had been unscathed but now its driver's side window was broken open, the result of a smash and grab thief. "Bloody criminals," observed Martin, under his breath. I asked him if break-ins were a problem in Bristol. "Oh, yes. It's become terrible," he says gravely. "They see a cell phone or a music player in a car and the buggers just take what they please. Those GPS systems have become really coveted." It occurred to me that Pete the Pirate, or anyone else for that matter who celebrates the lifestyles of pirates, wouldn't think pirates were so admirable if they had their valuables stolen by one. Most people forget that pirates, in reality, were no more than common thieves. Even Blackbeard.

Later, Martin and I were enjoying a plate of fish and chips in the corner room of the 1664 Llandoger Trow public house, at the very table, Martin tells me, where Daniel Dafoe met the former castaway, Alexander Selkirk, and where Dafoe conceived the book, *Robinson Crusoe*. (There seems to be no end to the Bristol fables.) I knew other historians have been unable to find any Thatches or Thatchers in the early Bristol records, so I asked Martin: "Has there ever been an attempt to trace Blackbeard's family history, the surname Thatch?"

"There's been a world-wide investigation," he replies. "We know that Edward Thatch was proud of his mother, and when he was 'had-up' for a bit of piracy he was embarrassed it would get back, so he changed his name to Teach so his mother wouldn't realize it was him." I thought to myself, she would have forgiven her son had she ended up with his diamonds.

Pete "the Pirate" Martin leads guided tours of Bristol's famous pirate haunts.

Martin continues: "But the older records in Bristol have all been destroyed. You've still got the libraries and various things. But London used to get upset with Bristol because Bristol wouldn't join in the fight when America became independent because Bristol had one-third of its population in Virginia. So London would come down and fire the place, so I'm afraid we don't have that sort of evidence [about Blackbeard]. I've researched all the graveyards around Bristol, but we can't find any evidence at all. Now, the important source of records would be in Lord Berkeley's private collection, 'cause he owned the *Berkeley Galley*, and I'm sure if the curators opened the locks to us one day we will find that James Teach, Edward's father, would be listed as crew. Then we could start the research in earnest."

Never mind that Edward didn't change his name to Teach until after he was caught 'a pirating, according to the same Bristol legend. I also knew that according to

Capt. Johnson's book, the *Berkeley Galley* was plundered by a pirate captain named Martel between Jamaica and Cuba in September, 1716, years after it supposedly sank with Blackbeard's father aboard. At the time the *Berkeley Galley* was captured by Martel, the ship was under the command of Edward Saunders. Ironically, Saunders is the sea captain for whom, Peter Martin says, Mrs. Thatch—Blackbeard's "mum"—cooked, above their basement flat in the Queen Anne house that could not have been built when Blackbeard was a boy because Anne was not yet a queen. It is all very confusing, and nonsensical. I imagine Bristol tourism officials hope the curators keep Lord Berkeley's private collection private. The pirate's professed Bristol connections seem to be doing quite well for the city's merchants, and Peter Martin's entertaining pirate walks, as well.

There was another connection Martin wanted to make between Blackbeard, Bristol and William Penn's Quakers of Pennsylvania, but it was time for me to move on.

It's a good story, in any event, of Blackbeard's Bristol roots, although I felt like I had been pitched a Hollywood screenplay. Peter Martin is certainly a charming guide and a true pirate at heart. I wouldn't hesitate to spend another day with him wandering the quays and pubs of Blackbeard's "hometown." If you are ever in Bristol, you should too—but I'm not sure I'd trust him around my woman, especially if she were a brilliant cook.

The next day, while waiting for the return train to London, I thought about the mystery of Thatch's true identity. We are left with the choices of believing Capt. Johnson, believing Bristol lore, or none of the above. I really didn't think the answer lay hidden in Lord Berkeley's private collection. I also didn't leave the West County feeling any more confident in Capt. Johnson's claim that "Edward Teach was a Bristol man born." In order to learn who Thatch really was, I knew it was time to enter the long, dimly-lit passageway of history.

The Llandoger Trow, circa 1664. According to legend, it was here where Daniel Dafoe met castaway Alexander Selkirk and conceived the book, Robinson Crusoe. *Bristol officials also contend that Blackbeard was an occasional patron.*

Kevin Duffus photo.

Four — Two Years A Pyrat

Should we restrict our narrative of Blackbeard's career to the indisputable facts preserved in the original sources of official correspondence, trial depositions and contemporary newspaper accounts, then his history as an officially-recognized pirate spans slightly more than a year and a half and would begin in the spring of 1717. It is a revelation that surprises many people—that the man who has been described as one of history's most infamous pirates was, strictly speaking, a pirate for no more than 20 months. By modern standards, a professional career path lasting fewer than two years would hardly be considered an achievement worth writing about. But Blackbeard's brief career was historically significant and his piratical accomplishments were sensational and many.

If history has been willing to accept the unsupported claims of Blackbeard's Bristol roots by the sphinx-like author Capt. Charles Johnson, so too have most historians acquiesced to Johnson's assertion that Edward Thatch's piratical proclivities were born in Jamaica. Even those historians who have impugned the veracity of Johnson falter, and typically begin their accounts of Blackbeard's sea-roving days out of Jamaica's Port Royal harbor as early as 1713, during the waning privateering years of the War of Spanish Succession (Queen Anne's War). They do so without verifiable sources other than the words of Johnson—partly because of Blackbeard's later association with the pirate pioneer and patriarch, Benjamin Hornigold.

In the absence of more reliable information, it has simply been assumed that Thatch served with Hornigold from the inception of the Golden Age of Piracy. The rise of piracy occurred during a post-war period when hundreds of disgruntled, out-of-work mariners, including Hornigold, fled the crowded wharves of Port Royal and other colonial entrepôts, for the freedom and felonious opportunities made possible by the ungoverned islands and harbors of the Bahamas. Hornigold is believed to have been among the first to lead raids against small trading sloops in the Florida Straits, dashing out of Nassau harbor on New Providence Island aboard small, armed sailing canoes called periaugers. But Thatch's presence in Jamaica or the Bahamas in 1713 is a hypothesis hanging on a non-existent thread. There is simply no corroborating evidence.

Not yet known by his alias, Blackbeard, Edward Thatch made his first appearance on the world stage of historical records when his name was included in a report to the British Board of Trade, dated July 5, 1717, written by

Capt. Matthew Musson. Musson had been hired by South Carolina Deputy Gov. Robert Daniel to assess the growing numbers of pirates lurking in the Bahamas and threatening the trade of Charleston. Before he reached Nassau, Musson was shipwrecked near Bimini, but he was still able to gather some intelligence on the pirate capital. Describing the situation as of March, 1717, Musson wrote that "five pirates [or vessels] made ye harbor of Providence their place of rendevous vizt. Hornigold, a sloop with ten guns and about 80 men; Jennings, a sloop with ten guns and 100 men; Burgiss, a sloop with eight guns and about 80 men; White, in a small vessel with 30 men and small arms; Thatch, a sloop six gunns and about 70 men."

Thatch could not have become a pirate captain overnight so it is a reasonable assumption that he had been in the Bahamas for at least a few months, if not for as long as one year. Unfortunately, until some previously unknown documents are found that can answer the questions of how, when and why Edward Thatch "went a-pyrating," his history prior to March 1717 will remain a mystery. We are left only with suppositions.

Perhaps Johnson was correct when he wrote that Thatch "had sailed some time out of Jamaica in privateers, in the late French war." However, a 1717 newspaper report (presumably more credible than Johnson's information) stated that Thatch had been a "mate" who had worked aboard a vessel sailing out of the port of Philadelphia. Actually, both statements could be correct. Many Philadelphia-based vessels that plied the merchant trade in American and Caribbean waters would have periodically called on the busy wharves of Kingston and Port Royal, Jamaica. And throughout Queen Anne's War, English merchant vessels hailing from North American ports such as Boston, New York, Philadelphia and Charleston were known to frequently participate in privateering raids against Spanish and French ships. So Edward Thatch could have sailed as a mate aboard a Philadelphia-based merchant sloop and still have, on occasion, entered Jamaican harbors as a privateer. Or history may have confused Thatch with someone else—a relative, perhaps.

Why would Thatch have become a pirate? According to University of Pittsburgh historian Marcus Rediker, most men became pirates by volunteering when their merchant vessel was detained by other pirates, generally to escape abusive captains, miserable conditions, meager rations and often non-existent pay. Generally, these disaffected volunteers were common sailors with nothing to lose, at the bottom of the barrel of humanity—uneducated, unskilled and uncivilized. Other men were forced aboard pirate vessels for their skills—tradesmen such as coopers, blacksmiths, carpenters, sailmakers, musicians, cooks and surgeons. Some of the Bahamian pirates came from the itinerant logwood cutters of the Bay of Campeche and Honduras, mostly rustic, drunken and ignorant men, who were driven from the area by the Spanish following the Treaty of Utrecht which ended Queen Anne's War. Also, of the nearly 4,000 men (and a few women) who were estimated to have been pirates between 1715 and 1726, a significant percentage were black Africans, although it is not always apparent whether they were free men and considered equal members of the crew, or if they were aboard pirate ships as slaves. In which of the preceding categories would Edward Thatch have belonged?

Tradition has it that Thatch had been Hornigold's pirate pupil. Of the future Blackbeard, Addison Whipple wrote: "As an eager young hand aboard Hornigold's pirate ship, [Thatch] showed that he had a marksman's eye, an ability at dirty infighting and a thirst for blood unmatched by any pirate of his time. Hornigold recognized this early and made the young man his protégé." Of course, there is absolutely no documented source for Whipple's characterization. Johnson wrote that despite Thatch's "uncommon Boldness and personal Courage, he was never raised to any Command, till he went a-pyrating, which I think was at the latter End of the Year 1716, when Capt. Benjamin Hornigold put him into a Sloop that he had made Prize of, and with whom he continued in Consortship." Johnson's version may sound plausible as far as the date goes. However, most pirate scholars would agree that more than boldness and courage, the attributes that produced pirate captains were the abilities to read and write, navigate using complex mathematical equations, understand and predict weather patterns, tides and currents, and manage and organize sailors of varying nationalities and temperaments—skills that would not likely have been "teachable" by Hornigold aboard ship. Pirate captains would not have had the time, motivation or patience for on-the-job training. As a result, we can rule out the possibilities that Blackbeard began his brief career of piracy as a lowly common sailor, a logwood cutter, a tradesman or a slave. We can furthermore conclude that Thatch probably entered the gravitational sphere of Nassau's pirate republic sometime during 1716, and he arrived already equipped with the experience and skills to lead men and the inclination to risk his life to gain a fast fortune.

On the other hand, history expects us to believe that Thatch had been an unemployed sailor in Jamaica who somehow passed unremarkably through the years between 1713 and 1717 and was "never raised to any command" before meteorically becoming a notorious and proficient pirate master with an unsurpassed "thirst for blood." Curiously, he never once was described as having performed the role of a subordinate officer for Hornigold, such as quartermaster or bo'sun—the ranks of sailors from which men were typically chosen to become captain. In the case of Blackbeard's early days as a pirate, history's pieces of the puzzle simply don't fit and have never been responsibly challenged by historians.

An alternative supposition may provide a puzzle piece that fits more neatly. There is a likelihood that Thatch participated in, or led as captain, one of the many small salvage parties from Colonial America that appeared off the coast of Florida during the winter of 1716, to collect gold and silver that had been spilled out of dozens of Spanish treasure galleons wrecked in a great hurricane the previous summer. Spanish authorities estimated that near the end of January, 1716, nearly a dozen English vessels were anchored over the wrecks scattered among the coral reefs of the Oculina Banks. Many of these treasure seekers and wreckers were young men who had heard about the Spanish gold from published accounts in the *Boston News-Letter*. They were simply looking for adventure and the chance to collect a vast and easy fortune by scavenging Florida's beaches and shallow waters, and then returning home to a hero's welcome.

One such treasure seeker was the romantic, daring, and dark-haired "Black" Sam Bellamy of Massachusetts, who, we will later learn, may have made a lasting impression on Edward Thatch. Bellamy, and his partner, Paulsgrave Williams, sailed a small boat from Rhode Island to Florida to "fish" the wrecks. There they encountered other wreckers from the English colonies, and Edward Thatch may have been among them. By the time many of these small crews had arrived on the scene in January, the Jamaican-based privateer, Capt. Henry Jennings, had already absconded with £87,000 of silver and gold that had been previously recovered by a small Spanish garrison guarding the wrecks. Jennings's success alerted Spain's authorities in Cuba, and soon, reinforcements were on the way. About that same time, Bellamy and others arrived on the scene, but they were quickly discouraged by the depths to which they had to dive to recover the gold and the determination of the Spaniards to protect their sunken cargos. Instead of becoming instantly rich and before returning home empty-handed, these wrecking parties dispersed in search of other money-making opportunities. Bellamy and Williams headed south for the Bay of Honduras, possibly to look for slaves or Indians who could be forced into diving for the submerged Spanish treasure. Other would-be treasure seekers sailed east to Nassau, where scuttlebutt among the sailors had promised their disappointments might be salved by the pleasures of lascivious women, wild drinking parties, games of chance, and men who knew of easier ways to become rich than to risk drowning off Florida's beaches. In this way, Edward Thatch may have met Benjamin Hornigold and become a pirate.

Many of the most familiar books about Blackbeard contain numerous and significant errors concerning his travels as a pirate. However, by piecing together fragments of information from the original sources, the most reliable secondary accounts, and research compiled by North Carolina archeologists David Moore and Richard Lawrence with the *Queen Anne's Revenge* project, it is possible to construct an accurate timetable and map of Edward Thatch's travels and captures from 1716 to 1718. Because this book is primarily concerned with Edward Thatch's last days, specifically the last six months of his life that began the day he sailed away from the scuttled hulk of his flagship, *Queen Anne's Revenge* at Old Topsail Inlet in late June 1718, the following is not a detailed account of Blackbeard's piracies prior to leaving the *Queen Anne's Revenge*.

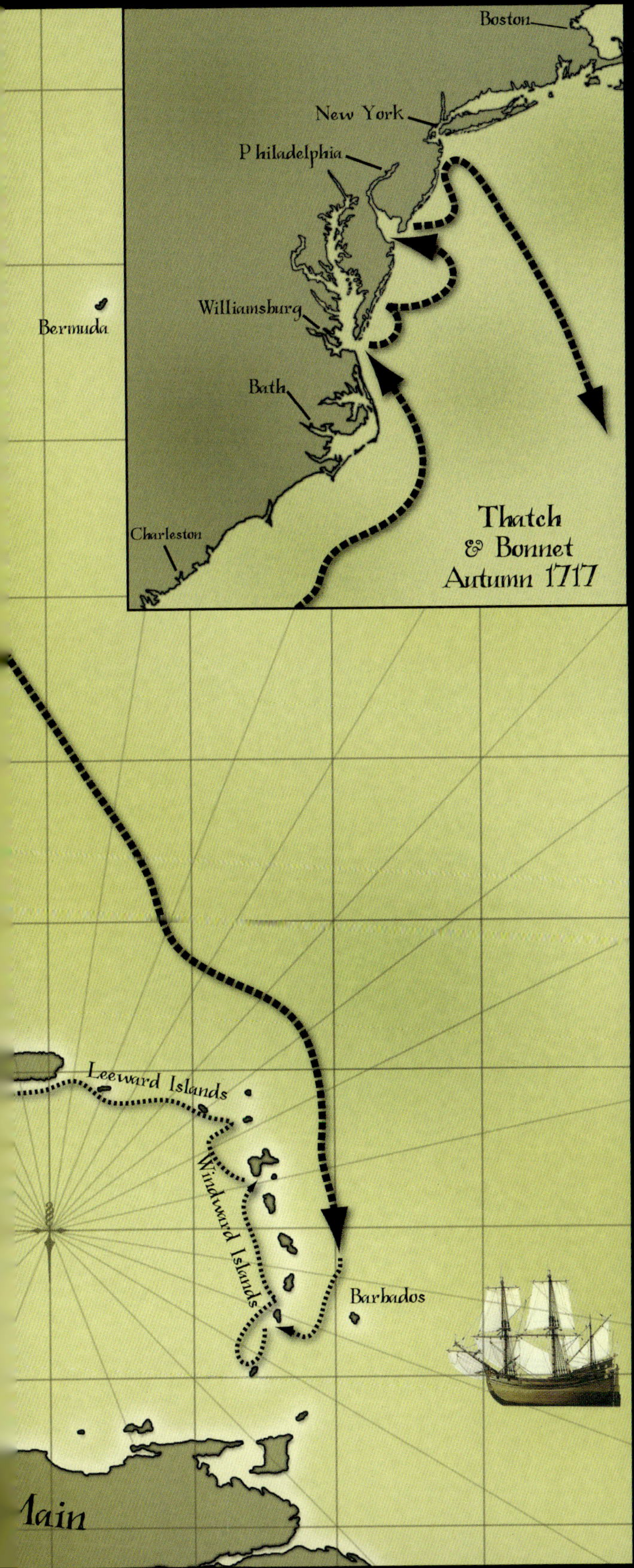

Blackbeard, or Thatch, is believed to have participated in, or commanded, four major piratical voyages or "cruises" (not counting brief sorties from Nassau), accounting for more than 100 prizes. As has been previously stated, official records do not identify Thatch as a pirate until the spring of 1717. However, even though Thatch's name is not mentioned in the records, there is sufficient reason to believe that he had become a member of Benjamin Hornigold's crew the previous spring, and set sail with Hornigold aboard the pirate leader's great sloop, narcissistically named *Benjamin*.

The spring 1716 cruise out of Nassau harbor was essentially a circumnavigation of Cuba. Near the Mariel Bay, Hornigold and his crew captured the French merchant sloop, *Marianne*, and successfully seized more than £12,000 in goods. After an unexpected encounter with his rival and nemesis, Henry Jennings, who made a failed attempt to chase down and capture Hornigold's sloop and his French prize, Hornigold fled around the western end of the island. Meanwhile, Jennings was double-crossed by Sam Bellamy and Paulsgrave Williams, who had only hours before helped Jennings capture more than 28,000 pieces of eight from another French vessel anchored nearby. Bellamy and his friends slipped away with Jennings's share of the loot, and they, like Hornigold, skedaddled around the western tip of Cuba. Sometime later, Hornigold, Bellamy, and, presumably, Thatch, gathered for the first time and agreed to work in unison as pirates. Bellamy accepted command of the *Marianne*. Reading between the lines, some historians have noted that Bellamy's promotion was significant because older Hornigold crew members were passed over, including Thatch. However, as we will learn later, Thatch was most likely Bellamy's age or younger and is believed to have admired and emulated the Massachusetts mariner.

During the next few weeks, the Hornigold-Bellamy consortium was joined by another pirate sloop skippered by a Frenchman named La Bouche, and together they hunted prey in the Yucatan Channel but captured little of significant value. It has been said that the three pirate captains made a peculiar team, since Hornigold wanted to limit his attacks to the vessels of England's former enemies—France and Spain. La Bouche was, of course, one of those former enemies. And Bellamy had no qualms about seizing the property of *all* nations and desired to openly wage war against the rich, as a "Robin Hood" of the sea. Arguments and dissension inevitably ensued, but so did the merriment typical of pirate societies. After putting into a sandy bay on Cuba's Isle of the Pines for fresh water and repairs, the diverse rogue fleet continued eastward to the western shores and coves of Hispaniola, which was an ideal place to hide and attack vessels passing through the frequently-used Windward Passage. By the end of May, Hornigold decided to leave his new partners and return to Nassau to cash in his share of loot, with the intention to regroup with Bellamy and La Bouche later that summer. When Hornigold returned to Hispaniola with a newly acquired sloop named *Adventure*, his partners were evermore determined to plunder English ships, in addition to those of other nations. Hornigold steadfastly refused, and the pirates had a falling out. A council was held, votes were cast and counted, and Hornigold was deposed as their commodore. He, and presumably Thatch, returned to Nassau by early September and spent the rest of the year making intermittent raids along the western fringes of the Bahamas.

The sources are silent concerning how Thatch and his closest friends spent the winter season of 1716-1717. One thing, however, had changed. They had been officially condemned as pirates—King George I declared them so in September. For many of the young men who had originally ventured out to comb the beaches of Florida for Spanish gold—an entirely honest pastime—they were now considered wanted criminals and enemies of the state. For men like Thatch, there was no turning back.

Based on Matthew Musson's report on the status of pirates at Nassau, we know that Thatch was captain of a six-gun sloop and 70 men in the spring of 1717. He was most likely not a subordinate of Hornigold, contrary to Johnson's version of their relationship in his book, but the two men and their pirate companies often sailed in consort, as they did in March, 1717, when they sailed far down the Spanish Main to Portobello on the Panamanian coast.

Along the way, the pirates had stopped a vessel and captured the physician, John Howell—one of Hornigold's crew was in dire need of medical help and a unique feature of pirate companies was that they strived to provide free health care for their members. Four and a half years later in Nassau, despite loudly protesting that he had been a forced man, Dr. Howell was put on trial for piracy and faced imminent death by hanging. Testifying as a witness on Howell's behalf was William Howard, who had been Thatch's quartermaster on *Queen Anne's Revenge*. Howard confirmed that Howell had been pressed into service against his will by Hornigold, and, as a result, Howell's neck was spared. The significance of the story is that it places Howard in Thatch's company during Thatch's early days of piracy. And, as we will later learn in greater detail, William Howard was also the son of a North Carolina landowner.

The Thatch and Hornigold cruise during the spring of 1717 was remarkable for another reason—how it strangely foreshadowed the future. Offshore of the historic treasure port of Portobello, the pirates captured a Jamaican-based sloop named the *Bonnet*, from which they recovered gold coins and other goods. Hornigold relinquished his sloop, *Adventure*, to the hapless former captain of the faster *Bonnet*, which Hornigold kept for himself. A week later in early April, south of Jamaica, Thatch and Hornigold intercepted the sloop *Revenge*, which yielded even more gold and silver. In a short time, and without a lot of effort or bloody engagements, the pirate team had accumulated an estimated £100,000 of treasure. But what was so remarkable was that they had plundered the two vessels, *Bonnet* and *Revenge*, because four months later, Edward Thatch would meet the man historians have described as the most unlikely and incompetent of all pirates, Stede Bonnet, captain and owner of a different sloop named *Revenge*.

Among those pirates returning to Nassau in August, 1717, was Paulsgrave Williams, and he brought bad news. His good friend, and Edward Thatch's role model, Sam Bellamy was dead, killed in a shipwreck. Bellamy had attempted to return home to show off his newly acquired flagship, the formidable 300-ton armed merchant galley, *Whydah*, but was driven ashore by a catastrophic storm onto the ragged cliffs of Cape Cod. Nine of Bellamy's shipmates had somehow survived, but they were captured and jailed in Boston, where it was virtually certain they would be convicted of piracy and hanged. The news so outraged Thatch that he vowed to wage a war of retribution against ships of New England. Soon after, when Stede Bonnet and his hired crew of pirates limped into the harbor after unsuccessfully attacking a more powerful Spanish vessel, Thatch evaluated the *Revenge*'s potential speed and firepower and decided it was just the vessel he would need to speed him northward into the familiar mid-Atlantic waters of English America. The sloop was perfectly named, and he knew just where to lurk to inflict maximum revenge—the capes of the Delaware Bay.

By the middle of September, 1717, a self-assured Edward Thatch stood on the quarterdeck of Stede Bonnet's *Revenge*, having assumed control as its captain. He watched as the bo'sun directed the helmsman to steer a course out of the Northwest Providence Channel, into the swiftly moving, sky-blue waters of the Gulf Stream and the Florida Straits. He had parted company and political philosophies with Hornigold—English vessels would now be among his prey. Aboard ship were his most trusted companions, 150 pirates including Bonnet, and 12 deadly cannon. Thatch had not shaved his face in quite some time and his extravagant beard, rarely seen on faces of men at the time, served him well as a grotesque disguise. He was now often called Blackbeard—a nickname partly inspired by his dead friend, "Black" Bellamy—and it suited him well.

During a three-week rampage of destruction beginning at the end of September, Blackbeard and his pirates captured 18 ships between Cape Charles, Virginia, and the entrance to the Delaware Bay. Uncharacteristically for "pupils" of Hornigold's style of gentlemanly piracy, the behavior of Blackbeard's men was malicious, arbitrary, and gratuitous, as was experienced by Capt. Codd of a ship from Liverpool. According to a news dispatch from Philadelphia, "They threw all Codd's Cargo over board, excepting some small matters they fancied." One merchant "begg'd for Cloth to make him but one Suit of Clothes, which they refused to grant him." The pirates wantonly tossed cargoes, including wheat, into the sea, chopped down the masts of one vessel driving her ashore, and sank another. They left the area sometime after the 22nd of October and headed south, announcing to some of their victims that they were on the hunt for a good ship "which they much wanted." Coincidentally, within a few days of their departure, Virginia's Lt. Gov. Alexander Spotswood passed the same way aboard the Royal Navy frigate, *Lyme*, commanded by Capt. Ellis Brand. Less than a year later, Spotswood and Brand would be plotting Blackbeard's demise.

Weeks later, on November 17, north of Barbados, Blackbeard captured the ship he thought he wanted: the 200-ton, 14-gun French slaver, *La Concorde*, in-bound from Africa. He and his crew took the vessel into Admiralty Bay on the west side of Bequia Island where they released the French crew and most of their slaves and proceeded to refit the 104-foot-long ship into a menacing 28-gun pirate flagship. They renamed her, *Queen Anne's Revenge*.

Between December, 1717, and March, 1718, Blackbeard's expanding flotilla, which included *Queen Anne's Revenge*, Bonnet's sloop *Revenge* (to which he was restored as captain), and at least one sloop that was captured off the Delaware capes and retained, proceeded up the Windward Island chain, then west across the Leeward Islands, along the north coasts of Hispaniola and Cuba and into the Gulf of Mexico as far as Veracruz. Previous historical accounts have generally failed to pinpoint Blackbeard's location during this time, vaguely stating that his ships vanished into Spanish-controlled waters. One published account postulated that they may have rested over the winter months in a secluded cove somewhere. Instead, they apparently kept moving. New England journalist Colin Woodard, author of *Republic of Pirates*, discovered new information in an issue of the London *Weekly Journal or British Gazetteer* indicating that a heavily-armed pirate ship known to Spanish mariners only as "the Great Devil" was lurking west of the Campeche Bank. There was only one pirate vessel in 1718 carrying the estimated 40 guns of "the Great Devil," and that was *Queen Anne's Revenge*. Most likely Blackbeard was hoping to intercept one of the silver-laden galleons departing from New Spain. It is presumed they were unsuccessful because by the end of March, Blackbeard, Bonnet and the rest of the pirates were on the other side of the Yucatan Peninsula, headed south for the busy shipping lanes of the Gulf of Honduras.

Two events took place during this cruise that seem to have significantly influenced Blackbeard's actions, attitude and future plans. From one of their captives, the pirates learned the appalling news (at least to them) that six of Bellamy's crew had been hanged from the gallows at Boston. The information must have produced two distinct thoughts in Blackbeard's mind. He would renew the vigor with which he would punish New England ships and their owners, and he would begin planning for his future, in order to avoid the same fate as Bellamy's men. If there was one thing pirates feared and loathed, it was the prospect of dangling by their necks from a hempen rope, fouling their breeches, and doing the macabre "dance of death" that so entertained the common masses in cities such as Boston, Charleston and London. And there was something else that terrified them. Popular conceptions of pirates fail to take into account that most were raised with the prevailing Christian mores of their time. The likelihood that they would be caught and convicted, and their unconsecrated mortal remains might be tarred and hung in chains as an example to the world, or their bodies dumped into unmarked graves between the low and high tides lines where their souls would roam restlessly for eternity, was an idea too abhorrent for most pirates to consider or allow. To avoid the fate of hanging, some of the more resolute and unrepentant men would choose to blow themselves up before being captured, while the rest would consider pleading for the king's forgiveness if they were ever offered a pardon.

As it happened, the other bit of news that came to the hundreds of pirates, forced men and African slaves of Blackbeard's fleet during the winter of 1717-1718 was that King George I of Great Britain had decided to offer the opportunity for pirates to accept his most gracious mercy, should they surrender themselves to any governor of the king's colonies in America or the West Indies. The terms of the king's pardon required pirates to turn themselves in by September 5, 1718. However, only acts of piracy committed prior to the 5th of January of that year would be forgiven—any after that date would not be eligible. The news of the king's "Proclamation for Suppressing Pyrates" no doubt sparked a divisive and unsettling debate among the men on board Blackbeard's ships. As the *Queen Anne's Revenge* and her consort sloops made their way across the breadth of the West Indies, it is likely that various factions of men assembled above and below decks and discussed their options. If sober, they may have made some attempt to be discreet, but if drunk, the debates may have become loud, ill-tempered and dangerous. Some of the men may have been wary to divulge their intentions to their commodore, the notoriously unpredictable Blackbeard. But he was holding his own private parlays and was making his own plans—plans that included none of the estimated 700 men of the company, but only 25 or so of his closest friends.

Unfortunately for some of Blackbeard's men, they continued to commit acts of piracy after the king's 5th of January time limit. One of those acts of piracy involved the burning and sinking of the 400-ton merchant ship, *Protestant Caesar* of Boston. The flotilla of pirate vessels had fanned-out in the Gulf of Honduras to cast a wide net for prizes, so Stede Bonnet and his *Revenge* were apart from the rest when he encountered the *Protestant Caesar* near the island of Roatán. Out-classed and out-gunned, the bungling Bonnet attempted to wage a running gun battle with the captain of the *Protestant Caesar* and failed. He returned to his bearded commodore with his tail between his legs. Two weeks later, determined not to allow the world to learn that his pirates had been bettered by a New England ship, Blackbeard tracked down and cornered the *Protestant Caesar* near the coast of Honduras. When the crew of the merchant ship saw "Death's Heads" and blood-red flags fluttering from the back stays of five vessels manned by pirates, including the cannon-studded *Queen Anne's Revenge*, they politely informed their captain, William Wyer, that they would not defend his ship. They then hastily escaped into the nearby jungle. Soon after, Blackbeard's quartermaster, William Howard, led a boarding party onto Wyer's ship and spent the next three days clearing her out of anything valuable. In a remarkable contradiction to the brutal and merciless image of Blackbeard portrayed by centuries of historical fiction, the pirate captain sent a message to Wyer who was hiding in the forest, telling him that he would be treated civilly if he would come aboard the *Queen Anne's Revenge* and talk. Blackbeard wanted to thank Wyer for not putting up a fight, for it would not have gone well for the Boston captain. Blackbeard also informed Wyer that he had no choice but to burn his ship as they would all ships of Boston for the execution of Bellamy's men. Wyer and his men were allowed to board one of Blackbeard's previously captured vessels, and they were sent on their way unharmed.

By mid April, 1718, the enormous burden of managing and feeding 700 pirates and supplying the vast quantity of alcohol consumed by them on a daily basis was becoming as oppressively heavy as the humidity of

the tropics. Blackbeard and his officers decided to head north and to find a way to shed themselves of their unwieldy forces. They set a course for Nassau harbor. On the way, they carried on some petty piracies, including taking freshly-caught turtle meat from some poor fishermen near the Cayman Islands. After rounding Cuba, they next took a rakish, 65-foot Spanish sloop, which they found sailing without a cargo. The unnamed sloop was turned into a tender—a consort vessel used to carry supplies. Believed to be Bermudian-built, she was nimble, tight and fair.

Blackbeard's fleet put in at Nassau for a few weeks and there, it is believed, as many as 300 of his pirates disembarked, presumably to seek the king's pardon from Gov. Woodes Rogers, who was expected to arrive during the summer and re-establish Royal rule over the lawless Bahamian archipelago. Benjamin Hornigold and 200 pirates residing at Nassau had already surrendered in February to Capt. Vincent Pearse of the king's frigate, *Phoenix*. Blackbeard, too, had decided to surrender himself to the king's representatives, but he had a different official in mind. In fact, it was so important for him to turn himself in to the governor of North Carolina, that he literally bypassed four other governors to get to him.

After a few weeks in Nassau, Blackbeard's slimmed-down retinue of pirates set sail again—now 400 men aboard *Queen Anne's Revenge*, Bonnet's *Revenge*, a sloop with the ever-popular name *Adventure* belonging to a forced man, David Herriot, and the smaller unnamed Spanish sloop. They first crossed the Florida Straits to the Spanish wrecks for another stab at beach-combing and free-diving for treasure. Presumably, they came up empty-handed. From there, they weighed anchor and rode the Gulf Stream up the coast to Charleston—Blackbeard's next conquest.

Blackbeard's arrival at the entrance of Charleston's harbor on June 4, 1718, may be one of the most puzzling chapters of his history. For four days, the pirates blockaded the port, intercepted and plundered as many as nine vessels offshore, held prominent South Carolina residents captive, and, ostensibly, had the city at its knees. Blackbeard's options were open: he could have remained offshore indefinitely, wrecking the colony's economy, starving its citizens and forcing the city's officials to hand over a king's ransom. All he demanded was a chest of medicine worth £400. However, contrary to suggestions in some recently published biographies, Blackbeard probably would not have entered the harbor and sacked the town. According to 19th century historian Edward McCrady, "it is altogether improbable that Thatch would have ventured his 40 guns against 100 which lined the fortifications of the town, and risked his vessels in the harbor where [the governor] would have had him under such disadvantage."

Next, Blackbeard's scheme was put into motion. Two days after leaving the Charleston bar, on June 10, 1718, the *Queen Anne's Revenge* unexpectedly wrecked at the entrance of Old Topsail Inlet in North Carolina. Before the majority of his pirates recognized what was happening—especially the dim-witted Bonnet—Blackbeard and about 25 of his most-trusted companions fled the scene with the company's communal chests of plunder. Some of the pirates had gone with Bonnet to surrender to the colony's governor, Charles Eden, only to discover upon their return to the inlet that they had been betrayed. Before he left, Blackbeard marooned 16 men on a nearby sandbank. Many of the hundreds of men remaining dispersed into the mainland and left the life of piracy for good.

It was a brilliant strategy. Blackbeard surrendered to Gov. Eden and appeared to return to an honest life with enough money to not have to work, at least for awhile. He came to North Carolina as if it was his home and all seemed well. But in a stunning reversal of fortunes, everything suddenly went wrong. Within six months, Blackbeard was dead.

Two years after becoming a pirate, Edward Thatch, alias Blackbeard, commanded one of the most powerful pirate fleets in history—an equal to the king's warships stationed in the colonies. Throughout his journey aboard the *Queen Anne's Revenge*, Blackbeard's pirates captured prizes, accumulated riches, supplemented their combat matériels, and added shipmates with valuable skills, including French cooks, musicians, and coopers, such as Edward Salter, who was forced from the sloop, *Margaret*, near Puerto Rico. But as quickly as Blackbeard rose in stature on the world stage of infamy, his career collapsed.

What happened during Blackbeard's last days that precipitated his demise? That is what this story is about.

An ancient live oak at Ocracoke Island's Springer's Point.

Five — Near the Old Watering Hole

THE BEST WAY TO ENVISION A HISTORICAL EVENT IS TO VISIT THE PLACE WHERE IT HAPPENED. FOR THAT reason, I went to the place where Blackbeard was killed, to try to better understand what took place there. I needed to know why the seasoned pirate captain was cornered in a place he seemed to know well.

As I sat on a small bench at Ocracoke Island's Springer's Point, about a dozen common grackles suddenly appeared from nowhere. The crow-like birds clamored about the gnarled limbs in the canopy of live oaks and interrupted my thoughts with their piercing, persistent chucks and chatter. One, in particular, seemed to be the leader. It was bolder and more vocal than the others, its iridescent black head twitching as it glared at me with its penetrating yellow eyes. Had I invaded their hideaway, I wondered?

I looked at the old well before me and concentrated, hoping to resume my effort to mentally travel in time back some few hundred years.

Springer's Point is an extraordinary place, not for its haunting beauty and rare ecosystem, not for its fragrant red cedars and hydra-like live oaks, nor because it was rescued from development in recent years by the North Carolina Coastal Land Trust. No, Springer's Point is most remarkable for its historical significance, a historical significance that is under-appreciated and often overlooked. There have been very few places like it along the entire east coast of America. And it is because of its well.

It is really not a well per se, not a true artesian well, but more correctly a fresh-water seep, known in the old days as a watering hole or watering place. These days it is lined with bricks of an undetermined age and capped with modern pressure-treated lumber held in place by a single galvanized rod. I saw the well for the first time about 30 years ago before it was covered, when Springer's Point was a much wilder place. Then, poison ivy and greenbriers guarded the well's stagnant, oily water. I didn't think much of it then. Neither can visitors today think much about it for there is no interpretive signage to indicate what it is or why it is there. I have heard that state archeologists came a while back and examined the well and surmised that it dates to at least the middle of the 19th century.

Maybe the bricks date to the mid-19th century, but I know the well is much older than that. Even when it was featured on a map published in London before the middle of the 18th century, it was considered an old well. Indeed, the well's significance is proven by the fact that it was, conspicuously, the only well identified by Surveyor-General Edward Moseley on his *New and Correct Map of the Province of North Carolina* in 1733. The well was most likely there before Walter Raleigh's first expedition arrived in 1584, before Verrazano's voyage in 1524. Who knows how many years, how many centuries the old watering hole has been around?

Sitting at the well I tried to imagine the various humans who have come there over the ages for its life-sustaining fresh water, dipping their containers made of shell, wood, pottery, pewter or silver. I wondered who they were and what they wore. I could picture native-Indian hunters and fishermen, Spanish and French explorers, Elizabethan colonists, shipwrecked castaways, all drawn to the watering hole.

My concentration was once more interrupted. In the distance I could hear the voices of men approaching from the nearby beach, apparently being drawn to the old watering hole themselves. Their words were muted but strident. Clearly they were discussing an issue of great consequence. I listened intently to determine who they were. I imagined they were pirates.

It was late on a Friday afternoon, the 21st of November, 1718, and the two men had been sent ashore to collect clams and oysters to supplement the meats of goat, beef, goose and duck for a supper the captain was intending to host that night in gratitude to his new friends. A farewell feast of sorts.

Along the wide, sandy bay, tattered and patched sailcloth, temporarily erected as canvas tents, fluttered limply in a light breeze. Everywhere one could see were empty bottles, broken ceramic jugs, piles of various animal bones, wide circles of ash from cook-fires and other flotsam,

The old watering place on Ocracoke Island. A well was marked in this location on a 1733 map of colonial North Carolina. As a source of fresh water, it attracted native-Americans, Spanish, French and English explorers, and pirates.

eleven casks of cocoa, a barrel of indigo, and a bale of cotton. Much of the cargo was labeled in French.

The wind was down and there was a chill in the air. No one else was on shore—the dying sea breeze, a southeasterly wind, allowed the infernal mosquitoes and flies to take flight, driving the company back on board their sloop. There were no taverns ashore, no women, no musicians, no parties, no soft pallets on which to sleep—a paucity of pirate pleasures. "Occocock," as it was known then, was a long way from Nassau, in more ways than one.

It was late, very late in the season to be so far north—"35 North" in the parlance of sailors. They were unaccustomed to the abbreviated length of the days. Weeks earlier the weather had turned and now periodic nor'easters had begun to blow, bringing cold winds and close, squally rains, one after the other. Winter at sea was for navy and merchant swabs, not for gentlemen of fortune like themselves. It was much too late to be there.

The approach of winter was the topic of conversation as the two pirates entered the forest along a narrow, sandy trail on their way to the watering hole. It was the topic of conversation anytime two or more of the pirate crew were out of earshot of the captain. "What are we still doing here?" they might have asked each other. Their money was nearly gone, provisions and rum were running low and their vessel was badly in need of careening and repairs. They had no suitable winter clothing. It had become quite a bone of contention. But no one was willing to press the captain on the issue. He had been exceedingly irritable for some time, but especially so since the two-masted French Martiniqueman had been brought in from Bermuda three months earlier. Some were so bold as to whisper that the captain was no longer in his right mind. He had become sullen, reckless and erratic.

The 19 or so pirates, thirteen whites and six blacks, were all that were left of their 400-head, six-ship, 60-gun pirate flotilla that just six months earlier had rivaled the strength of any buccaneer fleet in history. Even after the great separation at Old Topsail Inlet, the betrayals continued. Three crew members, accused of disloyalty by the captain, had just been left behind at Bath Town. Maybe after too much drink, some of the men might have derisively referred to their captain as "commodore," a rank saved for commanders of a fleet, and it would certainly have raised his ire. Still, the loyalty of the 20 who remained on board their single sloop was beyond measure, the last true friends of a once gallant, gregarious, hard-partying, convivial captain whose best days were behind him.

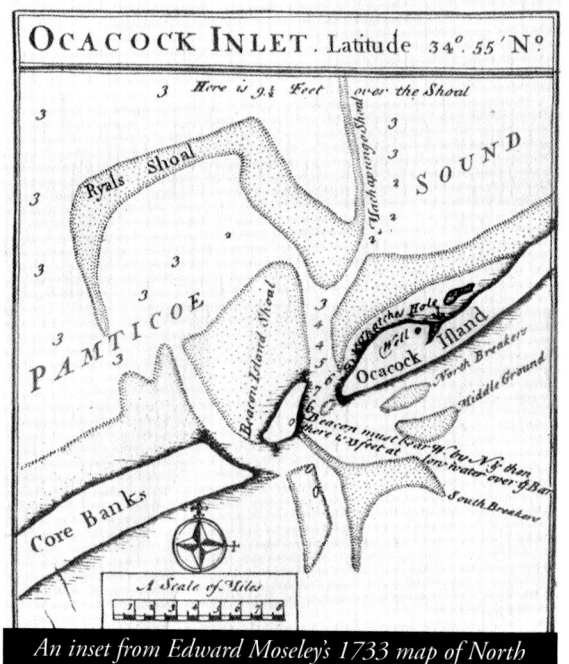

An inset from Edward Moseley's 1733 map of North Carolina shows a well on Ocracoke Island.

Their captain was Edward Thatch, remembered by history as Teach, who not long before had become notorious among the colonial governors and newspaper writers of his day by his double entendre-alias of Blackbeard—"Blackbeard the pyrat." The invention of his alias had been conceived as an ironic, trifling amusement—and a tip of the hat to his dead friend, Black Sam Bellamy—but to his, and the company's amazement, it caught on and spread like the plague. It was only a few weeks earlier that Capt. Vane had informed him that everyone in Nassau was now calling him

Blackbeard. They knew him as such in Virginia and up in Boston, too. The notoriety was no longer welcome.

He would have been the first to admit he was irritable, tired, and unhealthy. He had lost his confidence. He was ambivalent about his future. And the message he had just received from Bath Town did not make his plans any clearer. "Make the best of your way up as soon as possible your affairs will let you," said the message. Impossible, he must have thought, they had just been there, not much more than a fortnight before. He could not wait any longer or the Adventure's company would likely be forced to spend the winter in Carolina, a prospect none of them cared for. His men were intent on sailing to St. Thomas, eager to get back into the game. Besides, he had bid his farewells to the Governor, to his friends, to Knight. He did not care to repeat his emotional goodbye to his sister, Susannah, and her son—his namesake and nephew, Edward. He had resolved in his heart he would never see them again. He was not going back.

Nevertheless, the captain trusted Tobias Knight, the author of the letter, his friend and advisor and secretary of the colony. Knight had been like an uncle to him, gave him encouragement, legal counsel, a safe harbor, bought his goods, introduced him to the colony's society (for what there was to speak of), helped him sort out the problem with the French ship. But how long did Knight expect him to wait for the news from London? Why should he expect the untrustworthy English and their German-speaking, schnitzel-eating, Hanoverian King to do what was rumored they would do? His crew was anxious to go south, whether their ship was leaky and undermanned or not, whether England declared war on Spain or not, whether they had His Majesty's mercy or not.

Thatch was not so sure. He knew no vessels had entered the inlet since they had been at their mooring for the past week. But had word come to Knight by way of the Virginia road? It could have meant the difference between life and death.

Night was falling fast as a late autumn high pressure system and clearing skies promised a cold, star-filled sky. Wisps of gossamer clouds began to pick up a blush of pink and gold as the sun crept down over the western Pamlico Sound. The placid conditions meant the air was crowded with the noisy comings and goings of geese, brants, ducks, coots, gulls, great egrets, white ibis and brown pelicans. Such placid weather was sure not to last long and the birds knew enough to be moving further south.

"Sail ho," shouted a crew member. "Two sail, comin' from the Royal Shoal," called another, as the masts of a pair of trading sloops rose over the northwest horizon and approached the swash at the soundside entrance of Ship Channel. Some men ran to the rail to see.

"Strange ones, they are. I know not who they would be," said the captain, stepping out of the cabin and peering through the ship's spy glass. "We had just come that way ourselves, so they may be Chowan or Currituck traders from up Albemarle way. Twenty or thirty tonners at most. One looks larger than the other but they do not look familiar." The sloops appeared to round-up before the dying breeze and drop anchor abeam of the new tower on Beacon Island. He may have considered sending a boat over to determine who the sloops were, but chose not to. "No need to pay them mind in any case. We have nothing to fear of Carolina men," Blackbeard might have said to assuage his shipmates. Even if the visitors did mean him harm—had it been their former pirate friends Robert Tucker or Dick Richards seeking their revenge or that insolent planter, Bell—he thought, they could hardly do no worse to him than the double broadsides dealt to him by fate. He already felt cornered by life and defeated. Taking a mouthful of wine, he returned to his guests at his table.

If Capt. Thatch had experienced any premonition of danger, he would have kept his feelings from his shipmates. He would not, however, have been mistaken. He, and most of his men, had fewer than 24 hours to live.

Kevin Duffus photo.

The entrance to the National Archives of Great Britain at Kew, England.

Six—
Ragged Remnants of History

The National Archives of Great Britain holds more than 1,000 years of recorded history. Deep inside its climate-controlled stacks, and in its vaults, is stored some of modern civilization's most important writing preserved on original parchments, paper scrolls, documents, charters, laws, letters, royal declarations and decrees. Records in the collection include William the Conqueror's Domesday Book, the Magna Carta, the treaty ending the Hundred Years War, and Shakespeare's last will and testament. The sheer amount of information, knowledge and human experience contained within its walls is staggering to comprehend. More thought-provoking, however, may be the untold sums of lost facts, unknown truths, and hidden secrets, that remain buried within its collections—the untidy, ragged remnants and loose ends of history.

Formerly called the Public Records Office, the archives moved out of London to a modern facility at Kew Gardens on the river Thames, about a half-hour subway ride west of the city. The archives complex lacks the mausoleum-like monolith of the U.S. National Archives on Pennsylvania Avenue or the ornate Italian Renaissance design of the Library of Congress in Washington, D.C. But what it lacks in traditional ambiance, it makes up for in its design, efficiency, ease of use, cheerful and helpful staff, and well-equipped reading rooms with expansive windows—all things appreciated by harried, out-of-town researchers searching for their proverbial needle in a haystack.

I was assigned a place near the windows, a contemporary-style piece of furniture accommodating four researchers seated around a central column providing electrical outlets, light switches and other buttons I didn't have time to play with. The large room was busy with researchers and staff coming and going, patrons noisily tapping away on laptops and taking photographs of documents with digital cameras, their loud, artificial shutter sounds clicking unnecessarily. From across the room, I heard the grinding of an electric pencil sharpener. People were conversing in normal levels. In other words, it wasn't necessarily quiet, but neither are libraries these days.

After a surprisingly brief half-hour of waiting, the records I had requested were ready, stored neatly in a locker behind a clear-paned door. I approached the locker trying to appear nonchalant, but behind my facade, I was filled with breathless anticipation for the documents I was about to read. Reverently, I carried my containers of documents across the room, weaving among dozens of desks occupied by other researchers engrossed in their own mysteries. Back at my table and following a familiar procedure, I gently removed the documents from their boxes, unfastened the cloth bindings and began my descent into the mist and mysteries of the past.

Before me was a very old letter-book, its bindings broken, corners worn and peeling, and within its hard cover, dozens of pages of thick, brittle paper, their edges torn and darkened with the patina of age, and the whole collection warped and rippled as if the letters had been exposed to damp, salt air. They had. The letter-book contained the correspondence of the captains of His Majesty's Royal Navy who had served on board guard ships in the American colonies and the Caribbean during the second decade of the eighteenth century. Among them were the letters of Capt. Ellis Brand, captain of the sixth-rate, 24-gun frigate, HMS *Lyme*, which was stationed near the entrance to the Chesapeake Bay, Virginia. Brand is best remembered for having been appointed commander of an expedition to search for, capture and arrest, or destroy, the pirate Edward Thatch, aka Blackbeard. I began reading the 288-year-old script, which was written in Brand's own hand on a cold, blustery day in February, 1719.

"Sirs: This serves to acquaint you for their Lordship's information of my proceedings here, the notorious Pyrate Thach alias Blackbeard that I advised you of being lost in No. Carolina in June last has continued in that place with one sloop and about twenty men."

What follows is Brand's detailed and professional briefing of the expedition to apprehend Blackbeard. Reading Brand's handwriting requires patience—some words seem illegible, capitalization appears random, and punctuation is mostly nonexistent. But the story begins to flow, a story that is very familiar to me as I have read the sequence of events in numerous books over the years. I know the details almost by rote.

Blackbeard makes North Carolina his base of operations after wrecking his *Queen Anne's Revenge* at Old Topsail Inlet (Beaufort Inlet today), and despite accepting the King's Act of Grace from Gov. Charles Eden, he continues his piratical activities, bringing into the colony a ship loaded with sugar he claims to have found abandoned at sea. Some planters and merchants complain to Virginia's Lt. Gov. Alexander Spotswood of being abused or threatened by Blackbeard and his crew and report that North Carolina authorities are either cooperating with the pirates or are unable to control them. Spotswood decides to prevent the pirates' depredations from expanding northward into his colony and mounts a privately funded force to interdict Blackbeard and his crew. On November 17, 1718, in a classic pincer-like military strategy, the expedition is divided between a land force of up to 200 men led by Brand mounted on horseback, and two lightly armed sloops commanded by Lt. Robert Maynard. Brand's group travels by road and ferry directly to Bath Town, capital of the colony and a place believed to be frequented by the pirates. Maynard's force sets out by sea for Ocracoke Inlet, guided by two North Carolina pilots familiar with the intricacies of navigating in their home waters. As the traditional story is told, when Maynard arrives at Ocracoke Inlet on the 21st, he spies the masthead of Blackbeard's sloop *Adventure* beyond the sand dunes on the other side of the narrow island. Maynard's two sloops anchor offshore, choosing to delay their attack until the next morning, since it was late in the day and darkness was quickly coming.

As I am reading Brand's letter, a few old, persistent questions arise in my mind. Why, I have always wondered, have history books consistently said that it took Maynard five days to sail from Virginia to Ocracoke Inlet? The distance was, at most, a two day's sail. And why would he elect to anchor his small sloops in the ocean outside the bar of the inlet, a potentially dangerous place for vessels to ride? Further, a vessel anchored a safe distance off the island would be unlikely to be able to see the masts of two sloops anchored where Blackbeard is believed to have moored. The traditional story makes little sense.

Maybe you should know that I have been a sailor myself for nearly 40 years and have sailed the Atlantic waters off North Carolina's Outer Banks and throughout the tidewater region and tributaries of the Pamlico Sound—in Blackbeard's wake, you might say. In fact, for many years I docked my boat at Bath, not far from Blackbeard's favorite landing, and made the trip between Bath and Ocracoke more times than I can remember in weather fair and foul. Had I been Lt. Maynard, I would not have spent an uncomfortable night in the ocean just off Ocracoke's beach. I would have sought a safer, more placid and less exposed anchorage inside of the inlet. There were plenty of places to anchor without having to crowd the pirate and his friends.

Capt. Ellis Brand's letterbook at Britain's National Archives

Which is, in fact, exactly what Maynard did. History has been in error. Maynard dropped anchor on the soundside of the inlet. And what's more, he didn't even directly arrive there by way of the ocean.

I could hardly believe what I was reading. In Capt. Brand's credible and authoritative letter, there was a paragraph which seems to have escaped researchers for all of these years. As I read, the implications of the information became apparent, and I immediately had a sense of what really happened, why it took Maynard so long to get to Ocracoke, and, most importantly, why Blackbeard and his crew had no reason to suspect Maynard's two sloops were a threat.

Contrary to established history, Brand reported to his superiors that Maynard's sloops passed behind the Outer Banks through Roanoke Inlet on Thursday, the 20th of November, and they probably did so early in the day. Roanoke Inlet, now extinct, was located abreast of Roanoke Island, about 75 miles north of Ocracoke Inlet, and was at the time, a shallow, but navigable inlet for shoal draft

Ragged Remnants of History

vessels departing from, or sailing to, the settlements along the shores of Albemarle and Currituck Sounds. The inlet was especially useful for vessels heading to, or coming from, the north.

Upon entering Roanoke Inlet, Brand wrote, "They spoke with a vessel that acquainted them they had seen Thach's sloop the Monday before on Brant Island Shoals aground and a sloop with him helping him off."

Suddenly, all of the annoying, ambient noises of the reading room of the archives fell silent as I sat in my chair, stunned, incredulous—and amused. I had been there.

A memory floated to the surface.

It was 1985 and I had entered my sailboat in an overnight race from Oriental, North Carolina, on the Neuse River, to Bath, on the Pamlico River. We executed a perfect spinnaker start only to watch in horror as the colorful sail blew itself to shreds. We fell far behind the fleet trying to sort out the mess and raise a replacement sail just before the wind died. Some hours later, around 2 in the morning, we were tacking northward through the blackness and the heart of Pamlico Sound, a vast body of water, but which is no deeper than 25 feet at any point. I went below to plot our location (I was both captain and navigator—not a good combination when you are racing). And at the instant I determined we were headed for shallow water, the boat bumped, and then lurched forward in that peculiar, sickening way when a vessel runs aground on soft sand. We were stuck on Brant Island Shoals. I know the place well. I know what running aground there feels like.

Edward Thatch must not have been happy. "One of the greatest marooning freebooters" had marooned himself. It must have been an inauspicious start for the "lord of the Outer Banks," the notorious captain of a pirate ship setting sail for St. Thomas, shorthanded though he was. But then again, what was Blackbeard doing anywhere near Brant Island Shoals?

As we will see in a later chapter, Blackbeard probably left Bath Town both in haste and anger around the first of November, 1718. He left in haste because there were rumors of a potential new Indian threat emerging beyond the town proper and bitter memories of the deadly and devastating Tuscarora War of 1711-1715 were fresh on everyone's mind. He left in anger because there had been a dispute between Thatch and some of his men, including his one-time lieutenant, Israel Hands, who was wounded in the knee as a result. Later, in a closer examination of the letter from his friend, Tobias Knight, found in Thatch's possession after his death, we'll see that the pirate captain abandoned three members of his crew at Bath upon his departure. It was Capt. Charles Johnson who originated the story that Blackbeard had shot Hands beneath his mess table during an evening of drinking, simply to remind his crew who the captain really was. A more detailed look will reveal the faulty basis of Johnson's account.

Records fail to tell us how Blackbeard and his crew of the *Adventure* spent their time between the 1st of November and the 17th, the day he was reported to be stuck on Brant Island Shoals. The course for sailing from his moorings at the entrance to Bath Creek (called Town Creek in 1718) to Ocracoke is practically a straight shot—131 degrees, east-southeast. The distance is about 47 miles. Depending on the prevailing wind at the time, it could be a very fast trip, 10 hours or so with the wind out of the north, west or southwest; or it could take two days or more with a headwind out of the southeast. Of course, with little or no wind, or early winter squalls, it could take even longer to sail to Ocracoke Inlet. According to the log of HMS *Pearl*, a 40-gun, fifth-rate Royal Navy warship stationed at Lynhaven Bay on the south shore of the Chesapeake, the conditions there on the 4th of November were "fresh gales, close & squally weather." Regardless, the pirates were experienced, skilled sailors, who would not be deterred by poor weather. They must have taken a detour to account for the 17-day transit to Brant Island Shoals.

These days, the water of the Pamlico River is tinted a coffee-brown with sediment runoff from rampant development and millions of acres of tilled farmland upstream, but in Blackbeard's day the estuary was generally clear and colored slate-green. Ten miles southeast of Bath Creek, the river widens dramatically to a distance of five miles, plenty of room in which to tack a sloop like the 65-foot *Adventure* into a brisk headwind. Sailing along the north shore, he may have encountered a heavy chop at the confluence with the southward flowing Pungo River, but in bad weather the Pamlico could be uncomfortably rough most anywhere with its legendary short, blunt-shaped waves.

As the *Adventure* approached the mouth of the river, the shoreline on both sides began to vanish, although tall stands of old growth pines, cypress and juniper towered in the distance like great ethereal cathedrals. Lying low on the horizon were numerous green marshy islands, covered in white blankets of thousands of waterfowl. Then, the sloop entered the broad expanse and emptiness of the sound.

Brant Island Shoals is roughly 7 miles south of the rhumb line on the course from Bath to Ocracoke. The island itself has now been long submerged, but was marked on maps in the early 1700s, near the mainland; the shoals extend southeastward from the island's location to nearly the mid-point of the sound. Today, depths along the shoals vary to as little as two to three feet. In Blackbeard's time, the water would have been shallower.

Potential reasons for the *Adventure* grounding on Brant Island Shoals are interesting to consider, but, regrettably, none can be proven. Certainly, weather could have been a factor, forcing the sloop south of its intended course. Or, the pirate crew may have spotted a sail on the southern horizon, inducing them to head in that direction—pirates were known to sail out of their way for the prospect of supplementing their supply of rum and wine. For that matter, going off course and running aground may actually have been alcohol induced.

Another plausible reason is that the *Adventure* had been sailing out of the Neuse River on November 17. Brant Island Shoals stretches perpendicularly across the axis of the lower Neuse River, and is a navigational hazard that must be avoided for vessels sailing for Ocracoke Inlet, even today. Why would Blackbeard be on the Neuse River? Legend has it that he buried a chest of treasure beneath an oak tree near the present day town of Oriental, although it is possible he had other business in the area. If the pirate sloop ventured up the Neuse River after departing Bath Town around the first of November, it could explain the two-week gap before its grounding on the shoals. But it raises the question, what business would he have had in the area?

Had the *Adventure* sailed directly from Bath to Ocracoke, it is difficult to imagine the crew encountered Brant Island Shoals by accident. Blackbeard and his crew had made the same trip on many occasions and they knew the route well. Nevertheless, whatever the cause, and for other behaviors Thatch had exhibited that we will consider later, the mishap may have been symbolic of a pirate captain who was not sure where he wanted to go.

Roanoke Inlet, Thursday, the 20th of November, 1718. Lt. Robert Maynard had no reason to suspect his quarry would still be stuck on a sandbar after three days, especially since the small fishing boat he interrogated reported that they had seen another sloop helping the pirate off his temporary lodgings. Maynard could have chosen to split up his two-sloop flotilla, sending Midshipman Edmund Hyde in the smaller vessel, Ranger, back into the ocean and around Diamond Shoals to Ocracoke Inlet, in case Blackbeard had the mind to slip out to sea, while Maynard himself investigated the shoals off Brant Island.

Neither of His Majesty's small, hired trading vessels—Maynard's Jane and Hyde's Ranger—had cannon aboard. It was thought the additional weight would make them less maneuverable in Carolina's shallow sounds. Separated, their crews would stand no chance against the pirate's broadsides. Maynard was a cautious officer, intelligent and professional. He was intent on succeeding in the mission for which he was assigned—he cared not to be a lieutenant forever. He would lead both vessels to the last place Blackbeard was known to be. Yet, as smart as Maynard was, he couldn't have realized the brilliance of his strategy.

Around the north end of Roanoke Island they sailed, past the ruins of Fort Raleigh and the forgotten site of Walter Raleigh's lost colony, then south into Croatan Sound and finally, the northern waters of Pamlico Sound. It would be another day before they knew whether or not the pirate was still lurking about. On the calmer waters of the Pamlico, the men would have had a chance to check their powder, sharpen their swords and practice their fighting skills, which they must have done with utmost gravity.

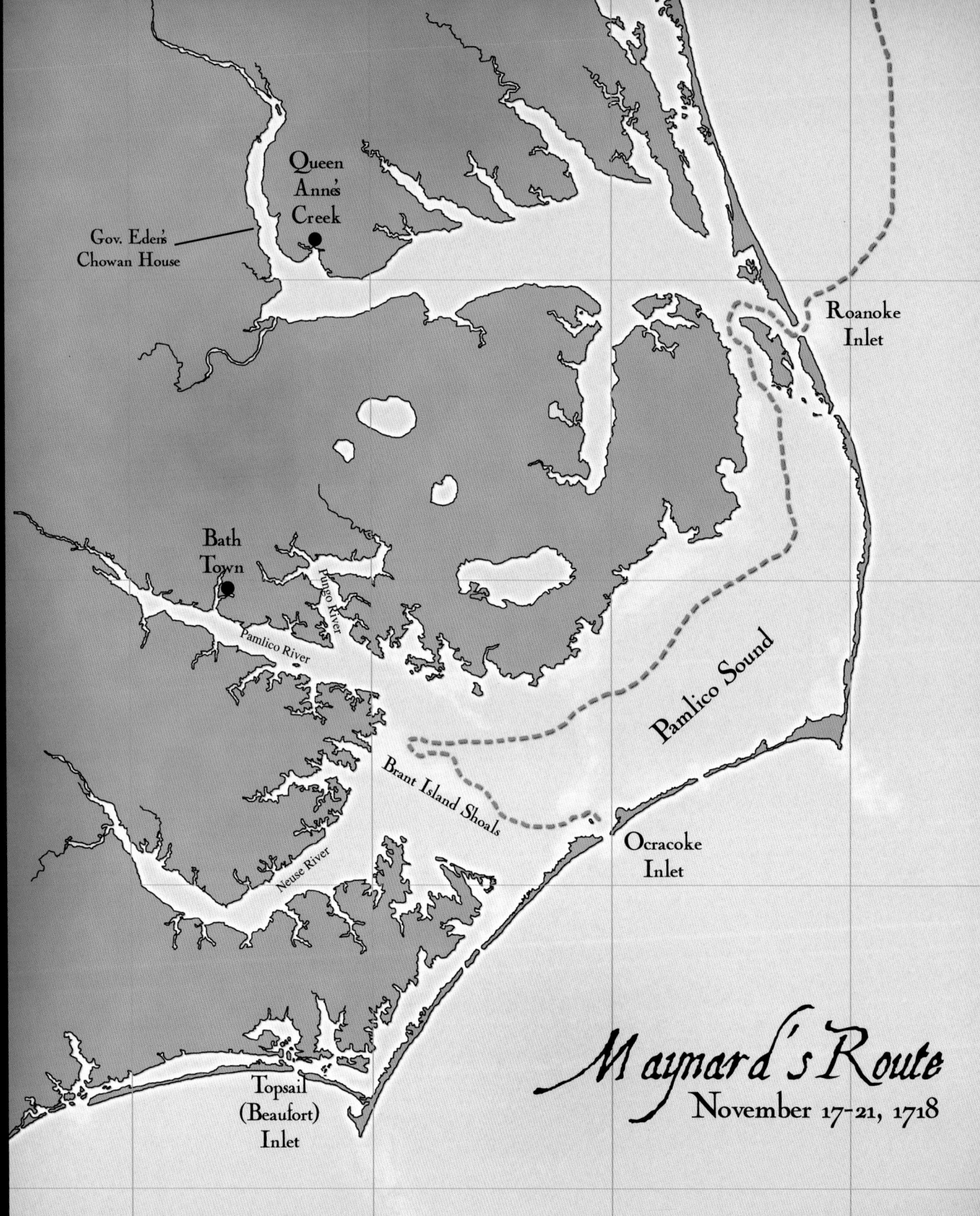

On Friday, the 21st of November, guided by their local pilots, Maynard's sloops cruised the length of Brant Island Shoals from the mainland to the middle of the sound, being careful not to run aground themselves. The pirate and his rescuers were nowhere to be seen. Maynard then commanded his helmsmen to steer a course for the entrance to Ocracoke Inlet, which required them to round the west side of the bulging mass of Royal Shoal. By following the crude but effective navigational markers recently established by the colony, they then had to sail the serpentine channel to the swash, the shallow demarcation at the opening of Ship Channel, the main route to the sea.

By late afternoon, Maynard's civilian-rigged sloops innocuously crept through Ship Channel to an anchorage on the east side of Beacon Island. At the time, there may have been construction underway of two wooden towers on the island which was later named for the towers' purpose. The unlighted beacons or range markers—the rear and larger of the two as much as 90-feet-tall—had been planned since 1715, when Ocracoke Inlet was designated the principal port of entry to the fledgling colony. The two beacons were to guide merchant mariners through the inlet and to let them know that North Carolina was open for business.

Maynard next gathered some intelligence. Either local pilots or subsistence fishermen living in the area, told Maynard what he needed to know. The two sloops visible to the east across the shallow tidal flats known as "Middle Ground," anchored near the prominent mound of trees and a small creek, were the vessels Maynard was looking for. The pirate often anchored there, near the old watering place.

With the wind down, sounds carried well over the water. Amidst the honking flights of waterfowl and the slapping of water against the hull of their sloops, Maynard's crew may have heard the muted sounds of voices, laughter and maybe even a musical instrument—a recorder. There seemed to be a bit of merriment going on over at the pirate's sloop.

Peering through his spy-glass, Maynard may have seen the glint of the setting sun's reflection off of a similar glass from the pirate sloop, someone spying on him in return. Knowing he was being watched, Maynard then wisely ordered most of his men to remain below decks until nightfall to maintain the appearance of two sparsely-manned merchant vessels. With any luck at all, the pirate would not perceive them to be a threat.

Mapping Ocracoke Inlet

The inlets of North Carolina's Outer Banks are considered to be among the most dynamic geologic features of the continent. As historian David Stick once wrote, "They are about as restless and unpredictable as bodies of water can ever be, for they are subjected to constant turbulence as the fresh inland waters and the salt sea waters collide, so that the inlets themselves are forever changing shape, size, depth, sometimes opening wider, at other times shoaling up and closing altogether." Stick has accounted for the appearance or disappearance of more than two dozen inlets between Cape Lookout and the Virginia border over five centuries of recorded history. The only inlet which has remained in place during the entire period, and therefore the most stable, is Ocracoke Inlet.

Through innumerable hurricanes, winter storms, floods, and tides, the masses of sand that form the inlet on both ocean and sound has been scoured, filled, shaped and reshaped on practically a daily basis. Through it all, historically speaking, the inlet has always been there, and so has its ageless sandbars, oyster-rock islets, tidal marshes, creeks, sloughs, hammocks and maritime woodlands. What has changed is the path by which billions of gallons of water transit the inlet each day. Since the early 1700s, there have been three different primary, navigable channels connecting ocean and sound and serving maritime trade: Ship Channel, Wallace Channel and Teaches Hole Channel. In Blackbeard's time, Ship Channel was the only navigable route between Pamlico Sound and the ocean for all but the shallowest draft vessels.

No one can say for certain how Ocracoke Inlet was shaped in 1718. However, it is possible to construct a reasonably researched notion. By combining six different nautical charts, USGS maps, 19th century U.S. Coast Survey charts, and two, more-primitively drafted maps of 1795 and 1733, and using graphics editing software, each of the maps were scaled so that certain consistently appearing geographic features, including Beacon Island, Springer's Point, and the creek known as "Old Slough," aligned. The result is the accompanying map that helps us to visualize what happened during that historic clash between Lt. Robert Maynard and Edward Thatch, aka Blackbeard.

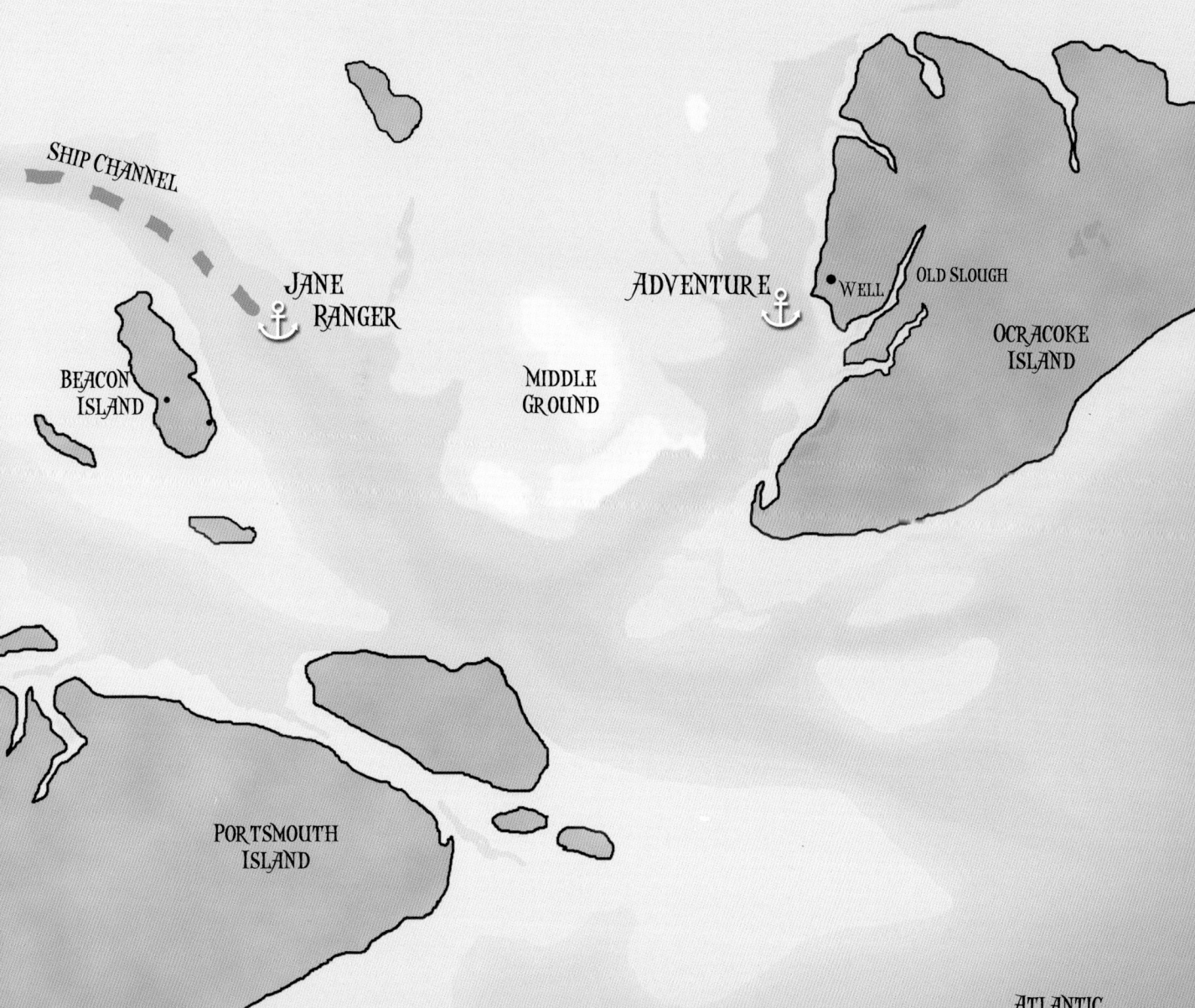

Seven—
Subtle Whispers of the Past

Teaches Hole Channel, Ocracoke Island, NC. Springer's Point is the wooded area above at the middle-right. The creek, "Old Slough" is directly below.

*H*ow do we seek history's forgotten truths when records are silent or never existed, relics and artifacts have vanished, memory has eroded like so many ancient places that wash into the sea?

In the case of the true identity of Edward Thatch alias Blackbeard, there is no cemetery to visit where we may press our ears to the portals of his tomb. Bronze bells, cannon or gold dust raised from the ocean's floor are of little help. There is no extant family Bible which contains his carefully detailed family relations; there are no census records, birth certificates, pension records, no DNA evidence. Is it possible for the man who terrified colonial America, and for a brief time became the obsession of the King's Privy Council, the Lords of Trade and Plantations, Royal and proprietary governors and Royal Navy captains, to have vanished without a trace from the face of the earth?

In his wake, the pirate left behind an unaccountably enormous legend, which has been transformed into someone who would not have been recognized by his friends and contemporaries. Blackbeard casts a long shadow over the centuries, but despite the shadow's shape we are still unable to peer through its blackness and see who he really was, or learn from where he came.

However, there may be a way.

Perhaps we can seek Edward Thatch's true identity by not looking directly at him but instead, by analyzing the seemingly unimportant details of his life, parsing his words and the records of his story, piecing together fragments of information about his relationships, behaviors, choices, travels and actions which have been deemed by historians to be accurate. We can pursue the authentic Edward Thatch by examining the events of his time that may have had an influence on his life. We can also turn to the people who surrounded him, his shipmates, and those who occupied the same place and time in history but who appear to not have had a connection to the pirate. Somewhere, hidden among seemingly unrelated records we may find a clue, a connection, a faint thread of evidence that will lead us in the right direction so we may discover who Blackbeard really was.

Our detective work will require us to entertain inferences, suppositions, and circumstantial evidence—uncertain waters that tend to make some historians and scholars queasy. However, it is not as if conjecture has not been a constant presence within the reams of books and papers written about pirates, and Blackbeard in particular. Historians have been willing to accept the singular statements presented by the mysterious Capt. Charles Johnson, like Edward Thatch's Bristol roots, without definitive sources and references. We know Johnson published numerous errors and missed some crucial facts such as Blackbeard's grounding on Brant Island Shoals, or Lt. Maynard's approach to Ocracoke from the west (and there will be many others we will reveal soon enough). So, why should we not employ powers of intuition and deduction, weigh circumstantial evidence, open our minds to the subtle whispers of the past?

We can start with something curious Blackbeard once said.

Near the Old Slough, Ocracoke. Saturday, the 22nd of November, 1718. The day dawned clear and cold with little wind. The high pressure system drifting eastward over the Outer Banks had provided a temporary reprieve from the increasing numbers of nor'easters but it was not going to last much longer. It would be a good day to begin the transfer of cargo from shore to the Adventure. *The French sugars and cocoa were needed to trade for food and rum if the right vessel came along, as they could not always just take what they pleased—not like before. They would begin preparations this day to sail for St. Thomas, and hopefully, a commission from the Danish governor there and a return to life as respectable privateers. The passage would be fraught with danger, however, were they to encounter His Majesty's Navy, Spaniards, or even some of their former pirate friends. Only six months before, Thatch's crew had sailed north from the Caribbean, powerful enough to stop any ship on the sea; now they would return, slinking like fearful puppies.*

Across the shallows of the Middle Ground, in the channel along Beacon Island, activity aboard the two recently arrived trading sloops indicated they were weighing anchor and putting to sea. Odd, though it seemed, that they were not waiting for more wind to send them on their way. And even more peculiar, they looked to be moving against the incoming tide. It was then that it was observed there were more men aboard the sloops than first believed, more than common traders typically carry. For the first time since the strangers arrived, Capt. Thatch and his crew became wary.

On board the sloop Jane, *Lt. Robert Maynard decided he could wait no longer for the wind to come up. If he tarried too long, the pirate could slip away. At 9 a.m., he ordered his men on both vessels to man the sweeps and begin rowing southward the mile and a half distance out of Ship Channel. "Uphill" they went, against the incoming tide, which tired the men when they most needed to conserve their strength.*

To the southeast, the sun was still low in the sky but it was to Maynard's advantage—he could clearly see the myriad patches of light-tan water that revealed shoal water. However, not taking any chances, the lieutenant called for boats to be launched to row ahead so his men could swing the lead and plumb the depths. This inlet, they were told, could be perilous to those without a local pilot, or without sufficient time to make their way cautiously. The channel's navigational markers, no more than de-limbed cedar saplings, were notoriously indifferent, and were sometimes known to be relocated by some local pilots under the cloak of darkness to discourage independent-minded captains from finding their own way and saving themselves a little money. But even the local pilots could run their master's vessels ashore as Lt. Maynard would soon find out. There were times when fair weather clouds under a high sun could be especially deceiving as their shadows made deep water appear where there was none.

For the time being, they were still headed toward the sea so no alarm had been raised by the pirate. But not for long.

At the bottom end of Ship Channel, at the junction of the inlet and channels to Portsmouth Island and Ocracoke Island, Maynard's little flotilla made a hard turn to port, making their way in the direction of the watering hole and the pirate lair. Now, however, the sun was off their starboard beam and the shoals were not so visible. Shimmering shafts of bright sunlight pierced the translucent emerald waters and vanished abruptly into the swirling sands below. The inlet seemed to boil with tiny wavelets as the incoming rush of tide met the outward flowing waters of the sound. The tide now increased the Jane's *and* Ranger's *speed and soon enough the engagement would commence.*

On the Adventure, *Blackbeard was not surprised when the strangers turned his way, but he still had no idea who they were. They had come from the sound. They did not appear to be His Majesty's biscuit eaters clad in blue coats. As a precaution, he ordered his crew to stand alert and prepare for a fight. But before matters became serious, Edward Thatch, notorious for scaring his victims into submission, must have decided to try a less aggressive approach and make friends with the rapidly approaching visitors. Maybe he hoped the sloops were delivering news of the new pardon from London.*

"Avast there, strangers," the pirate shouted through a speaking trumpet. "We are for King George! Hoist out your boat and come aboard so we may see who you are."

Pirates were liars if nothing else. Naturally, most criminally-inclined people during the 18th-century with a penchant to intimidate, steal, destroy, assault, and in some rare cases, brutally rape or murder, were easily capable of lying, too. Especially if their lives depended on it.

Blackbeard was not for King George. And whether or not Robert Maynard saw through the pirate's ruse was inconsequential. The lieutenant had not come there to discuss British politics. But Blackbeard's greeting may provide an important clue to his true identity.

George I became king of Great Britain and Ireland on August 1, 1714, succeeding Queen Anne who died without legitimate offspring to maintain the line of Scotland's Stuart monarchs. George I was a German of the House of Hanover but with ancestral connections to Stuart kings, James I and Charles I. His selection by the English Parliament had been preordained by the Act of Settlement in 1701, which had been passed to avert a succession crisis. George's accession to the throne created a crisis regardless and was not universally accepted. Anne's half-brother, Prince James Francis Edward Stuart, who was living in exile in France, was considered by many, including most Scots and King Louis XIV of France, to be the rightful heir to the throne. His supporters participated in the Jacobite Rebellion, an attempt to return the Stuarts to the throne. Opponents, however, questioned the legitimacy of Prince James's birth, claiming he had been substituted for a stillborn in the queen's bedchambers. Other intrigues had been afoot, including rumors of a "Popish plot" to assassinate Charles II and put his Catholic brother, the Duke of York (the father of Prince James), on the throne. Underlying the succession conflicts of the late-17th and early-18th centuries were the concerns and suspicions of Protestants and Anglican Church leaders of increasing Roman Catholic influence within the government of England, specifically as a result of theological differences among Christian churches over the sacrament of communion. Following numerous and complicated political maneuverings and compromises, including the 1707 Act of Union that united the kingdoms of England, Wales and Scotland, Great Britain found itself being ruled by a German who, it was said, could speak little or no English. Most pirates in 1718 were not fond of King George and were sympathetic to the Jacobite cause. A few were outright hostile to the king, including Blackbeard's close associate and fellow captain, Charles Vane, whose crew were heard to drink to the death and damnation of King George during at least one festive occasion.

Twelve months before Blackbeard was cornered at his Ocracoke moorings by Lt. Maynard, the pirate captain had captured the slave ship, *La Concorde*, north of the island of Barbados in the Windward Islands of the Caribbean. Once the French prize was manned by the pirate crew and secured inside the quiet confines of Admiralty Bay on the west side of Bequia Island and her crew and cargo of slaves landed on shore, Capt. Thatch began to consider names for what he planned to be his powerful, cannon studded flagship. From the tiniest dory to the largest ships on the seas, anyone who has ever acquired a previously christened vessel, by honest means or not, faces the dilemma of retaining the vessel's previous name or calling her something new. In the case of Blackbeard's slaver, *La Concorde*, he chose the latter—no French names for him. Besides, had she remained *La Concorde*, then people would know who her true owners were, although some pirates seemed not to care, like Blackbeard's friend, "Black" Sam Bellamy and his own captured slave galley, *Whydah*. Of course, mariners are famously superstitious and there is a common belief that renaming a vessel brings bad luck. In light of what troubles lay over the horizon for the lanky Blackbeard, superstition on his part would hardly have been unwarranted. Still, at the time, he must have thought it worth the risk.

At Bequia, Blackbeard next had to decide what to call his new prize, which is another process shared by masters of ships possessed both legitimately or piratically. Throughout the ages of maritime history, vessels have been named for countless reasons: for the owner, a mother, a wife, or a mistress; for a king or queen, a popular historical figure or a significant event; to declare a message of strength, an emotion or a philosophy; to trumpet national pride or to expound a political ideology. The records don't tell us how long Blackbeard deliberated on a name, or what the other choices were, but it seems as if he had planned his selection for some time.

At the pinnacle of his piratical career, Blackbeard chose to call his great ship, *Queen Anne's Revenge*. His choice says something about who he was, a choice for national pride and a political ideology. His choice suggests that, rather than having been an English "Bristol man born," Edward

Anne

Thatch may have really been a Scot.

The naming of *Queen Anne's Revenge* was not necessarily a timely declaration but more likely a broader political statement. When Blackbeard named his ultimate prize for the last of the Stuart monarchs, Queen Anne had been dead for more than three years. Even though she had been born in London, lived her early childhood years in France, married a prince of Denmark and was Queen of England and Ireland as well as Queen of Scotland, Anne represented to most Scots a symbol of their pride for the nearly 350-year-long rule of Scotland's royal House of Stuart.

Most pirate historians suggest that the 1713 Treaty of Utrecht, which ended the War of Spanish Succession, was the impetus that forced thousands of out-of-work mariners, including Blackbeard, into piracy. It has been estimated as many as 10,000 disgruntled sailors of the American and Caribbean colonies were crowding the docks of Boston, New York, Philadelphia, Charleston, and Port Royal, Jamaica, looking for work. However, what may have had a greater impact on their moral turpitude and ambivalent national loyalties were the political and religious machinations of the previous century.

By naming his flagship, *Queen Anne's Revenge*, Blackbeard was not simply tipping his tricorn cap to the death of Anne and the end of the Stuarts, but was signaling his intent to wage war on the commerce of the world in retribution for years of English contempt, incursions, interference and domination of his Highland homeland. For Edward Thatch, it was an attitude years in the making. We can be fairly certain he was not for King George.

To best divine Blackbeard's origins—his lost history, if you will—it would help if we could know the history he knew. We need to deduce what external influences and

events in his early life may have had a later bearing on what he did, or did not do, as a famous historical figure. Everyone's perspective about the world is formed at an early age, most often at their parents' side, listening, watching, learning. Young people in the days of old adopted the beliefs and attitudes of their parents and grandparents (unlike many youths today). They heard their elders speak, tell stories of the old ways, discuss the events of the day or of the recent past. What did young Ed Thatch hear?

"Customarily, very little can be learned of the childhood and youth of even the best-known pirates," wrote Robert E. Lee for the introductory chapter of his 1974 book on Blackbeard. "Pirates rarely wrote about themselves and their families. Each hoped to acquire a vast fortune and return to his former home without having tarnished his family name."

As a consequence, the official records say nothing about the early life of Blackbeard. It was, in fact, the intended result of his alias, and his famously extravagant beard for that matter, to disguise the tracks leading to his former life and family. So did Blackbeard succeed? Did he return home with a vast fortune? Did he protect his family name?

Since the records fail to provide the answers, we can only develop hypotheses and then weigh their plausibility. Working from the clue, "*Queen Anne's Revenge*," let's pursue the possibility that Blackbeard's forefathers were from Scotland. But before we can accurately assess what potentially shaped his thinking as a Highlander rather than a Bristolian, we need to know when he was born.

Despite the complete absence of evidence, Blackbeard's biographers have commonly portrayed his age in 1718 as being about 38-years-old, meaning he would have been born about 1680. That is most assuredly incorrect. It would have made the pirate about a decade older than his fellow captains at that time. And if true, his advanced age would have made him a fairly old sailor before becoming a captain late in his career. Prior to being recognized in the historical records as a pirate in 1717, Blackbeard was assumed to have served on privateering vessels during the War of Spanish Succession, and before that as a common merchant sailor. Life at sea was quite hard and men in those days aged quickly. Had he been born in 1680, Edward Thatch would have been quite old to be climbing the ratlines to the foretop in his late thirties. Historians also fondly imply that Thatch must have been fairly appealing to the ladies, which requires him to be a younger, more vigorous and virile man rather than a stiff-legged, leather-skinned, battle-scarred, old timer. This is an excellent example of how previous characterizations of Blackbeard are often contradictory.

George I

From his thorough research, the much-respected pirate authority, Marcus Rediker, found that "the average age of a pirate in the early 18th-century was twenty-seven," which was similar to the average age of a merchant seaman, as well as those in the Royal Navy. Rediker observed that "a sailor or pirate in his late twenties was not, by the standards of his occupation, a young man." Therefore, it is much easier to believe Blackbeard was in his late twenties when he took command of the *Queen Anne's Revenge*, which places his birth date close to either side of 1690, about the same age as his friend and role model, Black Sam Bellamy.

So, if young Edward Thatch, a Scot, sat fireside at his father's knee in the mid-1690s, what would he have heard? He likely would have been influenced by his parents' opinions of the wildly tumultuous events of the preceding decades. Those events included continuous inter-clan strife in Scotland, the Wars of the Three Kingdoms, the English Civil War, the Great Plague of London, the Monmouth Rebellion and the Bloody Assizes, the Glorious Revolution, and of course, the initial forays and failures of the Jacobite Rebellion. In nearly every instance, Scots found their lives and livelihoods threatened and property destroyed or confiscated. Some died for their convictions, and many fled their homeland or were forcibly removed as prisoners during the rebellions and became indentured servants, or even slaves, on the distant colonial outposts and plantations of the eastern Caribbean, most notably, Barbados.

Scots are a proud people, even today, so almost certainly young Thatch would have heard stories about the massacre at Glencoe in February, 1692, when 37 members of Clan MacDonald were murdered in the dark of night by their government-affiliated house guests. Another 40 women and children perished after their homes were destroyed in the bitter throes of the Highland winter. The barbarous plot was carried out with the sanction of King William of Orange because the MacDonalds had been slow to prove their allegiance to the new monarch, who had recently ousted the Catholic James II in the Glorious Revolution. Afterward, the Scottish Parliament declared the execution to be murder and the Glencoe Massacre became a rallying cry for Scottish nationalists and Jacobites—those followers of the deposed James II who wished to see the Catholic Stuart king restored to the throne. Hearing the story, the seeds of the future pirate's discontent with English authority would have been planted early in his life, as it was in many young men's lives.

As he developed into a young man in his teens, Thatch would have been further biased by news of excessive English authority through legislation such as the Alien Act of 1705 which placed an embargo on Scottish exports and also threatened to invalidate the inheritance of Scottish-owned estates in England. Even though Thatch and his family may not have descended from landed gentry, the outcome was just another intolerable affront of English hegemony.

Coincidentally, the same history influenced another Scot outlaw and folk hero who rose to infamy about the same time as Blackbeard. His Gaelic name was Raibeart Ruadh, or in the anglicized form, Red Robert. Some of his contemporaries called him Red MacGregor, but he is commonly known today as Rob Roy MacGregor. Red MacGregor was once a respected cattleman who became the victim of embezzlement and was forced by his creditors to turn outlaw. Instead of plundering Spanish gold and silver, casks of French sugar, Madeira wine and indigo dye as did pirates of the Spanish Main, the red-headed Rob Roy stole mostly cattle and raided noblemen's estates, becoming notorious as a sort of Robin Hood of Scotland. He also supported the Jacobite cause.

As a further coincidence, it was the writer Daniel Defoe who made Rob Roy famous through the publication of his sensational biographical story, *Highland Rogue*, in 1723. Those who subscribe to the theory that Capt. Charles Johnson was Daniel Defoe's nom de plume might find this fact a little ironic, since neither Robert MacGregor or Edward Thatch, with their "red" or "black" appellations, would ever have reached mythical status without the publicity of romanticists Defoe and Johnson. In retrospect, neither the pirate's nor the cattle rustler's exploits deserved the recognition they received from posterity—there were dozens more thieves, highwaymen, pirates and rogues who did far worse than they. It is simply that Red MacGregor and Blackbeard had catchy names.

Fortunately for MacGregor, the popularity of Defoe's book induced King George I to spare his life by one of His Majesty's gracious pardons. Blackbeard was not so lucky.

Naturally, a discussion of events and people that may have had a formative influence on young Ed Thatch's mind would have to include the subject of privateering and piracy. Any adolescent male of English, Scottish or Irish heritage growing up between 1690 and 1710 would have heard about or read about the fantastic treasures plundered by the likes of Sir Francis Drake and Sir Henry Morgan—two greatly admired privateers. It should be noted that the legal status of Drake and Morgan's raids have always been in question because they were often committed against Spain, which at the time was at peace with England. However, the same indistinct line between piracy and privateering prevailed among the next generation of sea-rovers during the Golden Age of Piracy—a generation that included Benjamin Hornigold, Sam Bellamy and Edward Thatch. Young boys such as Thatch who were able to read may have been able to study Alexander Exquemelin's *The Buccaneers of America*, which was wildly popular after its first English printing in 1684. They would have been captivated by the stories of life at sea and daring raids on Spanish treasure ports like Portobello, and unimaginably rich hauls of hundreds of thousands of gold and silver coins, and dazzling jewels.

By word of mouth, or from the few newspapers of the day, up-and-coming pirates like young Blackbeard would have followed the latest news of men such as Capt. William Kidd, and the pirate Henry Every, who both became legends within their own lifetimes. What young man wouldn't have been inspired by the success of Capt. Every who looted the fabulous riches of the *Ganj-i-sawa*, a ship owned by the emperor of the Mogul Empire? It has been estimated that Every's crew captured an enormous treasure which included 500,000 rials. With such stories in their heads, and role models such as Drake, Morgan, Kidd and Every, it is no wonder many young men at the dawn of the 18th century may have dreamed of becoming a pirate.

Near the Old Slough, Ocracoke. Saturday, the 22nd of November, 1718. Thatch and his friends found themselves in a woeful pickle. The pirates were cornered. The strangers approaching in the two trading sloops were His Majesty's men after all. Now apparent through the captain's spy glass, one of them on the quarterdeck of the trailing, larger sloop was wearing an officer's blue coat, its brass buttons gleaming in the morning sun and a modicum of gold braid trimming his sleeves.

It was a bad error in judgement, the pirate captain allowing himself to be trapped at their watering hole. The Adventure's company were unprepared, their cargo and spare sails strewn about the beach, guests were aboard, the ship unprepared to put to sea. They had waited too long; their time had run out.

When Thatch had called out his declaration for King George, the intruders answered that they were for King George as well by running-up their Royal Naval ensign, a field of red with the Union Jack in the upper left corner. They, in fact, worked for King George. No other words needed to have been spoken—they expressed their intent by flying their colors.

On board the Adventure not a second could be spared. Immediately, Blackbeard ordered the anchor line freed and the jib hoisted. The deck of the pirate sloop sprung to life as bo'sun Garret Gibbons and his men began to hastily haul on the jib's halliard and others scurried up from below with armloads of cutlasses, flintlock pistols, grenades, black powder cartridges for the cannon and a pair of grappling irons. Blackbeard and the ship's quartermaster, Thomas Miller, encouraged the crew to move sprightly. Gunner Philip Morton called for help as he frantically loaded the starboard guns with cartridges and swan shot—pieces of old iron, nails and other lethal odds and ends. Not all the men were sober or in tip-top fighting form but adrenaline provided an effective antidote for their hangovers.

The Adventure's guests, including Sam Odell—the trader who had helped the pirates get off Brant Island Shoals—quickly came to the realization that their convivial night of food and drink aboard Blackbeard's great sloop was not so much worth it. The pirate captain looked at them and immediately appreciated their plight. He suggested they go below into the hold and pretend to be prisoners in case they were boarded. The ploy would be unnecessary, however, if Blackbeard's next order was to be carried out—a strategy he learned from his friend, Vane. He grabbed a black slave, Caesar, and whispered in his ear, after which the young African man disappeared down the companionway. There would be no hangman's "hempen halter" in Blackbeard's future, that was for sure.

If the rest of the crew had been concerned about their captain's state of mind, his prior indecisiveness, his unpredictable nature, his lack of iron will, they were soon reassured. With speaking trumpet in hand, Edward Thatch grabbed the starboard shrouds and leapt upon the rail. The demonstration was mostly for the benefit of his men because he already knew the answers to his forthcoming questions. "Damn you for villains, who are you? And whence came you?" bellowed the bearded pirate.

Actually, we don't know for sure if Blackbeard really performed his, "Damn you for villains" soliloquy because the sole source of the information comes from the enigmatic and error-prone Capt. Johnson. It certainly sounds in keeping with the image of "a real, ranting, raging, roaring pirate," one who drove away birds, cats and dogs upon his arrival, who was as "grotesquely conspicuous a villain as can be found in the annals of crime." The truth is, the real Edward Thatch on that violent Saturday in November was not so courageous.

Noted pirate historians and authors have consistently stated that upon meeting Lt. Maynard and his two sloops, Blackbeard could have chosen to escape to the north, through the upper end of the channel that has ever since been named for his favorite hideout, Teach's Hole. One Blackbeard biographer, in particular, wrote that the thought of retreat never even occurred to the fearless pirate captain. Indeed, retreat was not an option, but not because Blackbeard was fearless.

Only since the Second World War has the continuously dredged Teach's Hole Channel been the primary route between the Pamlico Sound and the Atlantic Ocean, as the inlet's other historic passways—Ship Channel and Wallace Channel—had, over the years, progressively shoaled-over and for the most part disappeared. Navigation was different in 1718, when Blackbeard's channel narrowed and shoaled as it meandered around the north and west of Ocracoke Island, until there was practically no channel at all. At that time, the route was only navigable to those in shallow-draft vessels such as longboats, periaugers and light fishing sloops.

History has gotten it wrong, the error as dissonant as a badly played note in a violin recital. Blackbeard had no option to retreat. In fact, through a careful examination of the records, we know his preference was not to stand and fight at all, but to avoid the confrontation entirely. It is hard to believe but true. We become so obstinately devoted to an image and tradition that we ignore the real facts. What the pirate captain said after declaring his loyalties for King George as quoted in the reasonably accurate *Boston News-Letter* of February 23, 1719, was: "If he [Maynard] would let him alone, he [Blackbeard] would meddle not with him." Those were not the words of a bloodthirsty, fearsome pirate. Even Lt. Maynard alluded to the fact that Blackbeard had no escape when he later wrote to a colleague, "I should never have taken him, if I had not got him in such a Hole, whence he could not get out." (Some believe this was the origination of the name, Teach's Hole Channel.) Maynard's superior officer for the Blackbeard pursuit, Capt. Ellis Brand, also intimated in his official summary of the engagement that the pirate attempted to avoid the fight by fleeing toward the ocean, writing: "the Pyrate [endeavored] to get out of the same channel as our sloop [the *Ranger*] came in."

Blackbeard must have quickly sized-up his chances against the two sloops and their superior numbers—Maynard had 60 sailors, not counting himself and Midshipman Hyde, to the pirate crew of 21. On Blackbeard's side of the balance sheet, the *Adventure* had nine guns mounted while the King's sloops had none. The pirate captain may have also taken into account the health and sobriety of his men before he suggested the parties go their separate ways.

The source of the *Boston News-Letter* account of the engagement between Blackbeard and Maynard was a captain named, Humphrey Johnston, who had been in North Carolina at the time of the event, possibly anchored somewhere in the vicinity of Ocracoke Inlet. While it can't be proven Johnston was an eyewitness to the historic battle—he may have received his information second-hand, possibly from one of Maynard's men—the description he provided was extensive and many of the details match those reported by both Maynard and Brand in official documents.

According to Humphrey Johnston, when the pirate proposed his idea to not meddle with one another, May-

Teaches Hole Channel, Springer's Point, and the village of Ocracoke.

nard's response was, "It was him he wanted and that he would have him dead or alive, else it would cost him his life." Thatch then supposedly ordered a glass of wine—this was not done through his speaking trumpet so one wonders how close Humphrey Johnston, or his witness, was to the *Adventure*.

For his next declaration, the three common sources for the event—Maynard, the *Boston News-Letter*, and Capt. Charles Johnson's *A General History of Pirates*—all agree that Blackbeard used the word, "damnation." However, the two latter sources suggested that the pirate swore damnation to himself should he take or give mercy, whereas Maynard wrote that he was the subject of the pirate's censure: "At our first Salutation, he drank damnation to me and my men." Since Maynard was the principal witness, we should believe his account over all. Maynard also claimed that Blackbeard, realizing he was in danger of being apprehended, called His Majesty's sailors "cowardly puppies, saying, he would neither give nor take quarter."

With little or no wind for maneuvering and a contrary incoming tide, there were no other options but to fight. The deadly battle was on. But before we proceed further with the story we must go back a few months in time, to fully understand how these events came to be.

Subtle Whispers of the Past

sail and enormous mainsail proved her to be a fairly large, powerful sloop. Visitors were on the way in—perhaps the pirate commodore whose arrival had been expected for about a week. Scipio sounded the alarm, startling a cock who thrashed its wings and crowed defiantly.

Even though activity in the hardscrabble colony of North Carolina typically slowed to a crawl during the oppressive summer months, there had been some excitement of late. Not that peacefulness and normalcy were unwelcome to those residents of Bath Town, who had, during the past decade, survived disease, bloody political disputes, a devastating Indian war, drought and famine. Families were only just beginning to recover. But then something occurred in the summer of 1718 that had brought a golden glitter of hope to the impoverished precinct, like a rain after a long drought.

Among those residents surviving the previous troubles had been Tobias Knight, the long-time Secretary of the Colony, Collector of His Majesty's Customs, and planter. But now Knight was laid-up in bed with the marsh fever, able only to stir when official business required his presence, as happened about a fortnight earlier when pirates appeared in port. It was quite a sensation at the time—an exciting event for the sleepy town—even though the tired, hungry and haggard freebooters had come in rather innocuously, crowded in a ship's longboat. Had they not been so extravagantly dressed with swords hanging from their hips, they might not have been so believable as intrepid buccaneers of the fabled Spanish Main. The pirates asked for directions and began their walk, wobbling and weaving on their unsteady sea legs. Residents, young and old, gathered to gawk at the men, a safe distance away despite the pirates' deferential and uncomfortable demeanor.

A procession of sorts departed the town docks along Old Town Creek, growing in numbers as it crossed the commons and wound its way down the dirt path to the governor's townhouse at numbers 22-23 Bay Street. Tied to posts in front of the modest, two-story, wood-frame house were two horses—Gov. Charles Eden's and Tobias Knight's—tails swishing and swatting swarms of ravenous deer flies feeding on the horse's flesh.

The captain's name was Bonnet, of Barbados, and he humbly presented himself and his men to the governor in order to receive the benefit of His Majesty's Act of Grace. Becoming a pirate had seemed to be an exciting adventure, but things had gone awry. He recounted how a terrible misfortune had befallen them about a fortnight before when their great, 40-gun flagship wrecked when entering Old Topsail Inlet, down south in the colony. Another ship, a sloop, also went ashore and was lost when rushing to provide assistance. The company, as a result, was to separate. Many of its members desired to become legitimate citizens again, while a smaller number were not yet ready to give up the game.

Gold dust recovered from wreck believed to be Queen Anne's Revenge.
Photo by Wendy Welsh.
Courtesy NC Dep. of Cultural Resources

Behind closed doors the pirates made their plea. It was Bonnet's desire to go to St Thomas, where the Danish governor there was said to be hiring privateers to raid Spanish merchant ships. The King's pardon would make their passage safe. The eligibility of Bonnet and his men, however, became somewhat in doubt when it was realized that their company had taken a few trifling indiscretions—as they called their prizes—after the January deadline established by the King's Council. (The indiscretions were neither trifling nor few. They also

failed to mention that they had passed up the opportunity to surrender to at least two other colonial governors in their travels up from the West Indies but chose instead to sail to Bath Town.) When Gov. Eden explained the pirate's predicament, that they unfortunately were outside the bounds of the terms of His Majesty's forgiveness, they visibly lost their swagger and a bit of panic swept their faces. The Barbadian planter Bonnet shifted his weight from one foot to the other, looking twitchy and anxious. He was unsure of what to do next. However, the governor's secretary, Tobias Knight, weakened with fever but still clear of mind, spoke up and said it was not such a messy complication that could not be tidied-up with a handshake or two lined with some gold dust. All at once the leather-skinned sailors reached for their purses. Eden and Knight, two poorly paid proprietary officials ever in need of hard currency, were not about to refuse a kindness when proffering their expert counsel.

It would take a day or two to prepare the documents with the correct wording and all the proper flourishes, so, with their gold-filled purses, the pirates temporarily disbanded in search of accommodations and to whatever served for ale houses in the fledgling, five-street capital.

Later, pardons in hand, the pirates wasted no time casting off their longboat and rowing out to the river where they could raise the sail on the lateen yard to speed them on their way. They were in a hurry to get back to the greater part of their company at Old Topsail Inlet where the communal chests of plunder were to have been offloaded to safety from the sinking Queen Anne's Revenge and then shared out among the company upon their return. Before they departed they told Tobias Knight to expect more of their men, including their commodore, in the coming weeks. They would all be willing to pay handsomely for King George's little piece of parchment.

And then they were gone, leaving the Carolinians to their dusty streets, deer flies and summer malaise.

Just as Bonnet had promised, the commodore arrived, although maybe earlier and wealthier than Bonnet would have supposed. Within two hours of being spotted by young Scipio, the finely-rigged, nine-gun sloop Adventure turned-up smartly before the wind off Tobias Knight's landing—the place where all arriving vessels were required to report to His Majesty's Customs for the Colony of North Carolina. Sails were dropped and the crew lowered her anchor into the muddy bottom of the river.

A welcoming committee consisted mostly of Knight's slaves, summoned from their respective chores by the ringing of the bell by Scipio. They included 60-year-old Jack; 40-year-old Tom; Pompey, 27; Caesar, 24; and a young girl, Phillis. The Adventure's boat was rowed ashore, and stepping onto the dock was a tall, dark-skinned man with a long black beard neatly braided. The pirate captain and his officers were greeted by Jack and led up to the stately house which Esquire Knight had just exited, having used every bit of the two-hour warning to rouse from bed, wash the feverish sweat away and dress in his finest official clothing. Madam Katherine joined her husband at his side.

Arriving at the foot of the steps, Blackbeard the pirate bowed courteously. Knight asked him, "What would be your business here?" The pirate answered gravely, "We are here to meet with the government in order to apply for His Majesty's most gracious pardon." Knight responded, "Then, captain, you must enter my offices so that I may hear your story."

With all proper formality, Knight ushered Blackbeard and his men, including William Howard, John Martin, Nathaniel Jackson and Joseph Brooks, into a parlor where they sat at a small black walnut table surrounded by six yellow-colored chairs. Esquire Knight then looked intently toward the heavily bearded pirate captain and with an expanding smile said, "Well well, young Edward. I was not sure I would ever see you in Bath Town again. And you, gentlemen," as Knight looked at the other

An 18th century writing desk at the Palmer-Marsh House in Bath, North Carolin

pirates. "I know your families will be most glad to see you, too." Next, Knight turned back to Blackbeard. "Edward, you will be pleased to know your sister Susannah is well, and your nephew who shares your name has grown to be a fine young lad."

That we know Tobias and Katherine Knight possessed a small black walnut table and six yellow-colored chairs, as well as seven-year-old Scipio and his fellow slaves, is because the inventory of Knight's "goods and chattels" at the time of his death has survived the ages and is included in Beaufort County Deed Book I. These rare, extant inventories are especially enlightening and help us to understand and appreciate the material culture of the early colonists' lives. Just as archeological artifacts provide a physical, if not fragmentary, connection to the past, the words of inventories create vivid images of the lives of people who resided within a long-lost world. In the case of Tobias Knight, we can see him writing his pirate pardons seated at his favorite escritoire, or serving refreshments to Blackbeard and his crew on his tea table. When Knight traveled to the colony's council meetings or court sessions, which were almost always held 50 miles to the north in the Chowan Precinct, he may have packed his essentials in his seal skin portmanteau and rode horseback atop one of his two old saddles.

That we suspect Blackbeard had been acquainted with Tobias Knight before his arrival during the summer of 1718 and that the pirate had a sister and nephew residing within the colony is because of the determination and persistence of Beaufort County native, John H. Oden III. Oden had taken a particular interest in the 1720 inventory of Tobias Knight's estate because among those who signed the document as witnesses was his ancestor and namesake: John Oden, cooper of Bath Town.

A postal carrier for the U.S. Postal Service at Bath, John H. Oden III had an insatiable curiosity about his ancestors and a passion for the past. And like others in his county who could trace their roots to the earliest settlers of colonial North Carolina, Oden's family sustained an oral tradition that their forefathers had once been privateers in the early days. The story was like a cherished family heirloom, the possibility that kinfolk may have rubbed elbows with pirates of the Golden Age—or even had been pirates, themselves.

The idea dominated Oden's thoughts, leading him to pursue genealogical research in the mid-1970s at an age much younger than most people who take an interest in their origins. He was a co-founder of his county's genealogical society where he made lasting friends with dozens of like-minded souls. Together, they shared their knowledge, experience and tricks of the trade.

Along the way, John Oden read retired law professor Robert E. Lee's groundbreaking biography of Blackbeard, first published in 1974. The book recounts in vivid detail the suspicious relationship between Blackbeard, North Carolina Gov. Charles Eden, and the colony's collector of customs and council secretary, Tobias Knight. Lee described a long-held legend that a subterranean "tunnel" stretched from the cellar of Eden's mansion on Bath Creek to a landing, where allegedly Blackbeard often transferred his piratically-taken treasures to the care of the complicit governor. The precise location of the landing and the governor's mansion, although known to be on the west side of Bath Creek, had long been lost to memory. For a postal carrier driving the long, dusty farm roads in the neighborhood of Blackbeard's former haunts, John Oden must have had a lot of time to ponder the location of the infamous tunnel and the secret hiding place of Blackbeard's long-lost treasure.

A modest, humble and fun-loving man, John Oden lacked only a few credits toward completing his college degree but was the kind of person who believed the journey was always more fascinating than the destination; the process of learning more important than a diploma. A new journey presented itself when Oden was asked to be part of the planning for the upcoming 300-year anniversary of Bath, North Carolina's first incorporated town, which was scheduled for 2005.

It is a peculiar circumstance that some of the great advancements in historical knowledge during the past half-century have come about because of impending anniversaries—centennials, bicentennials, tricentennials, or quadricentennials. With the approach of these important milestones, small armies of historians and researchers descend upon libraries, archives, and courthouses to scour the records for documents and fragments of information that may have been overlooked by the historians of old. Then, upon the eve of the celebration, communities, organizations and publishers produce a flurry of historical research and publications. Such was the occasion that sparked John Oden's determination to abstract, index and publish Beaufort County Deed Book I, which contained a variety of documents, wills, inventories and depositions recorded between 1696 and 1729. Through his genealogical society acquaintances, Oden met a woman from Maryland named, Allen Hart Norris, who shared Oden's Bath Town privateering connections. Norris accepted Oden's challenge to transcribe the ancient book of deeds, now barely readable on faded rolls of microfilm in the North Carolina Archives.

Near the end of the long and tedious process of abstracting the old deeds, Oden asked Norris if she had read any descriptions of Gov. Eden's plantation on the west side of the creek with the possibility that they may be able to determine the location of the fabled tunnel. Norris searched the records and came across a deed that described the common boundaries of the Eden land in relation to his neighbors' property—Tobias Knight on the southern boundary and a plantation owned by a man named Beard on the northern side. Norris shared her information with Oden who could not have been

more stunned by the remarkable revelation. When he heard the Beard name for the first time from his colleague, Oden's initial reaction was that the implication could not possibly be true. Yet, there it was before him, a darkened 'rabbit hole' spiraling down into the unknown, enticing Oden to step through and discover a significant, yet controversial piece of lost history.

Was it possible that Edward Thatch, alias Blackbeard, was really Edward Beard? Was the correct form of the pirate's alias actually, Black Beard? Edward "Black" Beard, as in Robert "Red" MacGregor?

Most scholars who have thought deeply about the question of why Edward Thatch chose to surrender himself to North Carolina officials, and why he seemed to be so adept at navigating its confusing network of shoals and rivers, have considered the possibility that he had previously been to Bath Town. Lee touched on the issue in his book: "Blackbeard undoubtedly had been to Bath before...he knew the waters of the coastal rivers and the sounds of North Carolina. He was acquainted with the colonists of that section."

The more John Oden thought about the possibility of a man named Beard associated with a farm on the west side of Bath Creek in the early 1700s, the more he knew that he would have to get to the bottom of the mystery no matter where it would take him. Oden called Allen Hart Norris and another genealogy colleague, Jane Stubbs Bailey, who also lived in Maryland and who had Bath Town ancestors, as well. Oden proposed that they join in a quest—to prove or disprove the pirate captain's connections to the Beard of Bath Creek. Bailey recalls, at the outset, being startled by the far-fetched idea, as was Norris. But because of Oden's sincerity, generosity and impeccable analytical skills and intuition, the women were unable to refuse him. The three genealogists went underground, into their own "subterranean tunnel" of research. Even their closest family members and friends were unaware of their pursuit. And so began a thrilling five-year adventure.

Oden somehow found spare time from his mail carrier duties to make trips to the North Carolina Archives in Raleigh and East Carolina University's manuscript collection in Greenville. The rushed excursions were tiring but rewarding. In the true spirit of a pirate, Oden saw himself "plundering" the records for lost treasures—collecting bits and pieces of a grand puzzle—and his "treasure chest" of evidence began to fill. To this day, archivists in Raleigh recall Oden's enthusiasm and passion, and his whirlwind Saturday visits when he presented the appreciative staff with boxes of steaming-hot donuts before he disappeared into piles of records or the tight spaces of the microfilm room. Meanwhile, Bailey and Norris made trips together to the National Genealogical Society's research library at Arlington, Virginia. The women also did some plundering at the Daughters of the American Revolution library on the west side of the White House Ellipse in Washington, D.C. Each week, the three researchers shared their findings through dozens of letters and late-night phone calls. Norris collected and organized the research and then all three engaged in lengthy, lively and detailed discussions about their findings. Each took turns playing "devil's advocate," challenging the hypotheses of the others. To their shock, what seemed unbelievable, unlikely, outrageously implausible, was proving to be believable, likely, and plausible. The triumvirate of genealogists went deeper underground, having become suspicious of anyone looking over their shoulders.

Early in their investigation, Oden found the will of Capt. James Beard at the State Archives in Raleigh. At first, the possible relationship between James Beard, who owned 375 acres on the west side of Bath Creek as early as 1707, and Edward "Beard" was not evident. Oden hoped James Beard's will might offer a clue. Seated at one of the large oak tables in the search room of the Archives and while waiting for the document to be retrieved from the climate-controlled stacks, Oden's sense of anticipation must have been palpable. It was like digging for buried treasure in broad daylight in the middle of a crowded flea market. Oden might have stolen glances at his neighboring researchers to make sure no one was on to his secret.

The packet containing the will arrived. Nervously exhaling, Oden fumbled with the cloth ties which se-

This document in the collections of the North Carolina Archives is a claim by Thomas Peterson, Esquire, a merchant of Albemarle, against James Beard, deceased, who is identified as a mariner. As stated in the affadavit filed by Peterson's attorney, Edward Moseley, James Beard became indebted to Peterson for the sum of eleven pounds, twelve shillings and eight pence in 1707. Apparently, after promising to repay the debt, Beard later denied that he owed Peterson the money. James Beard died on Sunday, July 21, 1711 in South Carolina.

cured the papers and then opened the document, exposing its secrets to the world.

Capt. James Beard of Bath Town died on Sunday, July 21, 1711, while in South Carolina, most likely at Charleston. It had been a difficult year for settlers in the Pamlico region of North Carolina, where Beard resided. A bloody religious and political conflict between the Quaker-allied governor, Col. Thomas Cary, and his successor, Edward Hyde of the Anglican party, had only recently been resolved through intervention by Virginia's Lt. Gov. Alexander Spotswood. The local planters' inattention to their crops as a result of Cary's Rebellion, followed by a severe drought, left many in desperate need of food. Then yellow fever swept the land taking the lives of a considerable number of the Carolinians. It is likely that Capt. Beard succumbed to yellow fever while on a trading trip to Charleston.

As Oden read Beard's will, he must have felt like he had traveled back in time and was standing at Capt. Beard's bedside:

> We the under written on Sunday Night last ye 21st Instant about seven of ye Clock In the Evening, Capt. James Beard then very weak butt then very sensible did hear him declare that if itt pleased God to call him out of this world before next day when he designed to make his will, in such a case then he desired Mr. Jno. Morgan to take care of all his effects such of them were left to remit to his wife and son. Witnesses: Lewis Lansac, Stephen Sarazin, and Mary Brasley.

James Beard did not survive the night. He was never able to "make out" a proper will as he intended. His nuncupative will, or oral testimony, bequeathing his effects to his wife and son was the only indication that

he had heirs. It seemed to Oden to be a serious setback: the will failed to specifically name Beard's wife or son. But in a later search by Allen Norris through the receipts of North Carolina's Tuscarora War claims—compensation paid to landholders by the proprietary government for losses suffered as a result of the devastating Indian uprising which began just two months after Beard died—it was discovered that three years after his death, a Capt. Masten (or Marston) accepted Beard's claim on behalf of Masten's wife, Elizabeth. It could only mean one thing: the introduction of Masten's name in association to claims due the heirs of Beard's Bath Creek holdings suggests that Masten had married Beard's widow. James Beard's wife at the time of his death must have been Elizabeth. Throughout the colonial period it was customary for a woman to remarry fairly quickly after the death of her husband, and for the widow's new spouse to become the executor of the estate of her previous spouse. Unfortunately, no further research was able to attach a name to James Beard's son, or to determine his residence during this time. Life along the shores of the Pamlico River between 1711 and 1715 was chaotic, fluid and uncertain. The keeping of detailed records was abandoned for the sake of basic survival. And young men often left the colony in search of work elsewhere.

The will alone was not nearly enough evidence for John Oden to draw any conclusions. There would be no easy solution to the mystery of James Beard and his possible connections to Black Beard. How could they determine if Black Beard was really Edward Beard, son of Capt. James Beard of Bath Town? It became apparent to John Oden, Allen Norris and Jane Bailey that nothing less than tireless determination, personal sacrifice and complete faith in their work would be required if they were to succeed. And success did come, but at a dear price.

Plantation Row, Bath, North Carolina. Bath Creek is above and the Pamlico River is above and to the right. The route to the Pamlico Sound and Ocracoke follows the river out of the top of the photo.

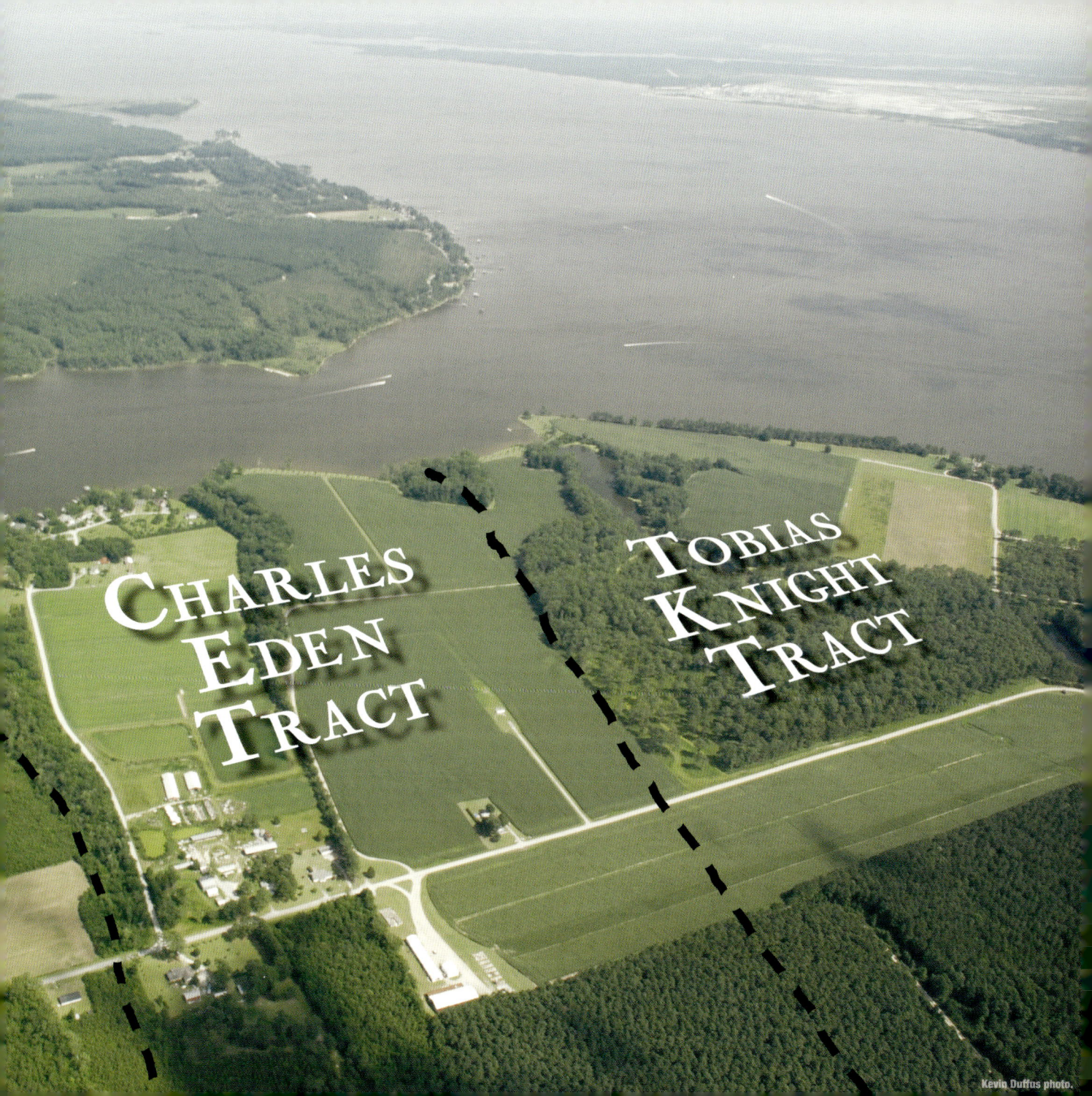

Ballast stones, Bath, North Carolina.

Nine — A Fruitless Vineyard

HISTORY TELLS US THAT HAVING DISPOSSESSED HIMSELF OF HIS UNMANAGEABLE, 400-MAN PIRATE COMpany at Old Topsail Inlet, the gallant Capt. Black Beard settled into a life of leisure along Bath Creek, North Carolina. Courtesy of the illustrious and imaginative Charles Johnson, we are supposed to think that "[Teach] married a young creature of about sixteen years of age, the governor performing the ceremony." Another of Black Beard's biographers says the pirate wooed his new love with a "lavish display of fine silks, jewels and gold" causing the beautiful, aristocratic girl to submit to "Teach's" desires. Of course, this "Teach" is the same honeymooner whom Johnson wants us to believe spent the days following his wedding sharing his new bride's charms with a select number of his crew. Even more sordid, Johnson wrote that "[Teach] and his companions often took with the wives and daughters of the planters." Johnson adds a final insult to early women of Carolina by remarking that he was not sure whether or not the pirates had paid for these romantic liaisons. Whoever Johnson really was (It is hard to accept that Daniel Defoe wrote such salacious material), he was not concerned about whether these scandalous anecdotes were true or not. They were selling books. And it is very obvious that the source of Johnson's information was somebody who had it out for Black Beard and his friends at Bath.

Local lore has insinuated itself into the pirate's traditional history, stating matter-of-factly that Black Beard bought himself a palatial house on a high vantage point known as Plum Point, across the creek from his friends, Secretary Knight and Gov. Eden. From his estate, the pirate was able to lordly watch over the approaches to the harbor. Before long, Black Beard somehow managed to become the bon vivant of Bath, eclipsing the fineries and social courtesies of the resident gentry formerly of England. It has been written by one respected author that "entertainments in his home were on a lavish scale." (This, we are expected to believe, is the same pirate host who had been having his way with his guests' spouses.) By reading some of the standard stories, we can imagine grand balls held on idyllic nights lit by moonlight and thousands of lanterns as Lord Black Beard and his teenage bride waltzed before the adoring residents of the Pamlico area plantations. Or so some want to believe.

The truth is that after his arrival in Bath in order to receive the royal pardon of King George I, Black Beard and his crew remained in the area for no more than two weeks. They were there a fortnight. A detailed and factual timeline of Black Beard's whereabouts during the summer of 1718 clearly requires the departure of the sloop *Adventure* and its pirate crew by around July 15, because fewer than three weeks later the pirate captain was walking the streets of Philadelphia.

There have been many attempts to recreate the lives and byways of Bath in the first quarter of the 18th century. Generally, descriptions of Bath in popular pirate literature as encountered by Black Beard and his crew are far from accurate, and at worst, make it difficult to determine the truth of what really transpired during the summer of 1718. Some authors have never even bothered to visit Bath before writing detailed descriptions of its surroundings. One wrote of a landscape so low and swampy that it could hardly be discerned where the water ended and land began. In fact, Bath Creek is mostly lined with ten- to twenty-five-foot high bluffs, which is what attracted the earliest settlers to that area of the Pamlico River basin in the first place.

Descriptions of Bath Town's raucous taverns and crowded ordinaries, thriving retail stalls, festive parties, pirates and planters reveling day and night, and "shotgun" weddings, are gross distortions of our history. For some strange reason, even scholarly writers feel compelled to embellish the truth when it comes to writing about pirates, and Black Beard in particular. It is as if, with an unseen wink and a nod from the author, readers are supposed to recognize when a narrative of history temporarily becomes a yarn. Even the venerable biographer Robert Lee fell victim, writing of the days when Black Beard converted his sloop *Adventure* into a "yacht, sailing the quiet inland waters and taking excursions on the high seas to break the tedium." Such writing is irresponsible and does a disservice to future generations of readers.

In reality, Black Beard and most of his men probably chose not to sleep ashore, avoiding the close quarters of stifling hot rooms and scant, straw-filled, insect-infested pallets of Bath's finest lodgings, preferring instead the familiar comforts, cool evening breezes and gentle rocking of their home, the sloop *Adventure*. As for their other diversions, the actual chronology simply does not allow enough time for all of the myths. It is most likely there were no "pirate castles on a hill," no parties or lavish dinner parties, no weddings, no crowded bazaars. Based on appraisals and inventories, even the wealthiest families of early Bath lived fairly frugal lives by modern standards. The colony had been on the brink of rack and ruin by the time the pirates arrived in 1718. The residents plainly lacked the capacity to "revel day and night."

As for the pirate's bawdy behavior, most minor violations of the law such as "breaking ye sabbath" or "swearing oaths" were prosecuted and recorded in the minutes of the courts. Sexual assault or even infidelity were considered high crimes and taken very seriously. Provost marshals and rangers were well established in the three primary counties of the colony. It is beyond reason that Black Beard and his crew "took up" with the wives of the planters without something being said about it in the official records. Besides, most pirates had a greater sense of propriety than popular mythology gives them credit for, especially in the presence of women and in civilized communities ashore. For the most part, Black Beard's honor and reputation have been unfairly sullied by history.

There is but one documented reference to any sort of unpleasantness perpetrated by Black Beard's crew during their brief visit in July, 1718. At a meeting of his Council at the end of the year, Gov. Eden reported, "Some disorders committed by them while at Bath Towne." It was revealed then almost as an afterthought; there had been four previous meetings of the Council since July and not once had anyone discussed the pirates or their "disorders." The minutes of the meeting also allude to the fact that the pirates were successfully "quieted" but the records do not tell us how. We also don't know what behaviors qualified to be considered "disorders." There may have been an occasion for some loud, profane disagreements or drunken brawls but, unfortunately, the records are mostly silent.

The published pages of the Colonial Records, court minutes and the entries of Beaufort County Deed Book I, are the best sources from which to accurately paint the landscape of Bath Creek in 1718. One of the first impressions you might have of Bath Town when reading the minutes of Council meetings or endless numbers of land patents and deed transfers is that it was a hotbed of real estate speculation, much as it is today, 300 years later.

According to the late East Carolina University historian Dr. Herbert Paschal, Bath Town was probably conceived and planned by adventurer, naturalist, author and surveyor, John Lawson. He was not the first to recognize the harbor's charms and potential, however. The Secotan nation had centuries before established its capital along Bath Creek. The second of Sir Walter Raleigh's three expeditions to establish an English colony in the New World visited Secotan in 1585. And, it was primarily the capital village, Secota, that provided the inspiration for John White's finely-detailed watercolors of native-American life.

Around 1706, Lawson laid-out 71 lots on a north-south axis situated on a pretty peninsula between what was then known as Town Creek (Bath Creek) and Adams Creek (Back Creek). Lawson was one of three founding town commissioners, along with planters Nicholas Daw and Joel Martin. Martin had been a plantation owner on the west side of Bath Creek since before 1702. Lawson and Martin began selling lots, serving as North Carolina's first real estate agents. Daw may have had better things to do as his name does not appear on the transactions. For a 250th commemoration of the founding of Bath, Paschal wrote the following:

> The first sale of lots under the terms of the act of incorporation, which the records disclose, was made on September 27, 1706. On this date conveyances were entered to thirteen different individuals. By the end of October at least twenty-five individuals owned lots in Bath. The names of these early lot holders are worthy of being preserved. They included: Nathaniel Wyersdale, Richard Odeon, Jr., Maurice Luellyn, Thomas Cary, Christopher

A Fruitless Vineyard

Gale, George Birkenhead, Thomas Peterson, John Porter, John Worsley, John Lawson, David Perkins, Henry Robinson, Simond Worsley, Nicholas Daw, James Beard, Daniel Mathews, Otho Russel, Giles Shute, Lyonell Reading, Thomas Sparrow, Thomas Worsley, James Walsh, Edmund Pearces, Joel Martin and one Capt. Raymond.

Despite a brisk volume of property transactions, the actual population of the town grew slowly. The majority of the property owners around Bath were only there a short time or they lived principally in other places, like the more established Chowan precinct in the northeastern sector of the colony. Other absentee land speculators spent much of their time in the region's largest cities of Charleston, Philadelphia or New York. Some of the other men involved in early Bath land sales are known to have been sea captains, mariners, and even privateers, and who purchased property as investments, just as people do today.

It was estimated that by 1708, only about 12 houses lined Front Street, the sandy lane that paralleled Town Creek. Nevertheless, the town fathers had high hopes for Bath, expecting it to become the provincial capital and possibly rivaling the size and economic output of Charleston. Then came disease, drought, religious zealots and Indian warriors, and the future for poor little Bath changed drastically. By 1715, normalcy was only just beginning to return to the village. But Bath's biggest impediment to becoming a great colonial capital could never be overcome—Ocracoke Inlet. While some have blamed the harbor's 55-mile distance from the sea, it was really the lack of a stable, deep water pathway through the inlet that prevented Bath from ever becoming a Charleston.

As for ordinaries being capable of lodging a 25-man pirate crew, it is unlikely. Accommodations in Bath were sparse even before the great catastrophes of 1711-1715. Out-of-town attendees to the Court of Pleas and Quarter Sessions at Bath once complained to the Lords Proprietors of the primitive nature of Bath's lodgings: "Ye ordinary keepers have not [beds] to Lodge us in which constrains us either to be burthinsum to ye gentel-men in town or Else to lay by ye fire side which y' Honrs cannot chuse but imagine to be great Hardship."

At another time, a visiting missionary named, Giles Rainsford, complained that "my lodging for the best part of my time in this government was in an old Tobacco house & exposed to even in my bed the injuries & violence of bad weather with infinite other inconveniences." Although, Rainsford's experience might say more about how clergymen were treated in the colony than its general quality of hospitality and lodgings. Maybe pirates were housed more kindly than vicars.

Another good source of information about the state of the self-styled capital of North Carolina comes from the rambling rantings of another missionary, Reverend John Urmstone. Urmstone was disliked practically everywhere he went in the colony, mostly for his constant complaining and annoying solicitations for food and money. He often referred to Carolina as a "fruitless vineyard," probably not because of his low numbers of conversions to the Anglican faith, but because he had so much difficulty filling his collection plate. As a result, we have to take the reverend's lack of popularity into account when reading his opinions. Nevertheless, Urmstone still gives us a contemporary description of Bath on the eve of Black Beard's arrival.

Bath was the target of Urmstone's favorite concern. In a letter to England in 1714, Urmstone wrote, "We expect to hear that famous city of Bath consisting of nine houses or rather cottages once stiled the Metropolis & seat of Government will be totally deserted." Making light of what must have been a tragic emotional toll on Bath residents as a result of the Tuscarora War, Urmstone remarked in another letter that they would soon abandon their town "for fear of 7 or 8 Indians."

The underlying reason for Urmstone's vitriolic disgust with Bath concerned the disputed possession and questionable safe-keeping of a library of books which had been gifted to the colony by the Reverend Thomas Bray. Bray was a representative of the Bishop of London who had authorized Bray to establish as many as thirty parochial libraries in the American colonies. According to Bernard Steiner, author of the *American Historical Review* article, "Rev. Thomas Bray and his American Libraries," Bath's library consisted of "thirty-eight folios, nineteen quartos, and 109 octavos. Its contents were much more varied than those of the average library. There were eleven works of history and travel, two geographies, five dictionaries, three works each on mathematics, natural history, heraldry, biography, and law, four ancient classics, the same number of works on grammar and language, three books of essays, two books on sports, and one each on medicine, mythology, and poetry."

Because of the great expanse of the county and the difficulty crossing the multitude of swamps, creeks and rivers in order to go to Bath to read a book, the collection was, out of necessity, a free circulating library, out of which "the inhabitants of Beaufort Precinct shall have liberty to borrow any book." Rev. Urmstone felt that as the senior clergyman in the colony, he should possess and manage Bray's library, but no matter how many times he demanded to have it, he was rebuffed. Throughout his many missives to the British Secretary over his twelve-year stay in North Carolina, Urmstone almost never failed to complain about the fate of the Bath library. He may have had good reason to be concerned for its safety, however, because, one by one, the books failed to be returned. In one of his most memorable statements, Urmstone wrote, "The famous library sent in by Dr. Bray's direction is in a great measure destroyed. I am told the books are all unbound and have served for some time for waste paper."

Had Urmstone's news reached the library's benefactor, it might have caused Rev. Bray a spot of bother, because in addition to being the Bishop of London's representative in the colonies, Bray was a member of the Society for the Reformation of Manners. Using his library for waste paper must have been considered quite a poor reflection on Bath's manners, indeed.

According to Dr. Paschal, as of 1955, only one volume of Bath's original library was known to have survived—a 1685 folio titled, *Applications of Church Catechism*—which was presented as a gift to the Episcopal Diocese of Eastern North Carolina in 1890. Apparently, defiling a church catechism is where Bath's library patrons drew the line.

In a postscript to the story of Rev. John Urmstone, life in colonial North Carolina must have had a more profound effect on his character than he had on his parishioners. In 1720 he was convicted of being publicly drunk. One year later he vanished, having returned to England without notifying his vestrymen who suddenly had no one to counter the spread of Quakerism in the colony. Fearing that the missionary had only taken a sabbatical, one of his parishioners sent an unsigned letter to the British Secretary asking that Urmstone not be sent back. "His life is so wicked and scandalous [he is a] notorious drunkard and swearing and lewdness is also what he is occupied for these and others of his vices."

So you can imagine, with men of the cloth like Rev. Urmstone setting the example, disorderly pirates in Bath Town during the summer of 1718 might have hardly caused a stir. No wonder Black Beard and his men skedaddled to the City of Brotherly Love after staying in the "fruitless vineyard" of Bath for just two weeks.

*Philadelphia's High Street (now Market Street) circa 1700.
Historical Society of Pennsylvania.*

Ten—
Lurking About High Street

After receiving their pardons but before departing from Bath about the middle of July, Black Beard indicated to Gov. Eden that it was his intent to sail to St. Thomas in order to apply for a privateering "letter of marque" from the Danish governor on the island. Instead, the pirates set sail for the Delaware Bay. The pirate captain did not intentionally mislead the governor; he just didn't plan to sail to the West Indies right away. The middle of July was hardly the time to be going south. Boaters, then as now, prefer the cooler breezes of the north during the dog days of summer. More importantly, Black Beard had people he wanted to see—a woman. And possibly a doctor.

It is odd that some pirate historians have chosen to exclude this episode from Black Beard's travels, one going so far as to say that the "theory" of the pirates going to Philadelphia makes little sense because there was not enough time for them to have accomplished everything Charles Johnson gave them credit for in *A General History of Pirates*. But we well know by now how unreliable Johnson was with his facts. The colonial records of Pennsylvania are a much better source of information and they clearly indicate that Black Beard was in Philadelphia by early August, 1718. On the 11th of that month, Pennsylvania Gov. William Keith addressed his Council members:

> Upon an Informacon that one Teach, a noted Pirate, who has done the greatest mischief of any to this Place, has been Lurking for some days in & about this town, I have granted a Provincial warrant for his being apprehended, if possible to be found, & several other petty Informacons of Late gives me Cause to suspect that many of the Pirates that have lately Surrendered themselves & obtained Certificates from this and the neighboring Governments, do still keep a Correspondence with their old Companions abroad.

To ignore Black Beard's mysterious Philadelphia connections would cause us to miss some of the most significant clues to his true identity, his years before becoming a pirate, and possibly, the origin of the name, Thatch, and its popular variation of Teach. Another conspicuous piece of evidence from Black Beard's August, 1718, cruise to the Delaware Bay and Philadelphia is that he and his shipmates did not molest or capture any vessels on the way in or on the way out, nor did they engage in any disorders. For a few weeks, they were model citizens.

They were no longer pirates. Stored safely in their sea chests were pieces of parchment garnished with a governor's signature and a wax seal proving their newly purchased innocence. They were but honest traders and aspiring privateers. At least for the time being.

About the first of August, the rakish sloop Adventure *tacked to port into the wide entrance of Delaware Bay, around the massive dunes of Cape Henlopen, and followed a north-northwesterly course headlong into the choppy waves of the bay. With a favorable wind it would take at least 36 hours to reach the wharves of the city—probably longer.*

As the bay narrowed northward of the Bombay Hook, near the point where the Delaware River spills into the bay, traffic of north- and south-bound vessels consolidated and the numbers of vessels jibing to and fro was a stunning sight for sailors accustomed to the wide-open spaces of the deep blue sea. Among the dozens of brigantines, snows, pinks, sloops and small fishing boats, the Adventure *appeared to be just another trading vessel plying the waters of the Delaware. They flew no "death's head" in the rigging. There were no name-boards on her bows. To further disguise the former pirate sloop, bo'sun Garret Gibbons almost certainly ordered the gun ports to be closed and rail guns and chasers stowed below deck. It must have been exasperating for the former gentlemen of fortune to be among so many fat, rich prizes, just there for the taking. What had it been, only a year since they had been there last and had captured dozens of ships? They had made merry of the fact that they could have captured the pompous governor of Virginia, Spotswood, aboard an English man-of-war, who, they were told had passed their way going south after spending some time in the great Quaker city.*

The captain had said this was not a pirating cruise, yet old habits were hard to shear. He had to remind them all that they had agreed to take the pardon—odd though it was to hear the roguish Black Beard ask his friends to control themselves for a change.

Past the marshlands of lower New Jersey and Delaware the land began to rise and so did the evidence of habitation along the shores. A few piers and landings may have been spotted jutting from the tree-lined shore and an occasional ferry crossing their path, burdened with horses and wagons. At the bend in the river below, the busy port of New Castle, the Adventure's *course altered to north by east, and the architecture of the Swedes and Quakers hove into view—meeting houses, churches and homes, and little villages springing up like the orbiting moons of a great heavenly body: the city of Philadelphia over the horizon. Unlike their Carolina counterparts down south, many of these structures were noticeably larger and built solidly of brick, sandstone or granite, with steeply sloped roofs of cedar shakes or slate.*

About 10 miles above New Castle, the tall, young, bearded captain became fidgety, pacing and preening himself before a looking glass. His crew exchanged knowing glances and began to prepare the sloop to anchor. Marcus Hook was coming into view and their captain, they knew, was especially fond of Swedish blondes. And one in particular.

In 1842, antiquarian, John F. Watson, completed a manuscript that was years in the making, titled, *Annals of Philadelphia—A Collection of Memoirs, Anecdotes, and Incidents of the City and Its Inhabitants and of the Earliest Settlements of the Inland Part of Pennsylvania from the Days of the Founders* (the subtitle goes on, but you get the point). Watson devoted quite a number of pages to Black Beard, whom Philadelphia claimed as their own, according to some accounts. Elderly citizens of the city shared with Watson many accounts told to them by their parents and grandparents of the days when Teach walked their streets. One of those oral histories concerned a Swedish woman named Margaret, who lived at Marcus Hook, on the western shores of the Delaware about 15 miles below Philadelphia. It was said that Black Beard and his crew "used to revel" at Margaret's house. Black Beard, according to Watson's sources, was accustomed to calling his lady friend, "Marcus," instead of Margaret, which must have been an easier way for him to keep his many girlfriend's names in order—he just called them by the name of whichever port he was in at the time. One wonders if there were other women he knew as Nassau, Port Royal, Havana, Bath?

Oddly enough, if you were to go to the township of Marcus Hook today, which is pigeon-holed between sprawling oil terminals, refineries and petroleum tank farms, you will find a street just one block off the river called, Discord Lane, a name that appears on maps 300 years old. And just a few yards west of Discord Lane is a tiny house that, in recent years, has been undergoing preservation and a good deal of scrutiny. Tradition has always said it was the house of Black Beard's mistress and it was identified as such on postcards going back 50 years or more.

The newest owners of the house, Michael and Pat Manerchia, had planned to renovate it for their own use but when they began to tear away gypsum board walls and rip out rotting floors, they began to find thousands of archeological artifacts from cannon balls to porcelain dolls, whalebone buttons, dishware and hundreds of bones of chickens and pigs.

At first, local authorities, architectural historians and archeologists took no interest in the property and would hardly give Manerchia—a heavy equipment operator—the courtesy of even a cursory examination. Now, some archeologists have changed their minds, and one expert has confirmed the origins of the house to early 18th century, just about the time Black Beard might have been there. Could the 16-by-20-foot, sawn plank house off Discord Lane be the former home of Black Beard's Swedish mistress Margaret? Had he smoked his clay pipe beside the stone hearth, or lain with his love in the tiny bed chamber? He certainly did not bury his treasure in the earthen cellar because it has yet to be found—or at least no one had admitted as much. Edward Thatch also failed to leave his calling card—a similar disappointment shared by the archeologists diving on the remains of the ship believed to be the *Queen Anne's Revenge*. So no one will probably be ever able to say, "Black Beard slept here." But we can be reasonably certain the pirate had a friend in Marcus Hook named, Margaret.

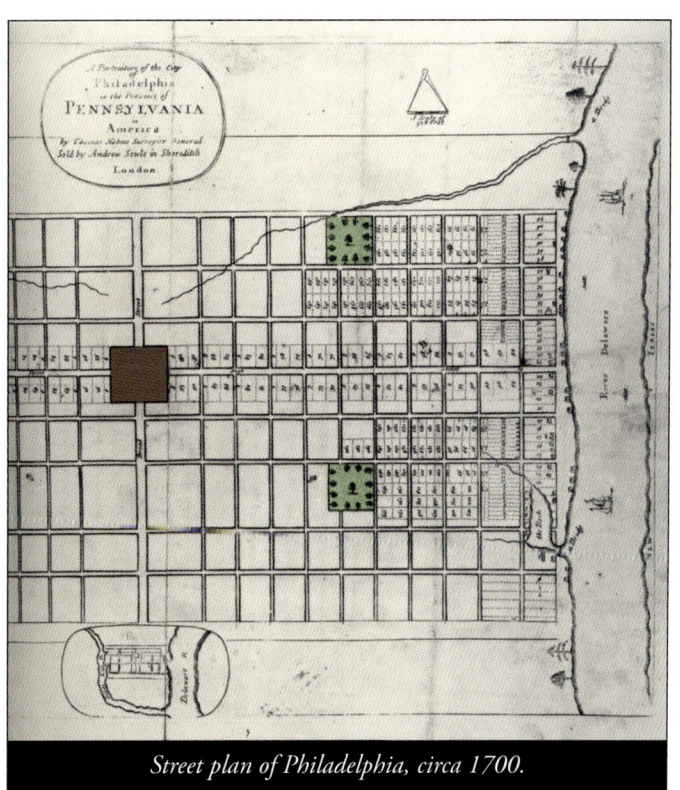
Street plan of Philadelphia, circa 1700.

Black Beard was also well acquainted with the Coates family of Philadelphia. Mrs. Bulah Coates ran a store at Number 77 High Street, not far from the modest brick and wood-framed, Christ Church, the future place of worship of Benjamin Franklin, George Washington and John Adams. The tall mariner was also known by Philadelphia's early residents to frequent an inn nearby, always "with his sword by his side."

In contrast to the dusty, tavern-less Bath Town, the streets and docks of Philadelphia during the summer of 1718 must have been awe-inspiring to young sailors. The city then was mostly dominated by Quaker influences, simple and unadorned—Queen Anne and Georgian styles had yet to arrive in the colonies. But Swedish and English

structures appeared here and there, such as the elegant Old Swede's Church beyond the southern outskirts of the city near the banks of the Delaware. High Street was the lively central east-west axis of the city where rows of two- and three-story brick buildings lined a cobblestone street. At the height of the business day a staccato of horses and drays, carriages and carts clattered along and echoed off the buildings. Along the wharves stretching northward, there was a constant frenzy of activity as cargos were loaded and unloaded. There were stacks of animal skins and lumber, and casks of dry goods, wet goods, wines and beers, rolling this way and that. Arriving and departing sailors loitered about and shared the news. Out in the river was a forest of masts, and clouds of luffing sails and standards drying in the light air as dozens of ships lay at anchor, and bobbing among them, longboats, barges and canoes.

According to John Watson, when the celebrated Black Beard came to town, he was recognized by some of the residents and was known to be quite a shopper. "He bought freely and paid well," it was remembered. Mrs. Coates told her grandson something fairly interesting about the pirate's persona: he and his crew were always "careful to give no direct offence to any of the settlements where they wished to be regarded as visiters and purchasers." There were other times, maybe during their visit in August of 1718, when Black Beard "was too politic to bring his vessel or crew within immediate reach."

Clearly, Black Beard had a familiarity with Pennsylvania's colonial capital and was comfortable roaming its cobblestone streets and alleys—as familiar with the city as its residents were with him. One can imagine him confidently strolling about High Street, hoisting his tricorn hat to passers-by—although probably not bothering to salute the uncocked brims of Quaker hats whose owners were known not to return the favor. Edward Thatch seemed to appreciate the refinements of the town destined to become, within the century, the colony's largest city—America's "London." But why? How did Black Beard know Philadelphia so well? Somehow, it is a question historians have neglected to answer.

Black Beard's familiarity with Philadelphia was certainly not as a result of his previous visit. He would not dared to have set foot anywhere close to High Street then. Less than one year before their August 1718 trip, in early October of the preceding year, Edward Teach was captain of Stede Bonnet's *Revenge*, ravaging and pillaging as many

The city of Philadelphia and the Delaware River in 1718 as depicted by painter, Peter Cooper. Black Beard's sloop Adventure *would have appeared much like the vessel on the far left of the preceding page.*

as 17 vessels off the capes of the Delaware Bay during an especially reckless rampage. Their actions were not just pirating but seemingly a drunken rage of retribution for the imprisonment of "Black" Sam Bellamy's crew in Boston earlier in the year—taking some ships, sinking others and indiscriminately tossing valuable cargos overboard. It was not during that cruise that Black Beard had roamed the streets of Philadelphia, forming the impressions and memories of its citizens like Mrs. Bulah Coates, endearing himself as a sagacious spendthrift. So the question remains, when during Black Beard's career did he spend substantial amounts of time in the City of Brotherly Love?

A story running in the November, 1717, issue of the *Boston News-Letter* may provide a clue:

> Philadelphia, October 24th. Arrives Linsey from Antigua, Codd from Liverpool and Dublin with 150 Passengers, many whereof are Servants. He was taken about 12 days since Off our Capes by a Pirate Sloop called the Revenge, of 12 Guns 150 Men, Commanded by one Teach, who formerly Sail'd Mate out of this Port.

The revealing reference, "Commanded by one Teach, who formerly Sail'd Mate out of this Port," has often been ignored by historians who preferred Capt. Johnson's unsupported claim that Black Beard "was a Bristol man born but had sailed some time out of Jamaica in privateers." It seems the authorities of Philadelphia, who kept meticulous records, would have known what they were talking about—or more correctly, who they were talking about. "Sailing mate out of this port" means that before he became Black Beard the pirate, Edward 'Teach' or 'Thatch' had served aboard a merchant or trading vessel hailing from the city of Philadelphia. Because of long-established traditions and shipboard hierarchies, being a mate aboard a ship sailing out of Philadelphia suggests that the future pirate captain had held that position for some time, possibly for five years or so, serving under the same master. It was a job for which he had been groomed from an early age.

In 1717, as has been previously noted, Black Beard could not have been elected captain of his first pirate command had he not possessed a rather extensive list of maritime skills, including the ability to navigate, read charts and piloting instructions, recognize tidal changes, evaluate currents, and understand varying weather systems. A captain had to be able to read and make fairly complicated mathematical computations. Usually, the selection of a pirate captain from a pool of prospects was fairly easy—he was among the few aboard who could read and was one of the few who could navigate. In Black Beard's case, it wasn't because "he had distinguished himself for his uncommon boldness and personal courage" as Charles Johnson wrote in 1724, but because the young man could figure out which way to point a vessel to get to where he wanted to go. Not too many men could in those days. Navigation by the sun and stars using a strange device known as an astrolabe or English quadrant was considered a "black art" by the average seaman.

Sailors like Black Beard were usually capable of navigating for two reasons—they had received a decent education in their youth and they had been placed aboard a ship for the purpose of learning the trade as a result of a connection, typically because of the influence of a relative or friend of the family. Some young men in the early 18th century, especially those of Scot or Irish descent were indentured or apprenticed to a merchant, a captain or trading master. Black Beard may have been sent away to Philadelphia as an apprentice at an early age by his father and "learned the ropes" in just such a way.

Why Philadelphia? Records indicate that there may have been at least one family connection between Philadelphia and Bath Town and there were probably more. Four brothers named Linton, originally of Scotland, emigrated to Philadelphia around the time of William Penn's second voyage to Pennsylvania in 1699, possibly aboard the same ship as Penn. The brothers—John, Jacob, Samuel, and Benjamin—had joined the Quaker Church, much to the disgust of their eldest brother, Roger, a Presbyterian, who proceeded to disinherit his siblings. A sixth brother, James, may have been Catholic, as it is known he moved to Ireland.

Fewer than 20 years after the arrival of the four Lintons in Philadelphia, a James Linton appears in the records of Bath County. Identified as both a captain and a cooper, James Linton is listed in the Beaufort County Deed Book as having owned, at various times, property in Bath Town proper, including lot numbers 13, 26 and 41.

The records fail to indicate when Linton acquired lots 26 and 41, leaving open the possibility the transaction had occurred during the 1711-1715 gap in the records caused by the Tuscarora War and its aftermath. Had he lived in a house on either lot 26 or 41, James Linton may have been the close neighbor of Gov. Eden. Lot number 13 presents an even more interesting connection for it had been previously owned by Capt. James Beard.

Although currently there is no proof, it seems plausible that one of the four Quaker brothers may have named one of their sons, James, after their brother in Ireland. The Philadelphia Lintons possibly had connections to the thriving Quaker community in early 18th-century North Carolina and other sons of the four brothers may have moved to the developing colony. A William Linton appears in the published *Abstract of North Carolina Wills 1690-1760*, having died in January 1726 in Bath County. Even today the Linton surname maintains a strong presence in the Bath Creek area, as well as in the nearby town of Pantego.

There is another intriguing sign that Black Beard may have had a long-standing connection to Philadelphia and it has to do with his name.

Thatch, Thatche, Tach, Thach, Thack, Theach, Theatch, Teatch and Teach are just some of the variations of the spelling found in contemporary records referring to the pirate, Black Beard. And the discrepancies spawned by the name's various forms has done as much to confuse and conceal his true identity as did his bountiful black beard. Consistent or standardized spelling, the orthography of the English language, had not yet been established in Great Britain and her colonies during the Golden Age of pirates. It would be another 30 years before Samuel Johnson began working on "A Dictionary of the English Language," which became the first widely published dictionary of the time. Until then, many words and names were spelled phonetically, the variations depending upon the common pronunciations of the writer. When Black Beard's presumed surname was written in official letters, council minutes, court records and newspaper stories of the day, it most often appeared as, Thatch. However, even within one letter, including the many written by the verbose Virginia lieutenant governor, Alexander Spotswood, for example, the name Thatch might have been spelled two or three different ways. Another reason for the confusion over the spelling of Thatch was because of the way the word was pronounced. In 18th-century England, Scotland and Ireland, words composed with a "th" were nearly always pronounced with a hard "t." Just as today when we say the name, Thomas, it sounds like "Tom-as." Another good example is how the river flowing through London is pronounced "Tehms" and not "Thaymes." Had you had the occasion to ask Black Beard his name, he probably would have pronounced it, Tetch or Teech, but he would have told you to spell it as Thatch.

Either way, he would have been lying to you.

On the second page of his biography, *Blackbeard the Pirate: A Reappraisal of His Life and Times*, Robert Lee wrote, "There are some indications that Edward Teach was born into an intelligent, respectable, well-to-do family, and, if so, he had all the more reason to abandon his real name and assume an alias." The statement rings as loud and as true as the peal of bells in a great cathedral. The truth is, even Thatch was likely an assumed name. Another likelihood is that the name Thatch might have been adopted by the future pirate when he was apprenticed to a sea captain as a young man, a practice prevalent, in particular, among Scottish families.

There has been another theory that Thatch's real surname was Drummond. It was John Watson who gave birth to the idea that Black Beard was, in fact, Edward Drummond, a native of Bristol, England. The only problem with Watson's theory of Black Beard's Bristol heritage is that Drummond is a Scottish surname and the Drummonds were fierce supporters of the Jacobite Rising of 1715. Nevertheless, in his *Annals of Philadelphia*, Watson makes an interesting point: "The name of Teach, it may be observed, seems to be a feigned name, because no such name can be found in the Philadelphia or New York directories." Watson had attempted to trace the Teach variation prior to the completion of his manuscript in 1842. In more recent times, numerous authors and researchers have gone to Bristol, England, to try and trace Black Beard's roots, searching for occurrences of the names, Teach and Thatch, in the extant records of the late 16th and early 17th centuries. None could be found. But no one seems to have looked into the early records of Philadelphia and its satellite communities and counties for Thatch or Thatcher, until now. Had they done so, they would have discovered the presence of Thatchers around the time of Black Beard.

Following the arrival of William Penn in 1682 and the establishment of his proprietary colony based on the principles of guaranteed democratic and religious freedoms, many citizens of Great Britain and Ireland made their way to Pennsylvania to avoid persecution at home. Among them was the family of Richard Thatcher, who shortly after Penn's arrival settled in Thornbury Township, Delaware County, about 20 miles west of Philadelphia. But it was Marcus Hook, fewer than 10 miles away, that provided the nearest gateway to the sea for Thornbury Township's farmers, trappers and tanners. Additionally, off the tongues of the early settlers of Pennsylvania, Thornbury would have been pronounced "Turnbury," a decidedly Scottish sounding place.

Richard Thatcher presided over the birth of many children and grandchildren before his death in 1722. One descendant, a William Thatcher, was known to have been born in North Carolina, which suggests some kind of connection to the southern colony, possibly through a trading account. Other records identify a Thatcher living in Philadelphia along Front Street at the north end, close to the wharves of the Delaware River during the third quarter of the 18th century, although many years after Black Beard's death. Nevertheless, the Thatchers of Pennsylvania provide an alternative source for the pirate's presumed name, or alias, Thatch. Had he known a Thatcher or had been apprenticed or indentured to a Thatcher, he may have adopted their name for his own, choosing to protect the reputation of the Beards of Carolina. It can be imagined that as a popular seaman aboard a coasting trader, plying the sea lanes between Philadelphia, New York and Charleston, his companions might have called him affectionately by the shortened nickname, Thatch, which, depending on the accent of the speaker, sounded a lot like "Teh-tch" or "Teech."

"A denizen of the Blue Anchor."
Illustration by Howard Pyle.

in colonial America's only newspaper at the time? Suddenly self-conscious, he might have discretely relocated into a dark corner, hoping he would not be recognized. And how could he have not been recognized? He was conspicuously tall, with the parchment-like skin of a sailor and with an extravagant, bushy black beard. He may have bundled and tucked the braids of his beard to make it look more trimmed, but still, beards were not the fashion in those days, and he would have been among the few men in Philadelphia to have one. Very likely, Black Beard may have paid something extra for the ale in order to buy a little anonymity and to be able to drink in peace.

The captain might also have eavesdropped on some of the stories coming from inbound crews, hearing that a pirate named Capt. Edwards was harassing ships off the Virginia and Delaware Capes. Upon learning the reports, Black Beard might have let slip a wry little smile because he knew that Capt. Edwards was none other than his former friend, Stede Bonnet. "Edwards" had been Bonnet's favorite alias. The information filtering in to the docks of Phildelphia and other colonial ports confirmed that Bonnet had returned to pirating after receiving the royal pardon. Black Beard probably assumed the angry Barbadian planter was out hunting for him. Hopefully, he might have thought, Bonnet wouldn't come bursting into the Blue Anchor at any moment.

In fact, Bonnet and Thatch had very nearly run into each other around the first of August. If Stede Bonnet's crew had not seen the sloop *Adventure* sailing north, on a reciprocal course, it may have been because they had recently captured two sloops in the entrance of the Delaware Bay, one loaded to the gunwales with more than 1,500 gallons of rum. One of the two captured captains, Peter Mainwaring, later testified at Bonnet's trial in Charleston that the pirates were thoroughly drunk. Possibly, at some dark hour of the night, Black Beard's single sloop and Bonnet's four ship convoy passed each other in the sea lanes off the Delmarva Peninsula, unaware of each other's proximity.

For whatever reason Black Beard came to Philadelphia in August, 1718, it must have been of grave importance because he could not have had complete faith in the protective qualities of Gov. Eden's pardon. He may have come to find a willing buyer for some of his ill-gotten gains. Quakers were well known to look the other way when the bizarrely-dressed gentlemen of fortune swaggered into their mercantiles with goods to unload. John F. Watson wrote in his *Annals of Philadelphia*: " I find among the scandals of the time, some one had set forth in a printed pamphlet, of 1703, that 'these Quakers have a neat way of getting money by encouraging the pirates, when they bring in good store of gold, so that when Avery's men were here, the Quaking justices were for letting them live quietly, or else they are bailed too easily.'"

Black Beard may also have been in Philadelphia to recruit competent sailors for his forthcoming reentry to life as a privateer. Prior to the end of the War of Spanish Succession, many Philadelphia-based merchant ships participated in privateering and it was then that Black Beard would have proven his " uncommon boldness and personal courage" so memorialized by Capt. Charles Johnson.

But if we had to bet our money on why Black Beard was in Philadelphia, it was because he desperately needed to see a doctor.

A few clues lead us to the conclusion that Black Beard had a serious medical problem. Eight and a half months before he visited Philadelphia during the summer of 1718, when the pirate captain captured the French slaver, *La Concorde*, Black Beard forced three French surgeons onto his crew. A couple of weeks later and 300 miles to the north, near the island of Nevis, the newly converted 40-gun pirate ship came within striking distance of the 30-gun British frigate, HMS *Scarborough*. Black Beard's crew decided they might like to try and engage His Majesty's warship for the singular purpose of humiliating the Royal Navy, or at least that is what they boasted to the crews of some of their later prizes. But

in a deposition later given to Gov. William Hamilton of the Leeward Islands by Thomas Knight, a temporary prisoner aboard *Queen Anne's Revenge*, the attack on the HMS *Scarborough* had to be called off, for "the Capt. being ill prevented it."

This incident is a treasure chest full of interesting implications about Black Beard and his crew. First of all, within the annals of piratedom, it is quite unusual for a captain to have called in sick for work. Secondly, it says something about Black Beard's command over his large crew at the time. Of course, pirate captains only really possessed ultimate authority when they were chasing or engaging an enemy ship or prize, but with three vessels bristling with cannon and hundreds of men in his modest fleet, it is curious that one man not feeling well caused the remaining company to call off the attack on the *Scarborough* if that was what the majority wanted to do. Most other pirate captains would have been subject to being deposed for such a weakness, even a temporary one. Not so with Black Beard. Whether by intimidation or affability, the captain had enjoyed an unusual influence over his crew. At least until the late summer of 1718.

Finally, there is the episode of the blockade of the port of Charleston on June 4, 1718. Even though Black Beard and his crews aboard the *Queen Anne's Revenge* and her consorts took as many as eight prizes off the Charleston bar, the primary mission for their five-day visit was to acquire a chest of medicines. Probably, one or all of the French surgeons pressed into service six months earlier had attended to Black Beard and his "affliction."

"Ah, mon Capitaine Teatche, you have an abominable distemper. See this pox, here on your hands. Your feet, too? Ah, oui. How should I say? Monsieur has a bad case of the clapoir," one of the doctors told their philandering patient.

"What may I do about it?" Black Beard asked.

"Well, monsieur, we need some special medicines; quicksilver and a syringe. Not something we carry on an Ivory Coast slaver. These kind of things you can only find in a large city."

"Like Charles Town?"

"Yes, indeed, they might have such a thing at your American Charles Town."

And so, at the entrance to Charleston harbor, when Black Beard had practically the entire colony of South Carolina at its knees, all he demanded was a chest of medicine. After some tense moments when his emissaries failed to return quickly enough, the chest of medicines arrived on board the *Queen Anne's Revenge*. Recently, some writers have postulated that the medicines were not for the captain but for some members of his crew and that Black Beard conceived the daring plan to hold the town for ransom out of concern for their health. Had Black Beard blockaded Charles Town for anyone but himself seems a little difficult to imagine.

Considering Black Beard's predilections, he was most likely suffering from a secondary stage of syphilis. Ironically, the disease was often referred to as "the French disease" in most every country but France. Symptoms may have included a rash, fever, sore throat, weight loss, headaches, disorientation and confusion, a general feeling of weakness and often, irritability—the sort of things that would prevent a pirate captain from leading an attack on a Royal Navy frigate as happened at Nevis, or serving as a pirate captain at all. Black Beard may well have strived to hide his symptoms from other members of his crew, even his closest friends, while at the same time he may have seen others on board with the same affliction. An irritable, disoriented, able seaman was probably not so remarkable on board ship, but when the captain exhibited those tendencies, it could be a matter of great concern for the other officers and crew.

As debilitating as syphilis could be, what was accepted as the most effective cure during the first quarter of the 18th century may have been perceived by the patient to be worse than the illness. In 1718, venereal disease was often treated by injecting mercury chloride into the patient using a pewter, urethral syringe. As the bo'sun of the *Queen Anne's Revenge* set her sails on a course for Old Topsail Inlet, Black Beard called for his doctor. Not long after, when the French surgeon came to the captain's cabin to administer the cure for his "problem," the patient—"the bravest and most daring corsair of them all"—saw what the doctor planned to do and probably decided to seek a second opinion. Which may be the real reason why Black Beard took such a risk going to

Urethral syringe recovered from the wreck of the Queen Anne's Revenge.
Photo By: Wendy Welsh. Courtesy of NC Dept of Cultural Resources.

Philadelphia in August, 1718. He never really trusted Frenchmen, anyway.

Had the August, 1718, visit to Philadelphia been the time when Black Beard "was too politic to bring his vessel or crew within immediate reach," it meant that his men aboard the *Adventure*, anchored amongst the ménagerie of vessels in the Delaware River, had some time to speak to each other freely. They may have even called a council and debated why they had to remain on their sloop and not enjoy the pleasures of the Quakers' ordinaries.

Did they not have the benefit of the King's pardon? Among the 25 men or so remaining onboard the Adventure was Israel Hands, who had lost his command and been demoted after the confusion of the Old Topsail Inlet separation—clearly, he and the captain had not been seeing eye-to-eye of late. William Howard, former quartermaster of the Queen Anne's Revenge, may have also been still part of the company. Among the others were some of Black Beard's most trusted friends, including John Martin of Bath Town. Black Beard and Martin had been together since their first days of pirating with Hornigold. The cooper, Edward Salter, was somewhat new to the crew, having been pressed from Henry Bostock's sloop, Margaret, the previous December, but Salter had exhibited an enterprising spirit and loyalty. Still, none of the men could deny that their captain was not well, their rum, food and fresh water were dwindling quickly, and for the time being, they had no income. They couldn't even be certain that the governor of the Virgin Islands would make them privateers, or that their captain would return from the Quaker town, for that matter. What would they do next? Most of the men were in agreement—their plans might have to change.

Meanwhile, somewhere in Philadelphia, probably near High and Front streets where Black Beard was known to frequent, the captain was tracked down by a messenger. A "friend" wanted him to know that Pennsylvania's Gov. Keith had just issued a warrant for his arrest. Black Beard may never have had the chance to see a physician. On the other hand, considering his behaviors over the next four months, maybe he had seen one, and the doctor told him that unless he took his medicine, his symptoms would worsen, he would lose his mind and then he would probably die.

With great haste, Black Beard hired a launch to take him out to the Adventure, probably leaving from the landing at Vine Street near the Penny-pot house, which was less frequented than the quay at the Blue Anchor and, therefore, had fewer prying eyes. Aboard the sloop, the captain asked the quartermaster, either William Howard or Thomas Miller, to make sail as quickly as possible. Black Beard had no intention of testing the validity of Gov. Eden's pardon while he waited in a jail in the colony of Pennsylvania. Within the hour, the Adventure weighed anchor and began to make her way down the Delaware and out into the open ocean.

Before the former pirate sloop reached the Delaware capes, the crew called another council, this time with the captain present. They told him they were not yet ready to go south to the Indies, and neither was their sloop—it had been some time since she had been careened. She needed some re-planking and re-caulking, her rigging was becoming worn and tired, sails needed to be *patched or replaced. They had not planned on using their own money to maintain the* Adventure. *They needed a prize, a sacrificial ship. And some of the men thought they knew where they could find one that might avoid entanglements with the government.*

For the first time in his two-year career as a pirate captain, Black Beard's vote was overruled. Rather than turning south or north, the Adventure *headed out into the deep blue sea. Their course was east-by-southeast, and the run to their destination was a little more than a thousand miles—about a week with a favorable wind. They were sailing for the eastern side of the Bermudas where French ships were known to pass on their way home from their plantations on Martinique. The plan did not suit the captain, but, c'est la vie. At least they were going after Frenchmen—he trusted them even less than before.*

Somewhere east of Bermuda on Friday, August 22, 1718, two French merchant ships were passed by a speeding school of dorado, flashing their luminescent colors near the surface between floating fields of sargassum. The ships were slowly working their way northward on a great circle course bound for home. They had departed Fort-de-France, Martinique, some weeks earlier, sailing close to the outer fringes of the Sargasso Sea and as far as possible from the depredations of Caribbean pirates. The ships were following an ocean passage usually traveled only by European-bound vessels departing from the Windward Islands and who had no reason to call on the American colonies. So it must have caught their attention when a Jamaican-rigged sloop came racing toward them from the northwest, on a perpendicular course such as pirates often do, flying fish scattering before its bow.

After three or four days of watching and waiting, Black Beard and the crew of the *Adventure* spotted two sailing vessels coming up from the south on an intersecting course. They immediately prepared to engage their quarry. However, they must have had a momentary doubt about their chances. It would have been the first such attempt on a prize since Black Beard had shed the greater part of his company at Old Topsail Inlet and his first engagement as captain of the *Adventure*. The two ships looked to be armed but Black Beard's sloop had the advantage of speed and maneuverability, and his crew were experienced, seasoned pirates. And he had Death's head flying in the rigging.

The engagement must not have gone well for the once-reformed pirates because the Frenchmen fought back—at least more than Frenchmen were expected to do. Apparently, in this instance, Black Beard's fabled supernatural glare and burning fuses in his hair did not sufficiently frighten his victims into submission. Or possibly, the two French captains thought their guns could discourage the marauders and fired a broadside or two. Eventually the pirates prevailed, and their victims struck their colors signaling their surrender.

Black Beard ordered all three vessels to be rafted together and his quartermaster boarded the prizes, inspecting the holds and spaces below decks. Black Beard would have interviewed the captains. They found one of the ships to be sailing "light," with no cargo in her holds, while the other was transporting a modest consignment of sugar, cocoa, cotton and indigo dye—a paltry catch. But the burdened ship had some other plunder the part-time pirates wanted—a veritable ship's chandlery of rigging, sails, anchors, spare masts, oakum, pitch and tar, and timber for repairs. The ship also had food and water and even a few French delicacies like casks of confectionaries. She was just what they had been looking for.

Black Beard's men transfered the French crew of the burdened vessel to the empty one and sent them on their way. They then needed to take their prize someplace where they could work in peace, someplace where they had friends to keep a weather-eye out for enemies behind their backs. They would be pirates again, just the one time, and all would be well again. Bermuda had to be avoided for the same reason they were unwelcome in Pennsylvania. They would take their prize back to their own government at Carolina, to Ocracoke, where they would feel at home (what would be an eternal home for some). They didn't realize it at the time, on that 22nd day of August, but what they had just done sealed their fate. Three months to the day, many of them would be killed, primarily on the basis of taking the French prize off Bermuda.

The remaining few days of August passed as the *Adventure* and the French Martiniqueman, as she has since been called, crept their way across the warm, cerulean waters of the Gulf Stream, clearly delineated by the parade of moisture-laden clouds above. Around September 1st, the two vessels entered Ocracoke Inlet and followed the right-hand channel up toward Old Slough and the watering place. But they did not have the privacy they had expected. Over the coming days, their activities were observed by someone who was not a friend.

In November, the *Boston News-Letter* issued a dispatch from Rhode Island quoting an Isaac Freeman who had been captain of a sloop captured near Ocracoke by another pirate named, Richard Worley, about a month after Black Beard and the French shipped arrived. Freeman reported that "Teach the Pirate has brought in a Ship to Ockrycock Inlet and Unrig'd her, and suffers no man to go on board except a Doctor to cure his wounded Men." So much for the design of Black Beard and his crew to dabble in piracy just once more in order to repair their sloop. Within six weeks, most everyone in colonial America who could read had learned of the French ship caper.

As clear and authentic as Freeman's observations were, they still raise some intriguing questions. Where did the doctor come from who was described as the only man allowed onboard the French ship to cure the wounded men? And who were the wounded men and how did they become wounded? No surgeon was listed among Black Beard's crew members when they were captured or killed a few months later. But there may have been another vessel at Ocracoke taking on fresh water at the time the French ship arrived, and the surgeon may have been a member of that crew. In fact, Freeman had described other vessels in the vicinity, including one from London with two doctors aboard—William Brigs and Thomas Taylor.

As for how the men were wounded, in the letter written by Capt. Ellis Brand on February 6, 1719 (described in an earlier chapter), Brand reported that he was notified by a paid informant that the surgeon attended to "two wounded men, which they said was done by shifting of a piece," or, in other words, a cannon had broken free on the voyage from Bermuda. It was a reasonable explanation that only marginally disguised the truth—but a necessary one, as we will later learn.

Someone might have asked Black Beard, although foolishly, why the doctor was the only one who was allowed to see the injured men. By a closer analysis of the evidence, the implication can only be that their wounds were obviously not typical of blunt-force trauma caused by a crushing weight of a loose cannon, but by the laceration-causing effects of gunshot or cannon shot during the engagement with the two French ships. If anyone whose confidentiality was not paid for with a little gold dust or by the threat of a painful death, observed the true nature of the injuries, they would have realized the truth—the French ship was acquired by way of a piratical action. But Black Beard had a plan. He hoped to be able to claim they had found the ship drifting and abandoned at sea.

Work began on the *Adventure* quickly. Careening a vessel during the Age of Piracy was a risky business—ship and crew were vulnerable to attack during the days and nights the vessel was on a beach—but it was absolutely essential two to three times a year. Below the waterline, wooden vessels were (and still are) vulnerable to the destructive, hole-boring powers of the shipworm or teredo, a warm-water mollusk that, unchecked, could perforate the hull of a ship in just a few months. Bottom planking had to be inspected and if weakened, replaced. Then the hull was scraped clean of barnacles and other bottom-clinging organisms that drastically slowed a vessel down—speed was the pirate ship's most cherished attribute. Finally, all of the narrow seams between the planking had to be re-stuffed with oakum, a mixture of individual strands of hempen rope and tar, and then sealed with heated pitch.

It was a tough job for the reduced numbers of the *Adventure*'s crew. The ship's officers, who had been accustomed to relax under tents on shore when their previous crews numbered in the hundreds, had to get their hands dirty once again, including the captain. Even so, it can be safely assumed the worst of the chores were done by the crew's African members.

Of course, before the *Adventure* could be hauled-over,

she had to be lightened. All of her cannon, the ship's stores of food, water and spirits, and much of her ballast stones had to be removed to shore, or possibly over to the French ship. During the careening process, the French ship was useful in another way other than for storage or for providing its parts. It was used to pull the *Adventure* over on her beam ends by a line running from the French ship's capstan to the sloop's mast. Using a second vessel during the careening process made the job significantly easier.

The work took the better part of two weeks. During that time, Black Beard and his men may have slept aboard the French ship or under tents along the broad beach near the watering hole and the Old Slough. In modern times, anyone who has ever camped, or spent any time at all on Ocracoke Island's neighbor to the southwest, Portsmouth Island, would have a reasonable idea of what sleeping under an open-sided canvas lean-to would be like during the late-summer on Ocracoke in 1718. If there had been no breeze blowing, it would have been impossible because of the never-ending torment of mosquitoes and biting flies. In fact, this may very likely have been where the legend of Black Beard's flaming face was born. Capt. Charles Johnson probably heard the story from Israel Hands and fashioned it into much more than it really was. Johnson wrote that Black Beard "stuck lighted Matches under his Hat, which appearing on each Side of his Face, his Eyes naturally looking fierce and wild, made him altogether such a Figure, that Imagination cannot form an Idea of a Fury, from Hell, to look more frightful."

Essentially, Black Beard's "lighted matches" were no more than an attempt to keep insects away—an 18th-century version of 21st-century insect repellent coils. It has been a well-known fact throughout history that smoke is an effective deterrent for undesirable flying insects, and for centuries in Far East cultures, incense was burned, not just for purifying the air in religious rites but also for driving away mosquitoes. We can easily imagine Black Beard and his crew seated on the soundside shore of Ocracoke around a cook fire, smoking their clay pipes and swatting and slapping at clouds of bugs. Irritated, Black Beard pulls out a pair of long tapers or slow-burning fuses, lights them, and tucks their ends up under his tricorn hat. His friends look at him and laugh merrily, for even though it keeps the mosquitoes at bay, it makes him look like the devil.

Common sense also tells us that the "lighted matches under his hat" in times of a pursuit or battle would simply be impractical. Had Black Beard stood among dozens of men upon the deck of his pirate ship as they were attempting to intimidate their prey into surrendering, his smoking face would not have been readily discernible, especially from hundreds of yards away on board a pitching, rolling ship. As his men would be preparing for a boarding action, their captain, most likely, would have been trying to keep his hair and hat from catching fire. He would have looked ridiculous. But had Black Beard been able to patent his invention to drive away Ocracoke's mosquitoes, he would have become far richer than by pirating, although he may have had to share some of his royalties with Capt. Johnson and Israel Hands.

There was one more curious bit of information from Ocracoke reported in the November issue of the *Boston News-Letter*. Isaac Freeman added that he was told that Teach the pirate had "gone up in the Country to Pimlicoe to Kill Beef for a Voyage but knows not where he is designed to go." This seemingly superfluous reference is an example of a "loose end" of history, a "throw-away" line that has more implications than at first appear. On face value, if Black Beard were indeed going up in the country to kill beef, it would be an odd thing for a pirate captain to do. Most would simply steal the food they needed, unless they were striving to not be a pirate anymore. Or, maybe Black Beard and his crew were, at least, pretending not to be pirates. And it also raises another question, whose beef were they going to kill? Pirates as cattle rustlers? In any case, they didn't need to go so far. According to Outer Banks historian, David Stick, Ocracoke was among the barrier islands used by mainland planters as open grazing grounds, and by 1700 it was populated with free-ranging livestock including cattle, hogs, sheep and horses. If the pirates needed meat, all they had to do was go ashore and hunt it for themselves, or hire one of the local pilots or subsistence fishermen to do it for them.

As it turned out, Black Beard's trip up country was not to hunt for beef, but to hunt for advice.

Crossing Pamlico Sound at Sunrise.

Replica of a 30-foot-long 18th century periauger at Historic Hertford, Perquimans County, North Carolina.

Twelve—
Midnight Run to Bath Town

As soon as they captured the French ship off of Bermuda and were bringing her back to the colony of North Carolina, Black Beard knew he had a problem, and it is a safe assumption he didn't know what the solution was. He and his crew had committed an act of piracy that most certainly would not be excused by King George's most gracious pardon. In the minds of the other men of the *Adventure*, taking the French ship was necessary for their survival—or at least necessary to keep their sloop afloat—but Black Beard knew the justification would fall on deaf ears. He needed a wise counsel, someone who could give him good advice, and he knew just who he needed to see—his family's long-time friend, Tobias Knight.

With the careening of the *Adventure* completed, cannon remounted, and the crew busy with sail repair, tarring-down the new standing rigging, and transferring the French cargo to the tents on the shore, Black Beard decided to take a little trip, up country, to Bath Town. He announced to his fellow officers he would travel alone, with just the four black men, Richard Stiles, Thomas Gates, James Blake, and James White. They would take the periauger and would just be gone for a couple of days. It would be a worthwhile courtesy, Black Beard probably explained, to take some gifts to the government so that they might determine if the *Adventure*'s company would be granted entry again into the colony.

Early in the morning on Saturday, September 13th, the captain departed Ocracoke Inlet on his solemn mission. It must have been an unusual moment. He was in the fewest company of men in more than two years at sea. Maybe he considered the significance of it all. He had as many as 400 men under his command just three months before, and now just four—Black Beard and the four black men, traveling together as brothers-in-arms, as they would become in death.

Before they departed they carried aboard the gifts: a few casks of sweetmeats, a bag of cocoa, loaf sugar and some other boxes which were not identified; sealed ceramic jars of water and food for the journey, most likely hard tack and salt pork, had already been stowed. Unbeknownst to the captain, however, bottles of French wine and a jar of rum were accidently left behind at Ocracoke—a most unfortunate mistake.

is doubtful. For one thing, it is hard to fathom that the pirate captain would assume he could simply drop in at the home of the colony's second highest official, unannounced, in the middle of the night. If we are to believe established history, Black Beard and Knight had only first met and were in each other's presence for about two weeks in early July, and had not seen each other since. For the pirate to leave Ocracoke, essentially alone and travel all the way to Bath to deliver his demands to a government official who was supposed to be practically a stranger is just completely implausible. Simply considering that Black Beard went without his other officers should raise some suspicion. We can only surmise the midnight encounter suggests there was more to the relationship between the two men than history has revealed. Furthermore, as shrewd and conniving as pirates are believed to have been and as cunning as they have been portrayed in cinema, it is unlikely Black Beard could have devised the complete scheme that would be played out in the coming days to legitimize his French prize. Because of the complicated nature of the plan, and because it required the endorsement of North Carolina's Vice-Admiralty Court of which Tobias Knight was the presiding officer, it could only have been resolved in its entirety by the feverish mind of Tobias Knight himself.

The scene is worthy of a cinematic treatment: the two men seated at a tea table at two in the morning—one short, bespectacled and feeble in his bedclothes, reeking of musty air and sickness, and the other tall and muscular dressed in boots, tarred-dungarees and muslin blouse with a long, braided beard, stiff and crusty with salt, smelling of the sea. Shadows danced about the painted white walls as candles flickered and the two men smoked long-stem clay pipes. Both the pirate and the customs collector were ill and gradually dying, their lives mostly behind them.

They were probably attended to by Knight's young slave, Phillis. Katherine Knight, Tobias's wife, remained in her bed chamber on the second floor, not wanting to interfere in her husband's business—especially business conducted in the middle of the night. The Knight's had a house guest, though. Edmund Chamberlayne had been residing at the house for a couple of weeks. Chamberlayne's "lodging room" on the upper story of the wood-framed house was very near Knight's and surely he heard the commotion when Black Beard arrived and lumbered into the parlor below. It is a distinct possibility that Chamberlayne was a party to the discussion. The historical record does not provide us an idea of who Chamberlayne was or what his relationship was to the Knights whom he stayed with for at least another 12 months. (Chamberlayne was a witness for the inventory of Knight's estate on September 15, 1719.) A reasonable assumption is that Chamberlayne had been retained to assist the Knights with the management of their farm or other affairs. He would prove his unwavering loyalty to Knight in the coming months.

Black Beard first had to explain why they had not yet gone south, how he had sailed instead to Philadelphia, hoping to find a doctor who could offer a remedy to the sores on his hands and feet, his headaches and malaise. He may have admitted his sudden bouts of anger and unpredictable reprisals, inducing Knight to ask his friend to remove his weapons so that the captain might be more comfortable. Black Beard got to the purpose of his visit and confided the truth to Knight, how his crew demanded they look for a prize, far out in the ocean where no one would know, in order to repair and resupply the *Adventure*. They took what he called a Frenchman—a small brigantine, perhaps—loaded with French delicacies. Black Beard then would have presented Knight with his gifts—the sweetmeats—which were most rare for a table in Bath Town. And at some point he would have again asked his friend Knight for a drink, something stronger than tea. Whatever Knight may have offered him, it wasn't enough.

It is plausible that the imposing but deferential captain asked his advisor if the French ship might be claimed to have been found by the *Adventure*'s company abandoned at sea—a derelict. Tobias Knight may have paced the room, thinking. He considered the potential outcome that if the second French ship had continued on its way to Europe, it could be months or years before an inquiry would find its way to North Carolina. If no one knew the prize had come into Ocracoke, the French would never be able to trace its whereabouts. If no suspicions were raised, then his friend Black Beard could successfully claim he found it abandoned at sea, its French crew possibly washed overboard in a storm.

Knight believed they had a solution—it could work. He then must have told his friend to go back to Ocracoke and wait, and next return to Bath in about 10 days and report his finding of the derelict ship to the governor. It would be absolutely imperative that no one know Black Beard had traveled to Knight's house on the 14th—Knight could not have stressed that requirement enough, lecturing to the wild-looking captain, nearly a foot taller than he. Eden would then request Knight to form a Court of Vice-Admiralty to formally hear the captain's claim to the rights of salvage. And after what would appear to be a diligent consideration, the court would adjudicate his prize. Knight advised Black Beard that he should then claim that the ship was leaky and in danger of foundering in the inlet where it would become a hazard to navigation. The governor, or Knight, would suggest Black Beard move it to a place out of the channel and burn it to the waterline, which, in effect, would destroy the evidence of the piracy—or so they thought. Also, there would be a tariff to pay to the governor as the representative of the government, a percentage of the cargo payable in sugars, Knight explained. And even though His Majesty's Customs could not require it in a case of salvage, a generous payment to Knight would not be refused. Secrecy was absolutely essential, however, and the captain must have the complete cooperation and confidence of his crew. Otherwise, the plan would fail and they all could be convicted and hanged for piracy.

When Black Beard walked out of Tobias Knight's house at about 4:30 a.m., the strategy was set. For some reason, Knight returned one of the kegs of sweetmeats to Black Beard and his four men, probably because they could use the additional food for the long voyage back to the inlet. But the mysterious boxes, "the contents of which were unknown" to the four black oarsmen—according to their depositions in Virginia—Tobias Knight kept for himself. As to what was in the boxes, history has provided us no clue.

As the pirate captain walked toward the sloping path leading down to the landing, Tobias Knight called out to him from the steps of the house.

"Don't worry yourself, Edward. You and your men cause no more trouble and all will be well."

Black Beard didn't look back but indicated his affirmation by lifting his hat.

He was still in need of a drink.

They had been awake for more than 24 hours since leaving Ocracoke the day before, and Black Beard and his men must have been exhausted. During the darkest hour before dawn and a few miles down river from Knight's along the northern shore, the pirate captain spotted the pale gleam of a lantern rocking gently from the mast of a similar periauger moored near a place known as Chester's Landing. Black Beard ordered his oarsmen to row in the direction of the light, stating that he wanted to go ashore at Chester's house, probably to rest or to find something to drink. It is also possible he could feel the familiar, dismal sensation coming on from his illness, a headache perhaps, and thought some rum or cider might settle his nerves or dull his pain.

As they rowed near the other periauger, Black Beard abruptly changed his mind about landing at Chester's house and ordered his oarsmen to come-up alongside the other boat, at which point he leapt aboard and asked the stranger in the darkness if he could offer him a dram.

The stranger in the darkness was William Bell, the son of a wealthy landholder and planter from Hyde Precinct. Bell was in transit to an unknown destination in the company of a young boy and an Indian. He had observed Black Beard's periauger making its way up the river toward Bath Town Creek earlier in the night, specifically recalling later having seen the five men aboard. When he saw the same men a few hours later heading back down river, the behavior appeared to be a bit odd to Bell. Who would head up river in the middle of the night and then row back down river before the break of day? Smugglers, perhaps? As the suspicious periauger suddenly began rowing in his direction, Bell was understandably nervous. When the tall stranger suddenly jumped aboard and asked if they had anything to drink, Bell, taken aback by the man's audacity, replied that it was too dark for him to draw from his barrel of brandy. His recalcitrance did not sit well with

Thirteen—
The Ides of September

"All along the crescent-shaped beach near the old watering hole on Ocracoke's sound side shore were sailcloth awnings and tarpaulin ground-cloths, open cook fires with large cuts of meats roasting on iron spits, stacks of firewood and driftwood piled here and there, small kegs for stools circled around games of dice or cards, ceramic jugs of wine, rum and brandy, and stacks of swords, cutlasses and muskets, ready for action."

WHILE THEIR CAPTAIN HAD BEEN AWAY UP THE Pamlico River plotting strategies with Tobias Knight and pillaging his neighbors, the *Adventure*'s company rested and worried. They probably kept a lookout up the rigging of the sloop to watch the inlet and the waters offshore because the *Adventure* was vulnerable without her captain. They also must have been uncomfortably wary of what trouble Mother Nature might have been brewing beyond the horizon. September has always been a worrisome time for mariners on the North Carolina coast. Historically during the months of August and September, tropical cyclones have had an increased probability of following the sweeping curve of the Gulf Stream, the warm water current that passes within 20 miles of Ocracoke Island.

On September 14, 1944, one of the most destructive hurricanes in recorded history struck the island, sinking some vessels, casting others on shore, flattening hotels and houses, and cutting new channels. Fortunately, no one on Ocracoke was killed. In the more recent memory of island residents, the names of Donna, Danielle, Floyd, Gustav, Isabel, Gloria, and Diana will always be associated with the month of September. It is a month to wait, watch and worry.

The possibility that a deadly storm could overtake their anchorage near the old watering hole at Ocracoke Inlet was a serious concern for Black Beard's men during those strange days when their captain was absent. Had a hurricane come while their leader was away up country, it could have spelled disaster for the *Adventure* and her crew. At the least, they could have lost all of the French ship's plunder piled haphazardly on shore; at the worst, they could have lost their sloop and their lives. They might have been forced to escape to the open ocean, even more shorthanded than usual, to distance themselves from the dangers of land. Without time or manpower to properly secure their heavy cannon, food stores or plunder, Black Beard's men would have likely been sailing into oblivion.

So when their mercurial captain returned to Ocracoke in the periauger after being gone for a couple of days, most of the *Adventure*'s company were probably relieved, while a few others may have had conflicted feelings. No doubt they were all curious to find out if Black Beard had found a way to explain the mast-less hulk of the French ship anchored inside the inlet and wondered if they were still within King George's good graces.

Keeping his thoughts to himself, Israel Hands, however, was probably not happy to see Black Beard at all. As the periauger hailed the *Adventure* and came alongside to board, the crew lined the rail to help unload the boat. Hands was particularly observant when the five men returned, since they had in their possession some items that they had not left with—"divers goods," as they were called. When his fellow pirates asked him how he came into possession of the items, Black Beard told the men on the *Adventure* the goods were things he had "bought in the country."

This turn of events, the instance when Black Beard sheepishly lied to his crew about how he came into the possession of the items formerly belonging to William Bell—the box of pipes, the yards of fabric, the barrel of brandy (which must have contained considerably less brandy), and the silver cup—is another extraordinary moment which has been overlooked by history. The facts are clear and were scrupulously preserved in the Virginia trial depositions and subsequently in the North Carolina Colonial Records. But some questions have never been asked. Why was it necessary for Black Beard to lie to his shipmates? Why would he have concealed the fact that he stole the items from the impertinent trader up the river? For pirates with a long résumé of depredations such as that of the *Adventure*'s company, you would think they would find humor in their captain's daring nighttime raid on the trader, the boy and the Indian. Instead, Black Beard wanted his men to believe he had purchased the items on his brief journey. No doubt, the four oarsmen—Stiles, Gates, Blake, and White—were under strict orders to saying nothing to the contrary.

The explanations for Black Beard's inexplicable behavior are few. He may have weighed the fact that his robbery was a criminal offense subject to the laws of the proprietary colony and not the Admiralty laws of the high seas, and he hoped he would not be discovered. He was embarrassed that his assault on Bell met with resistance, requiring the four black crewmen's help, or perhaps he wanted to conceal his sudden, irrational outburst against William Bell from his men, who had already developed a concern about their captain's mental health. Whatever the reason, Black Beard's imprudent heist would remain unknown for months to come, until one day when Israel Hands happened to discuss the matter with William Bell.

Even though no hurricanes struck Ocracoke Island in September, 1718, storm clouds of another kind were brewing beyond the horizon—at London, Nassau, Charleston, Cape Fear and Williamsburg. Throughout the summer and early fall, a series of seemingly divergent events involving the King's ministers, royal and proprietary governors, and unrepentant pirates were coinciding to have an important impact on the future of Black Beard and his crew—as well as for Black Beard's former friend, Stede Bonnet. For some of the participants, the events would determine whether they would live or die and would mark the beginning of the end of the Golden Age of Piracy.

One month earlier, Great Britain, France, the United Provinces of the Netherlands, and the Holy Roman Empire formed the Quadruple Alliance in order to counter the efforts of Philip V of Spain to claim the throne of France. Although war had not yet been declared, on the 11th of August, 28 ships of the British Navy engaged the Spanish fleet off the coast of Sicily. King George's navy prevailed but the action sent a ripple of concern through the offices of the Lords of Admiralty in London. Their navy was ill-prepared to fight a lengthy war after it had been significantly reduced in size for economic reasons following the Treaty of Utrecht in 1713. As war with Spain seemed inevitable, it was apparent His Majesty's Navy was going to need more men, more ships, and the outside assistance of privateers. And the ranks of privateers would have to be filled by pardoned pirates.

The Royal Proclamation pardoning acts of piracy had received unsatisfactory results. The deadline to surrender expired on September 5, 1718, and reports from the governors of the various colonies indicated that large numbers of suspected pirates had not surrendered or had taken the pardon and soon afterward returned to their old game, much as Black Beard and his men did. Even before the first pardon had expired, the King's Privy Council at St. James's Palace in London began to consider the possibility that an extension might be necessary if they were going to be able to recruit an effective privateering force to raid Spain's treasure fleets sailing from Central and South America.

Earlier in the year, when the HMS *Phoenix* arrived at New Providence on February 23rd with the king's proclamation and offer of pardon, hundreds of pirates turned themselves in, including Black Beard's former captain and mentor, Benjamin Hornigold. Most of the pardoned pirates dispersed, many going to their homes in the mainland colonies of the Carolinas, Virginia, Pennsylvania, New York, Rhode Island and Massachusetts, or south to other Caribbean islands. Some did not, and after accepting His Majesty's grace they soon returned to their old perversions, as was described once in a Charlestown courtroom "like a dog to the vomit." They included Black Beard's old acquaintance, pirate captain Charles Vane, a veritable storm cloud in his own right.

To the English authorities, Charles Vane was worse than a unrepentant pirate; he was a politically motivated sea rover and a die-hard Jacobite. The early formation of Vane's political ideology, however, may not have come from his family as Black Beard's probably did, but from Jamaica's governor. As a young, impressionable sailor, Vane had risen within the pirate ranks on the vessels of Capt. Henry Jennings, a one-time privateering master who sailed under a commission by Jamaica's chief executive, Lord Archibald Hamilton.

The Hamilton family represented one of the oldest Dukedoms in Scotland and were intensely proud of their heritage. Lord Hamilton's brothers, including James, the fourth Duke of Hamilton, were all ardent supporters of the Stuart dynasty and they were well-known for having participated in various intrigues to place Prince James Francis Edward Stuart, in exile in France, on the throne of Great Britain. Following the death of Queen Anne and the accession of George I of Hanover, Gov. Hamilton cleverly maneuvered his fellow Scots, pro-Stuart men and Catholics, into positions of authority, including command over Jamaica's defenses. Hamilton also organized a private navy of small, armed sloops, ostensibly to serve as a deterrent against the Spanish. But some pirate scholars, including Colin Woodard, author of *The Republic of Pirates*, have come to propose Hamilton's secret plan was to create a "colonial Jacobite navy," ready to defend the rightful king once the Stuarts were restored to the throne.

Sealed in secret packets sent to Port Royal, Jamaica, dispatches from France and Scotland during the summer of 1715 may have apprised Gov. Hamilton that a rising of the clans was about to commence; key London ministries were to be seized; James Stuart, the Old Pretender, would soon mount an invasion of the British Isles; and the Hanoverian king, George I, would soon be overthrown. This explosive correspondence must have emboldened the pro-Stuart leaders of Jamaica's government. Hamilton quickly needed to find a way to finance his ambitions to turn Jamaica into a Stuart-ruled colony, and in late 1715 there was no better place to raise money than the ocean floor off the Florida beaches where a staggering treasure had been disgorged by a Spanish fleet destroyed by a hurricane in July.

Treasure worth millions of pounds sterling was waiting to be recovered in the shallow depths off Sebastian Inlet's beaches and the news spread rapidly, like a new contagious virus, infecting men both virtuous and villainous. As much as any other root cause for the proliferation of piracy between 1715 and 1718, it was the irresistible lure of gold, silver and jewels from the Spanish wrecks off the coast of Florida that brought men from all over the American and Caribbean colonies—much like the California and Klondike gold rushes of the nineteenth century. But when the salvage turned out to be harder and more dangerous than expected, many of the treasure seekers found it too easy to make the transition into piracy. Nevertheless, they came in everything that would float from small canoes to large trading vessels—privateers, runaway Royal Navy sailors, merchant traders and destitute planters, "all mad to go a wrecking." Even governors weren't immune to the possibilities of supplementing their meager income. Jamaica's Archibald Hamilton was among them.

Hamilton turned to his trusted privateering captain,

Henry Jennings, for assistance. In December, 1715, Jennings left Jamaica with two sloops and 180 men, including experienced free-divers, to "fish" the fabulous treasures of the Florida wrecks. It is presumed that Charles Vane was on the expedition. Once Jennings arrived in the area of Sebastian Inlet, it occurred to him he wouldn't need his divers—some of the Spanish survivors of the maritime disaster had already done their work for them. Buried on shore were well over a quarter of a million silver pieces of eight. Landing on the beach with an overwhelming show of force, Jennings and his men convinced the shipwrecked Spaniards to show them where the treasure was hidden, and with hardly any effort at all, Gov. Hamilton's privateers soon returned to Jamaica with a significant plunder. However, it was not the happy occasion it might have been.

During the months following Jennings arrival with the Spanish silver at Port Royal on January 26, 1716, Hamilton learned the distressing news that the long-anticipated overthrow of the German king in London had failed, the Jacobite army in Scotland had been repelled at Sheriffmuir, Prince James Stuart abandoned his uninspired invasion of Scotland and was exiled in Rome, and some of Hamilton's relatives had been arrested and imprisoned in London. Compounding the governor's problems, Spanish and French authorities in the West Indies were complaining about his privateers and their unlawful raids on ships and the Spanish wrecks off Florida's coast. By March, the governor's opponents on Jamaica's council sent word to St. James's Palace in London of their suspicions of his Jacobite intrigues, and Hamilton's days as the island's governor were soon over. He was arrested and transported back to England to stand charges, leaving men like Charles Vane to carry on the subversion of King George's government in the West Indies and waters of colonial America during the years to come.

If history has provided us few facts on the origins of Black Beard, of Charles Vane we know even less. The author of *A General History of Pirates* doesn't offer the slightest suggestion as to his nationality, age or general background, and he began Vane's chapter deep into the pirate's career. Nevertheless, an eighteenth-century engraver depicted Vane as a somewhat distinguished-looking, middle-aged man wearing a shoulder-length wig, gentleman's buckled shoes and stockings, and posed with a sword in hand and pointing to something off into the distance. Almost certainly, the pirate never wore a wig or stockings, nor was he distinguished-looking and middle-aged but more likely of the same generation as "Black' Sam Bellamy and Edward "Black" Beard. History does preserve the facts that Vane was volatile, recalcitrant, audacious and prone to frequently drink to the damnation of King George.

Vane must have accumulated enough money from the Spanish wrecks to eventually leave Capt. Jennings's crew because he began an extended, if not unremarkable "pirate holiday" at Nassau on New Providence Island between the middle of 1716 and early 1718. If, during this period, his piratical activities were not significant enough to be remembered in the official records, Vane was, without a doubt, percolating his political views on the state of the British monarchy. Around the end of 1717, and soon after advance word arrived of King George's proclamation of a royal pardon, Vane and his fellow Jacobite pirates at Nassau composed a secret correspondence that was sent to former Royal Navy Capt. George Cammock, who had previously defected to France in support of Prince James Stuart. The message pledged the pirates' allegiance to James III as their rightful king and appealed to Cammock to come to the Bahamas to lead those pirates and mariners who refused to accept King George's pardon in an all-out effort to capture Bermuda for the Stuarts. But before Vane's ambitious plans could be carried out, HMS *Phoenix* arrived at Nassau from New York in February, 1718, with news that the lawless pirate republic was being reclaimed by the Crown. Former privateer and circumnavigating explorer, Woodes Rogers of Bristol, England, was soon to arrive to serve as Governor-in-Chief of the islands, and those pirates who did not surrender would be prosecuted and hanged.

The news of the pardon sharply divided the pirate camps on shore and the crews aboard ships at sea. At Nassau, Vane led a growing contingent of pirates who were vehemently opposed to the prospect of losing their autonomy, their freedom and their merry way of life. They were disgusted when dozens of their "brethren of the coast" presented themselves before the captain of HMS *Phoenix*, Vincent Pearse, to accept King George's pardon. They included many of the Bahamas' leading pirate captains and officers who had styled themselves "The Flying Gang," such as Josiah Burgess, Thomas Nichols, John Cockram, Paulsgrave Williams and Black Beard's friend, John Martin, who previously served as quartermaster on Benjamin Hornigold's sloops.

Black Beard was at sea during this time, in his newly captured and refitted *Queen Anne's Revenge*, making his way across the breadth of the Caribbean from the Windward Islands in the east to the Bay of Honduras along the Spanish Main, and he was regularly inflicting his revenge on New England vessels along the way for the imprisonment of Sam Bellamy's crew at Boston. Near Puerto Rico on December 5, 1717, Black Beard learned of the impending pardon from the captain of one of his prizes. He, like Vane, repudiated the reign of King George and would have been conflicted as to whether to submit to the Hanoverian's authority. There may have been numerous debates aboard his flagship regarding the pardon. The less committed pirates on Black Beard's crew—men who had been pressed or joined to escape harsh treatment by their previous captains—quietly raised the question as to whether the company should surrender before it was too late and the Royal Navy began to hunt them down. Black Beard himself probably began to consider his options and how he might surrender to the one colonial governor who would be most friendly and accommodating.

Meanwhile, rather than surrender, Vane and his Jacobite friends escaped in a sloop to a secluded island not far from Nassau but were soon cornered and captured. But rather than prosecuting Vane and his men, Capt. Pearse accepted the advice of Hornigold and Jennings and allowed the defiant pirates to accept the king's pardon as a sign of His Majesty's goodwill. Their names were added to the rolls of more than 200 men who promised to give up piracy and pursue more honorable professions.

Vane did not remain a reformed pirate for long. He re-formed a new crew of unrepentant, Jacobite pirates and other reprobates and ne'er-do-wells. Throughout March and early April of 1718, Vane and his angry band taunted

St. James's Palace, London

Coast of High Barbary

Look ahead, look a stern, look the weather in the lee,
Blow high! Blow low! and so sailed we.
I see a wreck to the windward and a lofty ship to lee,
A sailing down all on the coasts of High Barbary.

O are you a pirate or a man-o-war? cried we.
Blow high! Blow low! and so sailed we.
O no! I'm not a pirate but a man-o-war, cried he.
A sailing down all on the coasts of High Barbary.

We'll back up our topsails and heave our vessel to;
Blow high! Blow low! and so sailed we.
For we have got some letters to be carried home by you.
A sailing down all on the coasts of High Barbary.

For broadside, for broadside they fought all on the main;
Blow high! Blow low! and so sailed we.
Until at last the frigate shot the pirate's mast away.
A sailing down all on the coasts of High Barbary.

For quarters! For quarters! the saucy pirates cried,
Blow high! Blow low! and so sailed we.
The quarters that we showed them Was to sink them in the tide.
A sailing down all on The coasts of High Barbary.

With cutlass and gun, O we fought for hours three;
Blow high! Blow low! and so sailed we.
The ship it was their coffin and their grave it was the sea.
A sailing down all on the coasts of High Barbary.

relatively innocuous pirate gathering gave Spotswood the impetus to invade the colony of North Carolina, for which he had no legal right to do.

One of Black Beard's most recent biographers has suggested that the Ocracoke pirate banyan ended abruptly when the alcohol ran out. That is unlikely, for there may have been a more urgent cause that sent Charles Vane and his brigantine fleeing for the open sea. On September 27, 1718, South Carolina's Col. William Rhett engaged Stede Bonnet in a nearly stationary five-hour gun battle during which all three of the sloops involved were at various times aground on the shallows of the labyrinthine mouth of the Cape Fear River. Out-gunned and out-numbered, Bonnet and his crew eventually surrendered and were captured. While Bonnet's former colleague, Black Beard, and the two pirate crews partied on Ocracoke, the hapless Barbadian plantation owner was 180 miles away, shackled in chains in the brig of Col. Rhett's sloop *Henry*, on his way back to Charleston. News of the sensational capture of Stede Bonnet and his men would have taken fewer than 48 hours to travel from Cape Fear to Ocracoke, and Vane would have heard additional rumors that the intrepid Rhett had been intent on finding him, as well.

As Vane's men were recalled to their ship to weigh anchor, their captain called out to his counterpart. "Keep a weather-eye over your shoulder, Edward. Your enemies may be closer than you know."

Black Beard, watching the hasty departure of Vane's brigantine from the deck of the Adventure, stroked the long, stiff braids of his beard and thought Bonnet had been a fool for allowing himself to be backed into a corner. Even so, it was apparent that the numbers of safe harbors for pirates were dwindling. Considering the state of his health, if he ever found himself similarly trapped as Bonnet, he would use Vane's idea to light his powder magazine and blow himself and his attackers to hell.

Fourteen—
Colonial Chessboard

Following the sudden departure of Charles Vane and the end of Ocracoke's grand pirate ball, Black Beard put his crew to work in order to fulfill their obligations to Gov. Eden's Court of Vice-Admiralty. They planned to deliver at least 80 casks of sugar to Bath and it apparently would require two trips in the sloop *Adventure* during the month of October. We know this because Black Beard's movements were being watched.

Aboard the Royal Navy frigate HMS *Lyme*, the vessel assigned to protect merchant vessels from pirates on the approaches to the Chesapeake Bay, Capt. Ellis Brand wanted to assess the strength and whereabouts of the pirates rumored to be operating out of the neighboring colony to the south. Inbound vessels had previously brought news of the wreck of a 40-gun pirate ship at Old Topsail Inlet in June, and during the ensuing weeks many of Black Beard's castaways appeared in the Virginia colony on their way to new endeavors. Some remained in the Tidewater region of southeast Virginia while others sought passage on northern-bound ships. Dozens of skilled tradesmen had been forced into the pirate company over the previous year from vessels hailing from various colonial and European ports—among them carpenters, blacksmiths, surgeons, cooks, sailmakers, coopers and musicians—and they now had to find a way home. Other mariners were reluctant to give up their merry lives at sea and were observed in tippling houses and around the docks and landings in Norfolk and Kiquotan Roads (Hampton Roads today), attempting to entice honest men to form new pirate crews. Like spilling a box full of termites that scurry to the myriad crevices inside one's house, the dispersion and "retirement" of huge numbers of former pirates was a development that caused a great deal of consternation for colonial authorities.

Throughout the summer and early autumn of 1718, Brand hired a few mariners who regularly conducted trading trips in and out of the Pamlico and Albemarle sounds to gather intelligence on the remaining pirates' activities, moorings, and rumored ravages of North Carolina's population. Reports came back to Brand that the pirates, led by "the notorious Pyrat Thach alias Blackbeard," had brought in a French ship found abandoned at sea. Brand was also informed that the brigands frequently traded with the colony's inhabitants but the prices for the items purchased, primarily food, alcohol and tobacco, were almost always determined by the buyers. This was a practice employed by other pirates where they maintained a symbiotic relationship with their neighbors, particularly in the Bahamas. Despite these one-sided negotiations, it is important to note that for the most part after receiving their pardons, Black Beard and his men appeared to be trying their best to remain within the law—a few lapses notwithstanding. Some of the Carolina traders, however, must not have felt they got a fair deal when selling their goods to the pirates and complained to anyone who would listen. No doubt, among those determined to put an end to the pirates' unfair trading practices, and even worse outrages, was William Bell of New Currituck, Hyde Precinct.

It is not clear whether the abuses reported to the Virginia authorities were accurate, or whether there were many or few. Historical records mention only the one robbery of William Bell throughout Black Beard's brief stay in North Carolina in 1718. Could the robbery of Bell have been the only incident? The citizens of 18th-century Carolina were exceptionally litigious. The colonial records and county deed books are filled with disputes, lawsuits, warrants, summons and indictments. Had other citizens been robbed or assaulted, surely the crimes would have appeared somewhere in the records. There are none.

Bell obviously had friends with close ties to the Virginia government, including Gov. Eden's chief rival—the lawyer and former Speaker of the House and Surveyor General, Edward Moseley. At least one North Carolina scholar has characterized Moseley as the colony's finest citizen, primarily on the basis of his four decades of public service. For many years Moseley had been aligned with the Popular Party, a political faction that opposed those men of the province who supported the current administration of Eden's, known as the Proprietors Party. Eden's supporters included Tobias Knight, and Eden's trusted advisor Col. Thomas Pollock, a former acting governor who would fill the position again upon the death of Eden in 1722. Pollock and Moseley, who lived near each other on opposite shores of the Albemarle Sound near the mouth of the Chowan River, had disliked one another for some time. The mutual animus between the two men no doubt was forged seven years earlier when Moseley participated in an armed siege of Pollock's estate during the contentious and bloody Cary's rebellion.

Any opportunity to illuminate Eden's unsuitability as governor was capitalized upon by Moseley, who some historians believe had designs on the chief office for himself. From Moseley's perspective, the paternalistic treatment of Black Beard and his men by Eden and Knight was inexplicable, unless of course the colony's highest officials had somehow benefited financially from the pirate's presence. In his 1894 book, *The Carolina Pirates and Colonial Commerce*, Rev. Dr. Shirley Carter Hughson wrote, "The case of the French prize had by this time become notorious in the Provence, and whatever Eden and Knight pretended to think of it, everybody knew it was a clear case of piracy, and that instead of attempting the apprehension of the miscreants, the authorities had connived at their crimes, and had, it was generally believed, been well paid for their connivance."

Moseley was determined to prove the governor's collusion with the pirates, and he would go to extreme lengths to do so. The significance of this political wrangling and gamesmanship between Moseley and his friends and Eden and his supporters, cannot be overestimated in terms of the repercussions it had on the future of Black Beard and his crew. The Carolina pirates were no more than pawns on the colonial chessboard.

Moseley lived in Chowan Precinct, which had a good road leading northward into Virginia's Nansemond County and the ferries that crossed the James River to Williamsburg. No record confirms the event, but it makes sense that sometime after the adjudication of the French ship by the Vice-Admiralty Court and the robbery of William Bell in September, Moseley may have traveled to Williamsburg and discussed these scandalous events with Lt. Gov. Spotswood. The issue was not one that could be easily addressed in a letter. It was also not the first occasion Spotswood's assistance had been sought by citizens of North Carolina. Ironically, it was at the behest of Moseley's adversaries and Eden's predecessor, Gov. Edward Hyde, that Spotswood had dispatched a company of Royal marines to quell the violence of Cary's Rebellion during the summer of 1711. Historians have postulated that Spotswood was ever eager to extend his control and influence over his southern border, which he never considered to be far enough south. And in the early autumn of 1718, Edward Moseley and William Bell provided the Virginia chief executive with what appeared to be an open invitation.

The proximity of the pirates in the colony of North Carolina conveniently served Spotswood's political needs. He had been engaged in his own long-running dispute

Facing page: The Governor's Palace, Williamsburg, Virgini..

Lt. Gov. Alexander Spotswood

with members of his council and Virginia's House of Burgesses who had been agitating the Lords of Trade in London for the lieutenant governor's removal from office. Spotswood, his critics charged, employed heavy-handed tactics to control tobacco exports, accumulated expansive tracts of land through questionable practices and irresponsibly spent his colony's revenue on extravagant trappings for the palatial governor's mansion then under construction. Conversely, Spotswood cast aspersions on his adversaries by referring to each man by his particular behaviors of haughtiness, hypocrisy, inveteracy, brutishness, malice, conceitedness, and scurrility, "with about a score of base disloyalists and ungrateful Creolians for their adherents." Ironically, any one of the preceding adjectives could have been applied to the lieutenant governor himself. The former army officer must have been an exceedingly pompous and tiresome bore, which becomes evident by reading just one or two of his diffuse, long-winded letters to his superiors back in England. With a slight paunch, receding hairline and supercilious expression, Spotswood took enormous pleasure in his lordly station, even though he was merely a deputy governor for the absentee Earl of Orkney, George Hamilton. Incidentally, Hamilton was also the older brother of Jamaica's Jacobite governor, Archibald Hamilton, although it is not clear if the Earl had the same rabid passion his brother had for the House of Stuart.

During October 1718, a torrent of news dispatches, rumors, complaints and clandestine meetings dominated the lieutenant governor's agenda—or so history and Spotswood would have us believe. In reality, the torrent was mostly just a trickle.

A few weeks after Black Beard and Charles Vane learned of the capture of Stede Bonnet, so did Alexander Spotswood. The news that South Carolinians had pursued previously pardoned but recidivist pirates across the border into a neighboring colony and engaged them in a bloody and decisive gun battle must have commanded Spotswood's imagination. He was probably bitterly disappointed he had not been first to accomplish the feat. About the same time, informants on inbound sloops delivered the terrifying information that there was a large number of pirates industriously gathered along the northern shores of Ocracoke Inlet. It was an ominous turn of events that Spotswood characterized in a letter to London as, "a design of the most pernicious consequence to the trade of these Plantations, wch. was that of the pyrats fortifying an Island at Ouacock Inlett and making that a general rendevouze of such robbers." The ever-loquacious Spotswood found it advantageous to exaggerate the reports coming from North Carolina, to the extent that he would have others believe Black Beard and his cohorts were somehow building an impregnable bastion on North Carolina's Outer Banks—a feat that could not even be accomplished by hundreds of Confederate engineers, soldiers and laborers in the early days of the Civil War, 143 years into the future.

Furthermore, when we compare the actual evidence of Black Beard's escapades and whereabouts between July 1 and November 1 of 1718 and the purported offenses he committed during that time according to Spotswood, we find that the only connection that can be made is the pirate captain's pre-dawn assault on William Bell. Spotswood later tried to justify his intrusion into North Carolina's affairs in a letter to the 18-year-old Lord Carteret, one of the eight Lords Proprietors of North Carolina. In the letter he wrote, "The enclosed Affidavit of one of the Inhabitants of that Province, and [master] of a Vessell there, will best display Thatch's insolent behavior." Because no other incidents can be found in the records, Spotswood could only have been referring to Bell as the "inhabitant of that province." Then, Spotswood referred to "the repeated Applications of Trading People of that Province," which most likely refers to Edward Moseley. Moseley possessed one of the most extensive holdings of private property in North Carolina and the operations of his plantations depended greatly on the free flow of commodities in and out of the colony's sounds and rivers. All of those commodities had to pass in and out of Ocracoke Inlet, where the pirates had created a "nest" of sorts, like wasps in a door jamb. They might not attack, but you could never be entirely certain. Considering Moseley's extremely rash action in the months to come, it is not unreasonable to sus-

The Governor's Palace, Williamsburg, Virginia.

pect he was the one behind the "repeated applications" to which Spotswood referred. And there may have also been more to the relationship between Moseley and Spotswood than history has preserved. It is not inconceivable that the North Carolinian may have been favored with special privileges for the export of his tobacco through Virginia's ports, which was normally prohibited by Spotswood's policies, especially considering Moseley practically served Black Beard's head on a platter to Spotswood.

Teaches Hole Channel, Ocracoke, NC. "There were times when fair weather clouds under a high sun could be especially deceiving as their shadows made deep water appear where there was none."

Kevin Duffus photo.

Fifteen—
Mysterious Tides of History

Each day on Diamond Shoals, off Cape Point on Hatteras Island, opposing waves converge and crash into one another after hurtling their way from distant origins across thousands of miles of vast ocean. So, too, are there moments in history when the invisible undercurrents of time carry humans on an inevitable collision course with others. What may seem serendipitous is often the gravitational pull of an imminent historical event, inexorably drawing the participants along the untraveled paths of their futures, toward their destiny—and sometimes, their deaths. Such mysterious tides of history were at work during the unsettled autumn of November 1718.

Sometime, about two weeks after Black Beard had sailed from Bath Town, it is believed that Tobias Knight received a private message from Gov. Eden who was in residence at his plantation on the west side of the Chowan River. News had likely come to the governor by post road from Virginia that confirmed King George's second proclamation pardoning acts of piracy was aboard a ship making its way to the colonies and was due to arrive in mid-December. Knight was desperate to send word to the sloop *Adventure*—if she were still in port at Ocracoke—to alert the captain and his crew of the new certainty that their indemnity from past piracies would no longer be in doubt. The new proclamation, once it arrived, would prevent Black Beard from meeting the same fate as his unlucky friend Stede Bonnet.

Knight sat down at his desk in his library with a feeble but hurried hand to write his friend a letter, the contents of which have survived the centuries and have been described numerous times in scholarly accounts and folklore. Nearly every historian has characterized the letter as a warning to Black Beard that Virginia's Lt. Gov. Spotswood had launched an expedition to search for and to destroy the pirate captain and his crew at Ocracoke. Nineteenth-century scholar Shirley Carter Hughson wrote, "The pirate had received an intimation from Knight of the intended attack, but he had evidently treated the warning lightly, for he was wholly unprepared for a conflict when the Virginians hove in sight." Hughson and other historians could not have been more incorrect—the letter was by no means a warning.

Meanwhile, as Knight was composing his communiqué to his friend, the pirate captain and his *Adventure* were 30 miles away, stuck on the sandy shallows of Brant Island Shoals, outside of the entrance to the Neuse River. It was exactly one year to the day that Black Beard had captured his greatest prize off Barbados, the French slaver he renamed *Queen Anne's Revenge*. The pirates were probably not such good record keepers, or so sentimental that they would have remembered the date, but it was a bad omen just the same. Running aground had become somewhat of a habit since the pirates first crashed onto the North Carolina shore in June. Somewhere from a distance a trading sloop had seen the *Adventure* and the unmistakable signs of a sailing vessel struggling to free itself: a longboat off its bow sounding for deeper water, sails periodically luffing and the great main boom jibing wildly from beam to beam. Whether or not the trading sloop's captain recognized the vessel in distress belonged to pirates, he came to their aid. His name is believed to be Samuel Odell and his generosity was probably most appreciated and well-rewarded. Little did he know the trouble it would cause him.

And on that same day, when Tobias Knight was writing his letter and Black Beard was aground on Brant Island Shoals, Capt. Ellis Brand of the HMS *Lyme* was overseeing final preparations for his two prong invasion of North Carolina in search of the notorious pirate, as proposed and funded by Spotswood. The lieutenant governor hired two trading sloops, and Capt. Brand and Capt. George Gordon of the HMS *Pearl*, a 40-gun fifth-rate Royal Navy warship also stationed in the southern Chesapeake, provided the men: 35 sailors from Gordon's *Pearl* and 25 from Brand's *Lyme*. The two sloops and all of the men were commanded by Gordon's first lieutenant, Robert Maynard. At three o'clock in the afternoon on Monday the 17th, having been loaded with a month's worth of provisions, water, arms, ammunition and the pilots from North Carolina, the two sloops weighed anchor on their momentous mission.

Even before the two sloops disappeared below the horizon on their way to Cape Henry and the open ocean, Ellis Brand collected the necessaries required for an overland trip of an uncertain number of days and packed his kit in his cabin in the aft of the *Lyme*. Most likely the naval officer took extra care to include as many pistols, rounds and as much powder as was practical, and a saber or two. He must have dearly hoped they would not be needed. Within a couple of hours, after being rowed in his ship's launch across Kiquotan Roads and up the Nansemond River, Brand probably stopped for the night at the enticingly-named, Sleepy Hole Point, where he may have secured horses for the remainder of his mission. He was not in a particular hurry, since he was to arrive no sooner than Maynard in Bath Town. Nevertheless, at first light on Tuesday he was on his way by horseback for the capital of the colony of North Carolina. Sometime on Friday after making about 18 miles a day, Brand arrived at the burgeoning village of Queen Anne Creek (later to become Edenton) and was soon met by Col. Edward Moseley and his brothers-in-law, Col. Maurice Moore and Capt. Jeremiah Vail. For some days, the three Carolinians had been anxiously expecting the Royal Navy captain to arrive.

The number of forces accompanying Capt. Brand and the route they traveled varies in previously published accounts. Black Beard's most recent biographer suggests the main force of the expedition was a column of two hundred men, quite an astonishingly large number for even the greatest of early 18th-century Indian battles. Another historian has written that Brand's men had to hack their way through the Dismal Swamp, despite the fact there were as many as six roads on either boundary of the swamp in 1718 connecting southeastern Virginia with Bertie, Chowan, Perquimans, Pasquotank and Currituck precincts of northeastern North Carolina. Yet another noted author, also unaware of the existence of the roads, wrote that after passing through the cultivated (read civilized) fields and plantations of Virginia, Brand and his men entered "the trackless wilderness of North Carolina." The truth of the matter is most accurately told by Brand's colleague, Capt. Gordon, who wrote to the Lords of Admiralty on September 14, 1721, in order to clarify some of the facts of the event. Gordon wrote that Brand "went by land a single gentleman, and a Servant to apprehend Thatch with the assistance of the Gentlemen of that country who were weary of that rogue's insolence." It was not a column of 200 men but an expeditionary force of two—Brand and his servant. And had Brand been forced to hack his way through the Dismal Swamp and the "trackless wilderness of North Carolina," it would have taken him considerably longer to travel the 60 miles to Queen Anne Creek than the four days it actually required.

Brand spent Friday night at the home of one of the

Carolinians, possibly Vail's since his was closer to the landing of the ferry that would take them across the Albemarle Sound the next morning. The four men may have sat fireside on that cool November evening, and during a hospitable supper, discussed what might happen in the coming days. They must have appreciated the significance of their mission, its potential controversy and danger. Even so, they were well aware of what the Charlestonian hero, Col. William Rhett accomplished by engaging and capturing the pirate Stede Bonnet in the mouth of the Cape Fear River almost two months earlier. It had been accomplished once, and it could be accomplished again. And if any of the men expressed worry about the legality of their expedition, someone may have pointed out that the government of North Carolina lodged no protest against South Carolina Gov. Robert Johnson for invading his neighboring colony in September. Moseley may have interposed his expectation that they would surely reveal the shameful corruption of the administration of Gov. Eden and his chief justice Tobias Knight. Brand simply wondered where his sloops might be.

His sloops were near Ocracoke Inlet, within sight of their objective. At the same moment Capt. Brand and his hosts dined, Lt. Maynard's 60 Royal Navy sailors aboard their two sloops rested at their pre-battle anchorage in Ship Channel, where they had recently arrived after searching for the pirates at Brant Island Shoals. They, too, were emboldened by the success of Col. Rhett against Black Beard's former shipmates at Cape Fear. As they gathered together at the mess table below the main decks of the two sloops, the men likely discussed what their destiny might be upon the dawn of the next day. Would there be casualties? Would they be victorious? Would they recover a vast treasure of gold, silver and jewels?

Meanwhile, across the tidal flats of the Middle Ground, the crew and guests aboard the pirate sloop *Adventure* also dined and drank, and they no doubt enjoyed better fare than the Royal Navy sailors crowded aboard their small sloops nearby. The captain's mind, however, must have been preoccupied with the contents of the recently arrived letter from Tobias Knight, which he read over and over.

(*See a depiction of Tobias Knight's letter on next page.*)

The subtext of this seemingly inscrutable message, found among the effects of the slain pirate captain and preserved in the Colonial Records of North Carolina, has always been interpreted as proof of Tobias Knight's illicit interactions with pirates. Of that, there is no question. However, by winnowing of the words of the letter more carefully, there is still more to be learned.

First, the letter was no warning. Had Tobias Knight intended to warn his friend of Spotswood's impending attack, he would not have recommended to Black Beard to "make the best of [his] way" to Bath—instead, he would have told him to lay a course to sea as quickly as possible. In Bath, Black Beard would have been cornered, and there would have been no escape. The truth, lost to the ages as writers have been disinclined to delve beyond the standard story, could only have been that Knight wanted his friend Edward to know that an extension of the King's pardon was on its way. It was not a message the Secretary of the governor's Council could convey in writing, hence his sentence: "I have something more to say to you than at present I can write."

Secondly, by referring to the end of the "Indian Warr" Knight was alluding to the fact that the war turned out to be nothing more than a false alarm, a "villainous confederacy between some children and their servants" to prevent a slave from receiving a "punishment due him for past rogueries," as it was described in a meeting of the governor's council. But the threat of a new Indian war, real or not, may have been the impetus that hastened the *Adventure*'s final departure from Bath. Black Beard's sister, Susannah, and her family, would have been severely affected by the violence and devastation of the 1711 outbreak, especially since they were residents of Craven precinct which was particularly hard hit. With the panic of a new Indian war afoot, Black Beard would have wasted no time to leave Bath around November 1 to warn his sister. Since the 'war' turned out to be a false alarm, Knight knew Black Beard would want to be informed. Knight's sentence was not some passing reference or a casual comment regarding the latest news—it had a specific meaning for its recipient.

More mysterious is the identity of "Ganet." No one named Ganet was listed among the men killed or captured

> my ffriend, November 17, 1718
>
> If this finds you yet in harbour, I would have you make the best of your way up as soon as possible your affairs will let you. I have something more to say to you than at present I can write. The bearer will tell you the end of our Indian Warr and Ganet can tell you in part what I have to say to you so referr you in some measure to him.
>
> I really think these three men are heartily sorry at their difference with you, and will be very willing to ask your pardon. If I may advise be ffriends again, its better than falling out among your selves.
>
> I expect the governor this night or tomorrow, who I believe would be likewise glad to see you before you goe. I have not time to add save my hearty respects to you and am
>
> your real ffriend,
> And Servant
> T. Knight.

A depiction of the letter from Tobias Knight to Black Beard. The original letter is believed to be no longer extant.

during the engagement between the Royal Navy and the pirates aboard the *Adventure*. But there was a Garret (alternatively spelled as Garrat or Garrot) on Black Beard's crew—Garret Gibbons, the ship's bo'sun, who may have been related to a William Gibbons of Charleston who was known to have had ties to privateering. Considering the vagaries of handwriting and casualness of spelling at the time, it is easily conceivable that during an early court transcription of the Knight letter found among Black Beard's possessions, 'Garret' could have been misinterpreted as 'Ganet.' The "bearer" of the letter was not named by Knight but we will be able to deduce his identity later.

There is no mystery to Knight's mention of the three men who were heartily sorry at their difference with the pirate captain, only uncertainty as to who the three men were. It is doubtful one of the three men to whom Knight referred was Israel Hands. He was likely unwilling to ask Black Beard's forgiveness—much less ever trust him again—and Hands was in no shape to rejoin the company as it prepared to sail for the West Indies.

Knight's recommendation that Black Beard and the three men should be friends again suggests a relationship more close-knit than those between an ordinary captain and his crew. When Black Beard jettisoned the majority of his men at Old Topsail Inlet in June, 1718, he kept with him a core group of his best and most trusted friends, in addition to some other skilled sailors like Hands. It is possible this core group may have been acquainted with each other since their early teens, sharing the pride and kinship of community, religious beliefs and dissent against the crown. "It's better than falling out among your selves," implies a special union or fraternity, unlike the general associations among larger pirate crews. They may have been together for some time, much like many of the other gangs of young men from the colonies—New England, New York, Philadelphia and the Delaware Bay region, Virginia and the Carolinas—who had been drawn to the potential treasures of the wrecked Spanish galleons off the coast of Florida three years earlier. Knight's appeal to Black Beard to reconsider his decision to abandon the three men back at Bath, and their friendship, must have weighed heavily on the captain's mind. It's doubtful, but second thoughts by Black Beard may have even delayed his departure from North Carolina. On the other hand, he may actually have been secretly intending to save their lives by leaving them behind.

Also in his letter, Tobias Knight made it abundantly clear that he was Black Beard's friend—"your real ffriend," to be more precise. A cursory consideration might find nothing too remarkable about Knight's expression—maybe he signed all of his letters in that fashion. But consider the possibility that the salutation was sincere, that the relationship between the colony's second highest official and the pirate was more than casual. Knight also indicated that the governor "would be likewise glad to see you before you goe." These are extraordinary words which characterize a camaraderie among the three men that traditional history suggests existed for fewer than five months. Further adding to the improbability of their friendship, the records prove that Black Beard, at most, encountered the governor just twice since his arrival in Bath around the 1st of July, and the chief justice at least a few times more, including his midnight rendezvous with Knight on September 14. How is it that in such a brief time and in so few encounters, Gov. Eden and Tobias Knight became so bonded with Black Beard? Their relationship wouldn't seem so remarkable if we truly believed that Black Beard had thoroughly charmed the colony with "entertainments in his home on a lavish scale;" had bestowed on the population gifts of fine silks, jewels and gold; and brought into the colony a steady flow of much-needed hard currency. But we know now those distortions of history never occurred. Their meteoric relationship could not have been because the two government officials were star-struck by the pirate captain. His name and notoriety were just becoming widely known, but his celebrity in 1718 had not yet reached the stratospheric level it would until after his gruesome death and Charles Johnson published his *General History of Pirates*. Had Black Beard's friendship with Eden and Knight simply been purchased with gold dust and casks of sugar? The answer seems to be insufficient. That leaves us with only one possible explanation—the mysterious connection between the men precedes Black Beard's arrival in Bath Town on July 1, 1718. He had been there before.

On the morning of Saturday, the 22nd of November, 1718, Capt. Ellis Brand, his servant, Col. Maurice Moore and Capt. Jeremiah Vail boarded Bell's ferry to cross the Albemarle to rejoin the road to Bath Town on the southern shore of the sound. Col. Edward Moseley remained behind at Chowan, too dignified and righteous to confront those scoundrels in Bath who cavorted with rogues and robbers. Then again, perhaps Moseley went to work preparing his home to become the next governor's mansion.

At breakfast that morning at his house on the Pamlico River, Tobias Knight was fretful and may have gazed toward the horizon in the direction of Ocracoke. With a spyglass he could have seen the topmasts of ships far beyond the mouth of the Pamlico River, but the *Adventure* was no where in sight. It had been nearly a full week since he sent his letter down to the inlet. He most surely wondered why his friend had not yet returned to Bath Town, unless of course he was already on his way to St. Thomas.

At around ten in the morning on that fateful Saturday in November, near the old watering place at Ocracoke

Island, Knight's tall, bearded friend shouted at the two approaching trading sloops inexplicably crammed full of men armed with muskets and pistols glinting in the early sun.

"Damn you for villains, who are you? And whence came you? Leave us alone and we shall meddle not with you."

"It is you we want and we will have you, dead or alive, else it will cost us our life."

"Damnation to you, then, you cowardly puppies. We will give no quarter, nor take none! Mr. Morton, prepare your guns and fire when ready. Give them a taste of our hospitality."

The deadly Battle of Ocracoke Inlet, which commenced with the firing upon His Majesty's sailors by Black Beard's men, has been described in recent years as one of the most pivotal naval engagements in American history, a lofty distinction for which it may not rank. It was really more skirmish than battle, and some other pirate defeats were of greater significance. It was, however, pivotal as far as Black Beard and his company aboard the *Adventure* were concerned.

Naturally, there have been many attempts in literature to describe the event over the three centuries since it happened, and as can be expected, errors, omissions and fabrications have attached themselves to the story like a fungus to a tree. Some of the embellishments have, indeed, taken on a life form of their own. Capt. Johnson devoted quite a few pages to the battle, and he seems to have gotten many of his facts right. But in a close comparison, his account seems to be largely derived from the one published in the *Boston News-Letter* three months after the engagement. Lt. Maynard wrote his version of the action—a fairly concise version—in a letter to Lt. Symonds, a friend aboard the HMS *Phoenix* at New York. But before Maynard wrote to Symonds, he debriefed his superior officer, Capt. Ellis Brand. Brand subsequently wrote the official report of the hostilities to his superiors, the Lords of Admiralty in London. Three years later, Capt. George Gordon also wrote to the Admiralty in order to counter some glossed over statements by Maynard in his petition for a reward for his participation. By distilling the accounts of Brand, Maynard, Gordon and the *Boston News-Letter*, we can divine a reasonably accurate sequence of events, and at the same time, expose some of the more insidious inaccuracies.

Both of His Majesty's vessels, the "*Lyme* sloop" and the "*Pearl* sloop" (They were referred to by Brand not by their actual names, *Jane* and *Ranger*, but by the name of the warship in Virginia from which each respective crew came.) were forced to be propelled by oars because, as Maynard wrote, "it [was] a perfect calm." As the two sloops crept toward the *Adventure*'s anchorage but were still beyond speaking distance, Maynard's *Jane*, trailing the smaller sloop, ran aground and her crew began heaving her ballast overboard to lighten her load and reduce her draft. The *Ranger*, commanded by Midshipman Edmund Hyde, being smaller and drawing less water proceeded toward the pirate sloop. Then, the *Ranger* ran aground, and her crew had no choice but to stave her heavy, fresh water casks to re-float their sloop, recognizing that it was better to be thirsty than dead. The pilots hired for the navigation of North Carolina's intricate waters apparently were incapable of keeping their client's vessels in the center of the channel.

While the two intruding sloops struggled mightily to reach their objective, Black Beard ordered his anchor cable cut and his jib raised to make some headway, although there was little wind to generate much speed. The records don't tell us if the pirate captain deployed the *Adventure*'s sweeps for added propulsion, but he would have been significantly hampered by a shortage of personnel. Nevertheless, it is possible the four slaves—Richard Stiles, Thomas Gates, James Blake, and James White—were ordered to the arduous task of advancing the 65-foot, 50-ton sloop against the incoming tide.

At about this time, in Maynard's words, the two protagonists shouted their "first salutation," after which the *Adventure* began firing "several shots" at the smaller of the two sloops and attempted to escape out of the same channel. Mr. Hyde's sloop became free and bravely attempted to intercept the pirate by altering her course to leeward. As she closed the distance to "half a pistol shot" the *Adventure*'s gunner, Philip Morton, fired a deadly broadside and a hailstorm of iron and lead raked across the decks of the *Ranger* like Death's horrible scythe, killing Hyde and severely wounding the sloop's other officers, leaving no one to command the vessel. The die was cast. By the act of bearing arms, firing upon and killing sailors of His Majesty's Royal Navy, Black Beard's crew committed an act of treason for which no act of indemnity would ever forgive. One way or the other, they would die—at gunpoint, sword point or hangman's noose—for the men aboard the sloop *Adventure* had signed their death warrants. As for the sailors aboard Maynard's sloop who could plainly hear the screams of death and anguish from their fellow sailors aboard the stricken *Ranger*, it became suddenly evident they would no longer be fighting just for King and country but would be fighting for their lives.

Now comes one of the worst fictionalizations of the engagement that has regrettably wormed its way into accepted history. A recent biography states that Black Beard, who had seized the helm of the *Adventure*, suddenly began steering the sloop for shallow water, in the direction of the Old Slough, the creek used as a landing for trips to the watering hole in the woods. Quartermaster Thomas Miller supposedly recognized the mistake and warned Black Beard they were in danger of running aground, at which point Black Beard knocked Miller to the deck. The wily pirate captain knew what he was doing, for he was hoping to lure Maynard's sloop onto an intervening shoal where the *Adventure* could blow her to pieces. The depiction makes for a great dramatic scene but the problem is, it simply never happened. The biography cites the source of the anecdote as Charles Johnson's, *A General History of Pirates*, but nowhere in Johnson's account can the anecdote be found, nor is it found in the official statements of Brand and Maynard, nor in the *Boston News-Letter*. It does appear, however, as part of Robert Lee's version in his 1974 book, *Blackbeard the Pirate—A Reappraisal of His Life and Times*. But Lee cites the source as none other than Addison Whipple, who concocted the entire fanciful episode for his swashbuckling 1957 book, *Pirates—Rascals of the Spanish Main*. That is where the trail to the source ends, with the writer who warned his readers on the first page they were about to enter treacherous waters. There are no other historical sources that tell the story of how Black Beard attempted to lure Maynard's sloop ashore. The engagement at Ocracoke was summarized by Capt. Brand in one long paragraph—twenty-six lines. Lt. Maynard composed about the same number of words in his account. Whipple, an imaginative and entertaining writer, succeeded in stretching the pithy, primary sources into 17 exciting pages. Other writers, similarly compelled to make the most of the penultimate moment of Black Beard's story, have churned-out nearly as many words as Whipple. Where their information comes from, however, is a bit of a mystery. Such is the process in which mythology becomes history. "If you tell a lie often enough, it becomes the truth," Karl Marx once said, and his followers certainly knew something about revising history.

What we do know about the fight is there must have been a little wind because Brand's report indicated that after disabling the *Ranger*, "the pirate shot by them" and was maneuvering towards Maynard's sloop, *Jane*. As the distance closed between the two vessels, Maynard's men were able to fire their muskets to sever the *Adventure*'s fore-halliards, sending her jib—her sole means of propulsion—crashing to the foredeck in a tangled mess of canvas and snarls of tarred rope. In the confusion, who ever was steering the pirate sloop allowed her to slip onto a nearby shoal, which provided Maynard the opportunity to come up alongside and attempt a boarding. But Black Beard, despite making numerous tactical blunders, still had a trick or two up his sleeve and ordered his crew to strafe the deck of Maynard's sloop with swivel-guns and small arms fire loaded with "swan shot, spick nails and pieces of old iron, which killed six of his men and wounded ten," according to the *Boston News-Letter*. Maynard, in his letter, reported taking 20 casualties from the pirate's volley.

The air was soon choked with thick clouds of blue-gray smoke from the gunpowder blasts of cannon and small arms fire, and with little or no wind, the heavy pall added to the confusion of the fight. In a slow-motion but violent ballet, Maynard's sloop collided with the *Adventure*, and as the smoke began to clear, the deck of His Majesty's sloop was strewn with dead and wounded sailors. Black Beard must have thought his luck had turned. He rallied his men to leap over the rail of their sloop to board and finish off their attackers, of which only a couple remained uninjured, crouched in the aft portion of the *Jane*. But Maynard had been cautiously clever. Not wanting to

Mysterious Tides of History

Ocracoke Battle Sequence According to

1. Brand: "Weigh'd about nine there being little Wind... Lieut Maynard Ordered the Lyme's Sloop to make the best of their way for Thach's Sloop and Board him..."

2. Brand: "The Pearl's Sloop [Jane/Maynard] in following them run a ground and was forced to heave part their ballast over Board to get off again..."

3. Brand: "Before the Lyme [Ranger/Hyde] Sloop got near the Pyrate She ran a ground and was obliged to Stave her water to get of(f). The Pyrate Saw they design'd for him, cut his Cable and got under Sail..."

4. Brand: "The Pearl's Sloop [Jane] was off and rowing up after the other Sloop [Ranger]. The Pyrate had fired Severall Shot at the Small Sloop as She was Standing for him"

5. Maynard: "At our first Salutation, he drank Damnation to me and my Men, whom he stil'd Cowardly Puppies, saying, He would neither give nor take Quarter."
Boston News Letter: "When they came in hearing of each other, Teach called to Lt. Maynard and told him he was for King George...Teach understood his designs, told him that if he would let him alone, he would not meddle with him. Maynard answered that it was him he wanted..."

6. Brand: "The Pyrate had fired Severall Shot at the Small Sloop [Ranger] as She was Standing

Capt. Brand and Lt. Maynard

7. Brand: "The Pyrate Endeavoring to get out at the Same Channell as our Sloop came in put for it."

8. Brand: "The Lyme's Sloop [Ranger/Hyde] put her helm a Lee to Board Thach they then being within half Pistol Shott. The Pyrate at the same time fired his Broad Side Kill'd the Commander of my Sloop {Midshipman Edmund Hyde}, Wounded Mr Baker... and Killd my Cox'n whom had third Command and Wounded Several of my fellows."

9. Brand: "They [Ranger] had their Gibb and foresheets Shot away So the Pyrate Shot by them."

10. Brand: "Lieut Maynard was then pulling with his Oars for the two Sloops."

11. Brand: "Thachs fore Halliards and Gibb being Shott by the fire they reced from the Lyme's Sloop he flew to, which gave Mr Maynard an opportunity to board Thach."

12. Brand: "The little Sloop [Ranger] not being above her length from there Shott in between. The Pyrate and Mr Maynard. Enter'd their men, did good Service and Suffered much."

13. Brand: "The Pyrate had nineteen Men, Thirteen White and Six negroes, ten white men Kill'd and the rest of the Prisoners were all Wounded, they found at a Tent on Shoar about one hundred and forty Baggs of Cocoa and Ten Cask of Sugar which were belonging to Thach."

the story a little further, quoting the mariner Humphrey Johnston, who must have been anchored somewhere inside Ocracoke Inlet and heard the mêlée from a distance and collected details afterward. His account describes how Black Beard and Maynard immediately found one another and engaged in a sword fight. (Both men would have been easily recognizable to the other, one exceptionally tall and bearded, the other wearing the blue coat of a naval officer.) Published three months after the engagement, the news report captivated readers all across colonial America and copies could not be printed fast enough. It described the struggle between Maynard and Black Beard in these words:

> Maynard making a thrust, the point of his sword went against Teach's cartridge box and bended it to the hilt. Teach broke the guard of it, and wounded Maynard's fingers but did not disable him, whereupon he jumped back, threw away his sword and fired his pistol, which wounded Teach. [Abraham] Demelt struck in between them with his sword and cut Teach's face pretty much. In the interim both companies engaged in Maynard's sloop. One of Maynard's men being a Highlander, engaged Teach with his broad sword, who gave Teach a cut on the neck, Teach saying, 'Well done lad.' The highlander reply'd, if it be not well done, I'll do it better. With that he gave him a second stroke, which cut off his head, laying it flat on his shoulder.

And so it was that the mysterious tides of history swept two Scots along disparate courses of life and across the years and miles of time, to collide with one another in a deadly and historic clash near the old watering hole on Ocracoke Island on November 22, 1718. The great Black Beard was dead, but the legend was born.

It all happened quickly. According to Capt. Gordon's account, once Black Beard gained the deck of Maynard's sloop, the action lasted fewer than six minutes. For 360 seconds, the typically tranquil waters along the southwest shore of the island were pierced with a maelstrom of gunshots and the ringing peal of metal on metal—a carillon of death, punctuated with bloody screams, curses, shrieks, moans, and cheers. And then it was silent, save for the heaving breaths of the victors, the last gasps of the dying and the feeble, raspy pleas of the defeated: "Quarter, pray quarter, sir!" Thirteen pirates lay dead—nine bodies besides Black Beard's on the deck of the sloop, *Jane*, and three aboard the sloop, *Adventure*. Nine of Maynard's men were killed, and two from the crew of the *Ranger* were killed, all from cannon or gunshot—none by pirate cutlass.

One of the King's men had been killed by friendly fire. During the clash, the sloop, *Ranger*, which had been initially disabled by the pirate's volley against her, had come up along the opposite side of the *Adventure* where her men boarded and engaged the pirates who remained aboard their sloop, presumably the less skilled fighters. In the confusion of battle, one of the *Ranger*'s men was mistaken for a pirate and was shot and killed by one of Maynard's sailors from the *Jane*.

Despite all of their bluster and fearsome reputation, did Black Beard and his men turn out to be paper tigers? During hand-to-hand combat aboard Maynard's sloop, the King's men out-fought every single pirate, which implies there was greater swordsmanship among the Royal Navy sailors. However, they did have four extra men and their strength in numbers increased exponentially as each pirate fell to the deck. Another advantage Maynard's men may have had was the state of sobriety and poor health among the pirates. Considering their lifestyle, they probably didn't practice their sword fighting particularly often, and it had been at least 15 months since Black Beard had participated in a boarding action, except for his moonlight attack on William Bell. At that time, two months before the engagement with Maynard, he had been unable to subdue Bell without the assistance of his four black oarsmen at Chester's Landing. The pirate captain—the fearsome "Lord of the Outer Banks"—was clearly not the man he once was, or perhaps, never the man he was pretended to be.

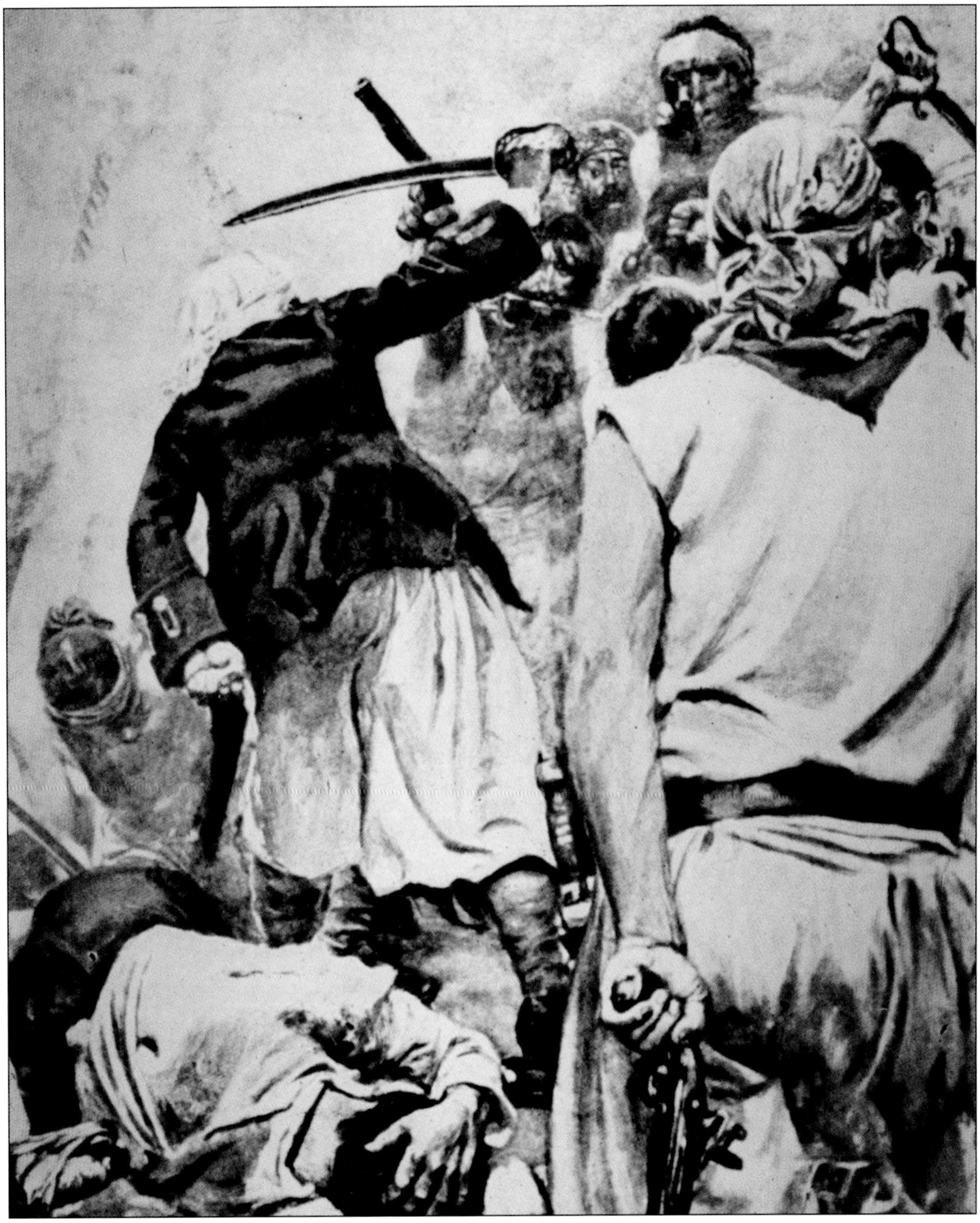

Lt. Robert Maynard and Black Beard engaged in hand-to-hand combat. Illustration by Howard Pyle.

the other "prisoner" below the deck of the *Adventure* is an even more intriguing revelation, as we will soon discover.

Destroying their own ship and thus committing suicide to avoid being hanged was a fairly prevalent idea among pirate crews at the time, and depositions attest to Charles Vane's threats to use the endgame strategy. During frequent drinking binges, pirates were known to swear oaths that they would blow themselves up rather than to be captured and "hanged like dogs." But when the moment actually arrived, as it did for many, most couldn't find the courage to light the match. Instead, they held out hope that a heartfelt confession, or a claim to have been the pirates' prisoner, or the arrival of a new Royal pardon, might yet spare them the noose. We know an attempt was made aboard the *Adventure* because it was verified in a letter written by Lt. Gov. Spotswood. But only in Charles Johnson's, *A General History of Pirates*, is the black man identified as Caesar. Johnson described Caesar as "a negro whom [Black Beard] had brought up," intimating a long-term, personal relationship between the two men. But there is a distinct possibility that by November, 1718, Caesar was no longer working for the pirate but for his friend, Tobias Knight.

Most historical accounts, including Johnson's, have Maynard and his men tidying things up and then setting sail for Bath Town within hours after the fight. The truth is, it took the Royal Navy sailors quite longer to recover, and Capt. Gordon's letters indicated that Maynard remained at Ocracoke for a "fortnight" or about two weeks. First, the prisoners had to be secured and guarded by the uninjured men. Then, Maynard probably had to begin triage to determine which of his men required the most immediate medical attention. Without a surgeon aboard—and records are unclear if Maynard had one in his company or not—the men would have had to provide their own medical assistance. The remainder of the first day was spent re-positioning and anchoring the three sloops which were probably rafted together. Then the crews began swabbing and clearing the decks of the detritus of battle. The corpses were removed from the sloops, including Black Beard's, but what was done with them remains an historical mystery. There is absolutely no mention in the records or other shred of convincing evidence that Black Beard's headless body was tossed overboard and, according to folklore, swam around his sloop. A thorough search of various Black Beard volumes for the source of the swimming corpse legend leads all the way back to Ocracoke where it was first featured in an island tourism pamphlet in the mid-1960s. Historians who have perpetuated this myth have failed to consider that had Black Beard's body been thrown overboard, so too would have been the remains of the other 12 pirates who were killed. As superstitious as sailors were, it is terribly far-fetched that the victors would have allowed the chance for so many putrescent, hideous bodies to drift about the anchorage, stranding on sandbars or bumping into the sloops' hulls and attracting hordes of sharks and scavenging seabirds over the two weeks they remained there. Also doubtful is the possibility that the 11 corpses from the King's sloops were taken back to Virginia under such crowded conditions—they were most likely buried in shallow, sandy graves on Ocracoke, along with the 13 dead pirates, including Black Beard (minus his head, of course).

While Maynard's men worked to restore the three sloops to proper sailing condition, including mending the spars, standing rigging and sails, the lieutenant entered the roundhouse of the *Adventure*—Capt. Thatch's personal domain—and began searching for items of value and incriminating evidence. It did not take long for Maynard and his men to discover with tremendous disappointment that there was no vast treasure to be had of glittering gold, silver and jewels. A small quantity of gold dust—literally tiny grains or small nuggets—and some silver plate was all the pirate plunder found aboard the sloop. Maynard did find the remarkable silver cup that was previously in the possession of William Bell. Also, among Black Beard's effects was his "pocket book"—a diary or private log book—and folded within it was the incriminating letter from Tobias Knight.

There has been some question among a few historians to the existence of Black Beard's diary, and they have based their doubts on the fact that the journal, described in some detail by Charles Johnson, has not been seen since.

Johnson wrote of Black Beard's "several memorandums... found writ with his own hand." The most remarkable of these memoranda was published in *A General History of Pirates*, and carries a surprising poetic cadence:

—Such a Day, Rum all out:
—Our Company somewhat sober:
—A Damned Confusion amongst us!
—Rogues a plotting;
—great Talk of Separation.
—So I looked sharp for a prize;
—such a Day took one, with a great
* deal of Liquor on Board,*
so kept the Company hot, damned hot,
then all Things went well again.

The idea of the haggard captain seated at his chart table during a rare private moment in the great cabin of his flagship, *Queen Anne's Revenge*, writing in his diary of his irritations with the never-ending pressures of commanding so many hard-to-please pirates, presents a fairly poignant and sympathetic portrait of Black Beard. History is unable to tell us when he wrote his "Such a day" diary entry, but it is generally believed to have been in the days or weeks leading up to the wreck of the 40-gun former slave ship at Old Topsail Inlet on June 10, 1718. Other documents, such as a letter written by Capt. Brand on July 12, prove that it was widely known that there had been a significant falling-out between the principal factions in Black Beard's company.

It's too bad we can't read more of his compositions but, although he referred to several, Johnson published only one. There can be little doubt the book once existed and that Johnson examined it personally. The author's transcription of Black Beard's unique use of punctuation alone is evidence he had access to the journal—which further suggests Johnson may have met Lt. Maynard after he returned to London. Capt. Brand confirmed that Maynard had recovered the "pocket book" and mentioned a memorandum within that noted the transfer of sugar casks to Tobias Knight's barn. We can only imagine what other interesting tidbits could be gleaned from Black Beard's personal diary—girlfriends' names, favorite taverns, locations of hidden treasure? If it survived the ages, the book has never resurfaced among public records, and were it to exist today, it would probably be worth at least as much as all the gold, silver and jewels ever to pass before Black Beard's eyes throughout his career.

Elsewhere on that historic Saturday in November, as he crossed Albemarle Sound aboard Bell's ferry, Ellis Brand was surely worried. He had no information as to the fate of Lt. Maynard and his two sloops but he well knew that five days after leaving Kiquotan, Virginia, the expedition could easily have been able to reach Bath Town harbor. Had they encountered the pirate along the way or cornered him at the colony's capital? Brand had no way of knowing.

He must have been frustrated, as well. The breezeless morning made the crossing of the Albemarle Sound painfully slow. Presumably, the vessel carrying him across was a form of shoal draft galley capable of being rowed when winds were light. Nevertheless, it ended up taking Brand and his companions, Moore and Vail, and their horses, the entire day to reach the landing at Kendrick's Creek on the south shore of the sound. Being the captain of a well-manned, 24-gun warship, Brand was probably unaccustomed to the rigors of overland travel, especially with only a servant to tend to his needs.

On the morning of the 23rd, Brand's little group set out again on the long, sandy road through uninhabited savanna and pocosin on their way to Bath Town, although at this point his entourage had increased in size. In his letter to the Lords of Admiralty, Brand indicated that they had been joined by several of the inhabitants who had heard he had come from Virginia to take the pirate "Thach." Perhaps the North Carolinians who joined the strange procession south were curious as to just how the Royal Navy captain, mounted on horseback with just a servant at his side, intended to defeat the fearsome pirate king and his sloop of nine cannon. There may have been some other men—Brand wrote that a few of Col. Moore's friends were along and they may have included a Provost Marshall, rangers or possibly members of the militia—but there is no specific information in the records.

Brand's anxiety and determination to get to Bath as soon as possible is evident by the fact that on Sunday they traveled into darkness, arriving at ten o'clock in the night on the north side of Rowland Creek about three miles from the village. Not wanting to prematurely spring his trap, Brand asked Col. Moore to ride into Bath Town to "learn if Thach was there." Moore soon returned with uncertain news: there was no sign of Maynard and his sloops, but there was word that the pirate captain was expected to arrive at any moment. (Clearly this expectation came from Tobias Knight, and he must have shared it with the governor.) Moore's information that Maynard had still not arrived must have really worried Brand. He reported in his letter: "I parted from Coll. Moore and went to the government [meaning Gov. Eden] and applied my self to him and let him know I was come in quest of Thach." Eden, apparently, did not sleep much that night.

The next morning, despite squally weather (The log of the HMS *Lyme* for that day at Kiquotan Roads shows that her crew was forced to strike her yards and topmasts because of high winds.), Brand hired two canoes, or periaugers, to search the river and Pamlico Sound for signs of Maynard and his expedition. Again, Brand's patience was tested as two stormy days passed without any information, any hint of what might have happened over the distant horizon. Finally, on Wednesday, Brand's scouting party was spotted coming up the river. As the boats solemnly made their way up Bath Creek to the town landing, dozens of citizens must have gathered and waited with bated breath. By then, everyone in the precinct knew of Capt. Brand's mission, and of the two sloops that had been sent by Virginia's Lt. Gov. Spotswood in pursuit of Black Beard and his men. But to which side had the tide turned? Regardless of their respective loyalties, whether for the pirates or the King's men, the extent of the tension and worry among the bystanders must have been palpable, even audible as whispers were passed about. Perhaps even bets were cast as to the potential outcome. The drama of the moment simply cannot be overstated. Imagine some of those present: Gov. Eden, Brand, Moore, Vail; merchants, traders, and ale-house owners who may have done a fair business with the pirates, and a few women who may have traded with them as well; Israel Hands and the three other pirates whose difference with their captain probably saved their lives (at least for the time being); and although Tobias Knight was not likely present because he was bed-ridden, in his stead, one of his servants, or even Edmund Chamberlaine, may have observed the event on behalf of his master.

The boats were rowed within hailing distance.

"Oy there, Master Brand. It was a bloody fight but ye King's men have prevailed. Capt. Thatch is dead!" shouted the men from the canoes as they neared the dock. Gasps rose from the crowd on shore. A lady swooned. *"Mr. Maynard had on his side kill'd 11 of his men, and 12 more dead are pirates. Many more are wounded. They are all too wrecked to come up for now, your lieutenant told us."*

At once, shock swept the stunned crowd as the gravity of the news settled in. The great Black Beard dead? Capt. of the Carolina pirates gone? Whoever he was, servant or Chamberlaine, Tobias Knight's man on the scene flew-off in great haste, either on horseback or boat, to deliver the terrible news. Gov. Eden probably did his best to appear emotionally unmoved, but his thoughts turned to the realization that the impending arrival of the extension of the King's pardon could no longer help his friend. Israel Hands no doubt smiled, despite his painful knee. Capt. Brand breathed a great sigh of relief.

Tobias Knight slumped into a chair in his parlor and could hardly believe the news. His friend, Edward, dead? It could not possibly be true. He had just seen him, hardly a fortnight before in the very room where he just received the news. The captain was expected to come up to Bath Town at any moment to make amends with his friends.

How could it have happened? An abomination by that meddling, pompous arse, Spotswood, who Knight knew had designs on taking the Carolina government for his own. It was murder, is what it was. The Virginians had no right. If his health would hold, Tobias Knight would see to it that Spotswood and his henchmen would be sued for murder. As he thought more about it, the presence of Moore and Vail in town meant that the vainglorious Anglican Moseley must be involved as well. They would all pay. Be damned! Poor Edward. And to think that his salvation—the King's extension of his act of forgiveness—could only be a few days away, on a ship not far from the Carolina coast.

While he had been waiting for the news of his sloops in Bath Town, Ellis Brand had not been idle. There were plenty of people around who were willing to talk and to inform the Royal Navy captain of some peculiar business doings about town involving the governor and his collector of customs. Some of these informants included those who may have had a grudge against Eden, Knight or Black Beard himself. Certainly, one of those eager to see justice prevail was William Bell, who was partly responsible for Spotswood's incursion into North Carolina.

Someone told Brand that a generous amount of the cargo taken from the French ship captured by Black Beard and his men could be found in a couple of barns in the precinct, notably 60 hogsheads of sugar in the governor's storehouse in town and 20 located at Knight's out on the plantation by the river. On Brand's first trip out to the Knight place at the mouth of Bath Town Creek, the feeble but defiant council secretary and customs collector absolutely denied knowing anything about casks of sugar and swore vehemently that he had nothing to do with the pirate Black Beard. Knight was sick, but still capable of putting up a fight, especially against the man who shared in the responsibility for the death of his nephew-like friend and protégé. In a letter to London, Brand said that Knight had made an abundance of difficulty and advised the governor not to assist him. In a curious statement, Brand claimed that Knight was "constantly justifying the pirates." It would seem that the collector knew he had to continue to maintain Black Beard's innocence in order to protect his own reputation.

Once more, imagination can hardly do justice to the potential drama at Tobias Knight's when Capt. Brand first came calling. Col. Moore and Capt. Vail probably came too, along with a few other men. As frigid rain beat down from blustery November squalls, Knight may not have even allowed the men to enter his house leaving them to stand out in the elements, so seething mad he must have been over the brutal death of his friend. An astute veteran of many years of legal disputes in the colony, the collector was not going to make things easy for the Royal Navy officer. But when Brand returned the next day armed with new evidence, Knight's resolve began to crumble. We don't know exactly when this occurred, but it was probably after Maynard came up to Bath in command of Black Beard's sloop, *Adventure*. The reason being that on Brand's second visit to Knight's house to demand possession of the casks of French sugar believed to be stored in Knight's barn, Brand was holding Black Beard's "pocket book" that had an entry in the pirate's own hand detailing the delivery of the sugar to Knight's storehouse. Knight quickly admitted the casks were indeed in his barn where they were being stored for the pirate who had planned on removing them at a later date. Knight had no suitable explanation as to why the casks of sugar were hidden beneath piles of fodder.

Before Maynard had departed Ocracoke for Bath, he moved the worst of the injured to the smaller sloop, *Ranger*, and ordered her crew to make rapid sail for Virginia for one of the wounded was critical and in need of a competent surgeon. Maynard was also anxious for the *Ranger* to deliver the news of their victory over the pirates to his superior, Capt. Gordon of the HMS *Pearl*, as well as Lt. Gov. Spotswood. The sloop arrived at Kiquotan Roads on Sunday afternoon, November 30th, and their report was welcomed with pride as reflected in the *Pearl's* log entry of December 1:

Moderate gales & fair weather; yesterday in the afternoon the Ranger sloop that was man'd Arm'd &c by Capt. Brand of His Majesty's Ship Lyme on the Expedition against Edward Thach commonly call'd blackbeard a pyrat, anchored here from No. Carolina, who acquainted us of the destruction of the aforesaid Thach & most of his men, and the seizure of their Effects, by our men.

As the days passed at Ocracoke and his remaining men recovered from their wounds, Lt. Maynard completed the process of counting the dead and wounded among the pirates and collecting information from the survivors: recording their name, rank, home port, and possibly a cursory statement or deposition. During the height of the action a couple of the injured pirates were reported to have slipped overboard where they were soon discovered and either killed or captured, although one, somehow, was able to evade detection and make his way ashore. The man crawled some distance into the nearby tidal marsh where he eventually died of his wounds. Days later, scavenging sea birds marked the location of his remains. No other pirates were believed to have escaped the King's men. Or did they?

By a careful comparison of the head counts provided by Lt. Maynard and Capt. Brand, and a list of the pirate's names on the King's warrant for reward payments issued a few years later, there appears to be a discrepancy of two men. Maynard wrote that the pirate "had on board 21 men," but that he killed 12, besides Black Beard, and took nine prisoners. Hopefully, Maynard had been more proficient with his math than his grammar, and he actually meant that he killed 12, including Black Beard. More confusing, Brand reported "the pirate had 19 men, 13 white and six negroes," and that Maynard had killed nine with the remaining prisoners all wounded. The King's warrant agrees with Brand's figures. But Maynard was there—should not he have known better than anyone? Humphrey Johnston's version as published in the *Boston News-Letter* is of no help because the newspaper reported "Teach's men being about 20 were all killed in the engagement, excepting two carried to Virginia."

The discrepancy may have resulted from some confusion over the status of two of the men on board the *Adventure*. One we know was Samuel Odell, who after the engagement loudly protested his innocence and claimed not to be a member of Black Beard's crew despite having as many as 70 wounds according to Charles Johnson. (Maynard may have said to Odell that had he not been a pirate, he should not have borne arms against the King's men, which thus made him a combatant.)

Also present aboard the *Adventure*, apparently hiding below decks, was the Bath Town mariner and planter, James Robins. Robins was listed on a roster of Black Beard's crew members by Charles Johnson in *A General History of Pirates*. But his was not one of the names appearing on the King's list. The variance leaves one possibility. Robins was one of the men who had come from Bath, maybe along with Garret Gibbons, at the behest of Tobias Knight to deliver Knight's message and advice to make amends with the three crew members Black Beard abandoned back in Bath. When Maynard interviewed Robins, the Bath Town resident claimed to have been imprisoned aboard the *Adventure* the night before the battle, and because he could prove he was a landowner in Bath County, Maynard must have accepted his story as true. But there is more to James Robins's past than, so far, history has managed to reveal—until now.

Seventeen—
The Bath County Pirates

CONTRARY TO THE POPULAR LEGEND, THE SEVERED HEAD OF THE PIRATE CAPTAIN DID NOT HANG FROM the bowsprit of the sloop *Adventure* when Lt. Maynard sailed triumphantly from Ocracoke to Bath Town harbor. Instead, his crew most likely removed it from its protective, scented container, and then rigged the macabre trophy to the *Adventure*'s bowsprit shortly upon their arrival. As much as the the head was worth in Virginia—a bounty of £100 was offered by Lt. Gov. Spotswood—Maynard would not have displayed it when there was no one around to see it and risk the chance of it falling from its precarious perch and disappearing somewhere below the murky depths of the Pamlico Sound.

The last of autumn's leaves reluctantly fluttered to the ground. At Bath Town, December had come, cold, wet and dreary, and a low pall of chimney smoke hung over the scattered plantations, town houses and slave quarters like Death's forbidding shadow. To escape the slanting winter rains and the appalling turn of events, the residents of the colony's troubled little capital hid behind closed doors, so there were probably few to see Maynard's arrival and the pirate captain's grisly head swinging to-and-fro as the sloop *Adventure* lay at anchor outside of the entrance to Bath Creek on or about Saturday, the 6th of December. Except for Tobias Knight, whose bedchamber window looked out upon the awful scene. Tobias Knight saw it, and it compounded his sickness and rage. He moved to his writing desk, took out a quill, and began to write an impassioned letter to his governor, replete with technical questions and challenges as to the legality of Lt. Gov. Spotswood's invasion of their colony, and the killing and arrest of its citizens. The letter was handed to a trusted servant who rushed it to Eden's residence on Bay Street. Eden, himself, had not the wisdom to know how to answer Knight's questions so he wrote a postscript at the end of the letter with his own question or two and summoned a messenger with a speedy horse and sent them galloping 37 miles north to his esteemed counsel, Col. Thomas Pollock.

On Monday, Pollock did his best to advise the governor on the issue but admitted in the first sentence of

when ownership of the sloop *Adventure* was awarded to Thatch, declarations from the hearing of the pirates' appeal for His Majesty's pardon, depositions from the Vice-Admiralty Court in September for the adjudication of the French derelict, as well as receipts and other correspondence. Eden knew those papers could not be allowed to fall into the hands of the Virginia authorities.

Even before Knight had finished writing his letter to the governor, a longboat brought Lt. Maynard up to the town where Capt. Brand was ready to greet him and to offer his hearty congratulations on a job well done—a muted victory celebration on the home field of an opponent. Brand was surely relieved to see Maynard and his sailors, mangled as they were from the fight with Black Beard and his men, for the Royal Navy captain finally had a show of force to support his investigation into Bath Town's residents' connivance with the pirates. Brand's informants led him to the whereabouts of five more of Black Beard's crew, in addition to the angry, limping Israel Hands. The former sailing master was not hard to find—his doctor lived just seven lots down the street from the governor. With Maynard finally in Bath, they were able to round-up and arrest the suspected brigands to be delivered to Williamsburg where they were to stand trial for piracy.

Who were they, these pirates who remained in Bath after their captain had left them behind? That's what genealogists John Oden, Allen Norris and Jane Bailey wanted to know. What they discovered did nothing but strengthen their conviction that Black Beard, alias Edward Teach or Edward Thatch, was none other than Edward Beard, son of Bath planter and merchant, James Beard.

Oden, Norris and Bailey each could trace their families back to the earliest days of Bath County, so there was nothing remarkable about the fact that all three genealogists had grown up hearing oral traditions of ancestors who had been suspected of being privateers—or pirates. As a young girl in the late-1930s and '40s, Allen Norris can remember her grandfather, respected North Carolina educator and historian, William C. Allen, telling her such stories, and also that the pirate Black Beard had once lived on a farm near Bath. She had no reason to question the likelihood of such a legend in her youth. But as an adult, Norris was not someone who could easily accept the veracity of an outlandish urban myth. She worked for 39 years at the National Security Agency, retiring in 1992 as a senior cryptanalyst. So when her analysis of the research collected by her partners, Oden and Bailey, consistently confirmed her childhood Black Beard stories, she realized her grandfather had not been spinning a yarn. Norris recalls "bells going off in my head as the truth flashed before my eyes." Black Beard was Edward Beard.

One of the fundamental reasons for their theory that Black Beard, and a number of the men who were known to have been on his crew, were related to established Bath area families was the repetition of certain surnames in the Beaufort County Deed Book and on the crew list of pirates captured or killed. John Martin and James Robins, suspected pirates on Charles Johnson's list of Black Beard's wounded crew members, both appear in the deeds of Bath County prior to November, 1718.

Martin is an especially interesting subject. Records prove his father was Joel Martin, owner of a plantation on the west side of Bath Town Creek since 1702 and one of the three founding Bath Town commissioners, along with adventurer John Lawson and planter Nicholas Daw. Over the years, the elder Martin accumulated vast tracts of land in Bath, Hyde and Craven counties on which he grazed his herds of cattle and flocks of sheep, all of which are mentioned in his last will and testament proved shortly after his death, sometime in early 1716. To his son, John, he bequeathed a horse, a bed, a gun and 220 acres of land on the north side of Matchapungo Creek, about eight miles east of Bath, known today simply as Pungo Creek. But the younger Martin's inheritance may not have been enough to satisfy his desire for wealth, because it was about the same time that it is believed he set out to fish for gold and silver on the Spanish treasure wrecks of the east coast of Florida. Somewhere along the way, John Martin fell into the company of the "father" of so many famous pirates, Benjamin Hornigold. According to pirate historian, Colin Woodard, author of *The Republic of Pirates*, Martin eventually served under Hornigold as his quartermaster and surrendered with Hornigold to Royal Navy Capt. Vincent

Pearse and accepted the King's pardon at Nassau in February, 1718. Of course, Edward "Black" Beard also served with Hornigold, and it is plausible that Martin and Beard were together from the start, on what began as a relatively innocent treasure hunt, that eventually led them into piracy. The actual evidence is meager. John Martin appears on Capt. Pearse's list of surrendered pirates and a John Martin appears on the King's warrant for pirates captured with Black Beard. Also, there are many instances in which John Martin appears in the Bath County records. Are they all the same man? Intuition seems to say they are, even if there is no proof—no smoking pirate flintlock pistol. Although, according to Joel Martin's will, there was a "buccaneer gun" in the family.

As we already know, other Bath County names appeared on pirate crews, including William Howard, who prior to serving as quartermaster for Black Beard, was quartermaster for Hornigold as well, according to Colin Woodard. A further coincidence shared by William Howard and John Martin, besides their second-in-command stints on Benjamin Hornigold's pirate ships, was that their families' Bath County landholdings were less than five miles apart.

Genealogists Oden, Norris and Bailey were able to trace even more connections. Other pirates, either killed or captured at Ocracoke or apprehended at Bath, include Joseph Curtice, Joseph Brooks, Joseph Brooks Jr., Thomas Miller, Nathaniel Jackson, Stephen Daniel, and John Philips—all surnames appearing in the Bath County deeds, although the men themselves are not listed. In addition, Garret Gibbons and John Gills (or Giles) appear to share surnames with other men who had business transactions within Bath County. Remarkably, the number of suspected pirates from Black Beard's crew who matched a surname, or both first and last name, of citizens listed in the Bath County deeds, is more than 75 percent. Three out of four men (excluding either free blacks or slaves) who remained with Black Beard after his surprise downsizing of his company after the wreck of the *Queen Anne's Revenge*, were, in all probability, Bath County mariners, neighbors, and friends.

They were the Bath County pirates.

Two events of particular interest occurred in the neighboring colonies of South Carolina and Virginia, around the middle of December, 1718. At White Point in Charleston, on December 10, Stede Bonnet was delivered, kicking and screaming to the gallows, where he was hanged, and then buried below the high tide line in the nearby saltmarsh. A day or two later at Kiquotan Roads, Virginia, a ship arrived from London and delivered King George's new proclamation, extending his "Gracious Pardon." The pardon arrived about 20 days too late for Edward "Black" Beard. It would have spared his life.

Meanwhile, before his business was concluded at Bath Town, Maynard had to transfer 80 casks of sugar from the storehouses of Tobias Knight and Gov. Eden back into the cargo hold of the *Adventure*. More of a challenge was subduing and confining the six suspected pirates who no doubt were extremely reluctant to take a trip to Virginia—even Israel Hands, who was certainly not looking forward to being shackled and jailed with his former mates.

Capt. Brand curiously chose to return to Virginia by horseback, as confirmed in his letters. As a naval officer, it seems he would have preferred the rocking motion of the sloop, *Adventure*, to the gait of his steed and the long muddy road. Brand may have wanted to confer with Edward Moseley before he departed the colony, potentially about the disappointing pittance of evidence recovered by his lieutenant linking the pirates with the government of the colony. On the way north from Bath County, he was accompanied by Gov. Eden, who happened to be returning to his estate on the west bank of the Chowan River. Eden was a widower with no children of his own and had not remarried after his wife, Penelope, died in January, 1716. If Eden felt the sudden desire to leave his house in Bath Town and return to Chowan County, it could have been to celebrate the Twelve Days of Christmas with friends, neighbors and his two stepchildren by Penelope. Or he may have decided it would be better if he distanced himself from Bath, Tobias Knight, and the odor of piracy that would linger long after the *Adventure* disappeared over the horizon for the final time. Or he may have

had once been an army officer and had seen his share of gore. So it was not the pirate captain's head that may have caused him to feel a bit bilious in early January of 1719. Instead, it was what had arrived by ship from St. James's Palace in London just a few weeks before—the latest proclamation from King George I, which graciously extended the dates for which pirates would be eligible to surrender and receive the Crown's mercy and clemency.

Spotswood must have had his most astute legal advisors read over the document with a fine-tooth comb. Something about the proclamation worried the lieutenant governor. Or more accurately, his concern was with something absent from the proclamation. Unlike the King's Proclamation of the previous year which specified a date—January 5, 1718—after which acts of piracy would no longer be eligible to be forgiven, the subsequent Proclamation listed no such date. This is how the first pardon was worded:

> ...we do hereby promise, and declare, that in Case any of the said Pyrates, shall on, or before, the 5th of September, in the Year of our Lord 1718, surrender him or themselves, to one of our Principal Secretaries of State in Great Britain or Ireland, or to any Governor or Deputy Governor of any of our Plantations beyond the Seas; every such Pyrate and Pyrates so surrendering him, or themselves, as aforesaid, shall have our gracious Pardon, of, and for such, his or their Pyracy, or Pyracies, by him or them committed, before the fifth of January next ensuing [January 1718].

This is how the second pardon was worded:

> We have thought fit, by and with the Advice of Our Privy-Council, to Issue this Our Royal Proclamation; And We do hereby Promise and Declare, That in case any the said Pirates shall, on or before the First Day of July, in the Year of Our Lord One thousand seven hundred and nineteen, Surrender him or themselves to One of Our Principal Secretaries of State in Great Britain or Ireland, or to any Governors or Deputy-Governors of any of Our Plantations or dominions beyond the Seas, every such Pirate and Pirates, so Surrendering him or themselves, as aforesaid, shall have Our Gracious Pardon of and for such his or their Piracy or Piracies, by him or them Committed before such time as they shall have received Notice of this Our Royal Proclamation.

Spotswood probably read the words more than once to be certain of what the King and Privy Council intended: "every such pirate...shall have Our Gracious Pardon of and for such his or their Piracy or Piracies, by him or them Committed before such time as they shall have received Notice of this Our Royal Proclamation." The implication couldn't be clearer. The new Proclamation was worded to encourage more men to surrender and return to honest, productive lives. There was no specific calendar date after which acts of piracies would no longer be eligible to be forgiven—only those piracies committed after the pirates received notice of the Royal Proclamation would be ineligible. In other words, every piracy committed before a pirate heard about the new pardon would be forgiven. Black Beard's men, who had been arrested at Ocracoke or in Bath Town, did not receive notice of the new Proclamation until after they were incarcerated in Williamsburg. Every piracy they committed prior to that time should have been set aside by Spotswood.

Instead, the lieutenant governor forged ahead with the process of extracting statements from the pirates, or at least from those who would talk. Based on evidence and depositions later forwarded to a North Carolina court, we are fairly certain that Israel Hands and the four African men who accompanied Black Beard to Bath on his midnight visit to Tobias Knight in September were the only former pirates to cooperate. Hands provided more than enough detail about the capture of the French ship and its cargo, and Richard Stiles, James Blake, James White and Thomas Gates offered a thorough account of their trip to Knight's house and their captain's assault on William Bell. Spotswood's investigation proceeded quickly and his prosecutors prepared for a trial before the Court of Vice-Admiralty for determining the guilt or innocence of Black Beard's crew. But, in reality, the evidence for the convictions was not based on testimony.

What history has failed to reveal to us is that Spotswood was already certain of the outcome, that some of the men would be found guilty, while others found innocent. The pre-trial depositions were not about collecting damning evidence against Black Beard's pirates. The depositions were about fishing for damning evidence against Black Beard's patrons, the two top officials of North Carolina: Charles Eden and Tobias Knight.

Among the many errors contained in books and scholarly accounts published in the past 50 years on of the life and times of Black Beard the pirate, one of the more significant but egregious concerns what happened to his shipmates after his death. The traditional story is essentially this: 15 men suspected of being pirates under the command of Capt. Edward Thatch were tried in Williamsburg on March 11, 1719; 13 were convicted and sentenced to death, while Samuel Odell, who was not a crew member, was acquitted and Israel Hands was pardoned for testifying on behalf of the Crown. Some authors have waxed poetically as to how the condemned 13 pirates were strung-up in succession, every few hundred feet along the road between the Virginia capital and the landing on the James River, and there, all 13 were purportedly hanged.

The key aspects of the traditional story are incorrect. Some of the prisoners were pardoned and released before the trial. The trial of the remaining white pirates took place about six weeks earlier than believed. Not all of the pirates thought to have been hanged were executed, and the few hangings that did occur did not happen at Williamsburg.

To some degree it is understandable how modern historians have failed to get the story right. There are practically no extant records with which to research the Williamsburg pirate trials in order to find the truth. No depositions, no recorded testimony, no motions or judgments—nothing has survived that would have been able to tell us exactly what happened during Black Beard's last days, such as is available in the very detailed records of South Carolina for the trial of Stede Bonnet and his crew. While North Carolina's records pertaining to Black Beard's five-month, on-and-off stay in the colony seemed to have vanished into thin air, Virginia's records are believed to have been destroyed in one of three fires. Williamsburg's first and second Capitol buildings burned to the ground in 1747 and 1832, respectively, although there is some reason to believe the Admiralty Court records may have survived and were transferred to Richmond. Then, in early April, 1865, the State court building was destroyed by fire during the final stages of the siege of Richmond, and the "great mass of records" of the colonial era courts were thought to have been lost.

As a result, the single source of information to which historians have turned over the years for what transpired at Williamsburg regarding the Bath County pirates has been the problematic Capt. Charles Johnson and his book, *A General History of Pirates*. While many writers have exposed Johnson's errors in other matters, not a single one has questioned his facts concerning the hanging of Black Beard's crew. It is just too easy and expedient to draw on Johnson when no other facts seem to be available.

So, without primary source records and only Johnson to fall back on, we again have to find the answers the hard way, by collecting shards of clues, dates, and names, and searching references in the deed books, Alexander Spotswood's letters, North Carolina's colonial records, and the ship's log of the HMS *Pearl*. As an archeologist reassembles an elaborate earthenware jar without prior knowledge of its original shape and appearance, so too must we cobble together what facts we have to gain a reasonably accurate vision of the past. We can start with the whereabouts of the suspected Bath County pirate, James Robins, in January, 1719.

There is no better way to say it: James Robins got caught with his pants down. And thanks to the genealogists John Oden, Allen Norris and Jane Bailey, we know about his indiscretion. On the faded microfilmed page, number 262, of Beaufort County deed book four, is a salacious but otherwise revealing bit of information. As part of a legal dispute over the paternity of a child born to a Beaufort Precinct woman named, Elizabeth Goodin, a deposition from a Thomas Unday was written into the records for the purpose of proving Ms. Goodin's looseness of character. Unday testified that sometime in January, 1719, at the plantation owned by James Robins, the "said Robins lay with both

years after his "hanging" in Williamsburg, cooper Edward Salter had become one of the largest landholders in Bath County, if not the colony of North Carolina. At the time of his death in 1735, Salter also owned a sea-going brigantine, more than one periauger, and many slaves. In deeds and records, as well as on the sandy streets of Bath Town, Salter was referred to, not as a pirate or cooper, but as a merchant and gentleman.

Why were the Bath County pirates Edward Salter, John Martin and James Robins not hanged as history has been so resolutely determined to claim? In the case of Salter and Martin, it could only be because they were among those men who were arrested in Bath Town and who were not aboard the *Adventure* during the engagement with Lt. Maynard, and thus were eligible for the King's pardon which arrived in mid-December. Robins is believed to have been aboard the *Adventure*, although not as a combatant, because his name appeared on a preliminary list of pirates captured and taken to Williamsburg but was not on the King's warrant for payment of rewards to Capt. Brand's and Capt. Gordon's men for capturing the pirates. He was able to prove his ownership of a plantation on Bath Town Creek since early September, so it was not possible for him to have been on Black Beard's crew when they brought the French ship into the colony. However, had he been aboard the *Queen Anne's Revenge* during the months before she grounded at Old Topsail Inlet, then Robins would have been guilty of piracies occurring after January 5, 1718, and would have been subsequently, and reluctantly, pardoned by Spotswood rather than acquitted by the court.

As it turns out, our shards of clues, dates, and names, and other references, lead us to conclude that of the 13 pirates who were hanged according to historians, only six were actually executed—two whites and four blacks. Even though the court records have been lost, there is still enough evidence to draw a conclusion.

On Saturday, February 14, 1719, Lt. Gov. Spotswood wrote a letter to Lord Cartwight, a proprietor of North Carolina, in which he attempted to explain his justification for invading his lordship's colony. In Spotswood's words, he rescued "the Trade of North Carolina from the Insults of Pyrates upon the Earnest Solicitations of the Inhabitants there." Spotswood wrote that the "prisoners have been brought hither and Tryed, and it plainly appears that the Ship they brought into Carolina was, after the date of His Majesty's pardon." Some historians have taken these words as proof that the pirates were found guilty and executed, but Spotswood never actually said so. In fact, the true message Spotswood was trying to convey was not the guilt or innocence of Black Beard's men for bringing in the French ship, but that Lord Cartwright's senior representative in North Carolina, Gov. Eden, had been collaborating with, and harboring unrepentant pirates, and that he had no business finding on behalf of Black Beard that the French ship was legal salvage.

Because we know that at least one of the Bath County pirates, James Robins, was back home before the end of January, and Spotswood confirmed that a trial had already taken place in his letter of February 14, we can be confident that at least part of the judicial process had been concluded by the first of February. In fact, a piece of the puzzle coming from the ship's log of the HMS *Pearl* falls neatly into place. Capt. Gordon, in his entry of remarkable occurrences for January 28, 1719, writes: "Yesterday in the afternoon the longboat came... This morning sent 2 condemned pyrats ashore to Hampton to be executed, which about 1/2 past 11 was done accordingly." These two condemned pirates had to have been the two surviving white crew members from the *Adventure*—everyone else has been accounted for. In addition to confirming that two of the survivors of the engagement at Ocracoke were hanged, Capt. Gordon lets us know that the executions took place at Hampton, not Williamsburg, contradicting what every Black Beard scholar has written.

The cases of the white prisoners were processed separately and earlier than those of the five black men taken from the sloop, *Adventure*, because Spotswood was not confident whether or not the black men, believed to be slaves, should be tried as pirates. He had to wait until after the winter weather began to abate before he could summon his council to Williamsburg to consider the issue. At a meeting of his council on March 11, Lt. Gov. Spotswood

continues on page 176

Gov. Eden's remains were moved to the cemetery of St. Pauls Church in Edenton, NC, in 1889. His original slate marker has survived the ages (inset above).

Today, the remains of Gov. Charles Eden rest on the grounds of St. Paul's Church in Edenton, NC. The epitaph on his slate marker states that Eden "governed this Province Eight years, to ye satisfaction of ye Lords Proprietors, and ye ease and happiness of ye people." However, history's interpretation of Eden's complicity with Black Beard and the Bath County pirates has not been so set in stone. After his death on March 26, 1722, there was an effort made by his family and friends to restore the governor's reputation, which was believed to have been tarnished by the letters of Lt. Gov. Spotswood, and the first edition of Capt. Johnson's *History of Pirates*. In a later edition, Johnson retracted his earlier aspersions of Eden, writing that there had been no written proof of the governor's dealings with Black Beard and his cohorts. No surprise, there. And no one has ever been able to explain how Eden could have legally pardoned the pirates in the first place, or awarded Black Beard ownership of the *Adventure*, or the cargo of the French "derelict."

Tobias Knight was brought before the Council and charged as an accessory to acts of piracy. Having been allowed plenty of time to prepare, Knight mounted a masterful defense and was found not guilty by men who were essentially his friends. The fact that he was near death may have contributed to his acquittal. Knight's will was probated just two months later in July, 1719. He is believed to be buried near his house on Archbell Point at the mouth of Bath Creek.

The Bath County Pirates

Eighteen —
Black Beard's Blood

Kevin Duffus photo.

Much more n[...]
Beard, so Oden, [...]
other colonial pro[...]
tling in North Ca[...]
toms documents [...]
James. Records fro[...]
cargo between Virg[...]
James Beard. In al[...]
for its captain but f[...]
exiled Stuart Prince[...]

Prior to becom[...]
ince of Carolina, Ja[...]
rons of Charleston. [...]
Cooper River wher[...]
nancial assistance fr[...]
state that 12 Charle[...]
locally built, sailed [...]
New England to th[...]

In the Charles[...]
in the colony prior [...]
seems to have had [...]
dies. However, there[...]
tain or mariner at th[...]
early records of Sou[...]
ers, Matthew, James[...]
who is believed to [...]
suspected that this [...]
James Beard's brothe[...]
William Beard sold t[...]
ceased wife, Susanna[...]
deed, Beard referred [...]
Susannah Beard, wh[...]
when married wome[...]
was especially true [...]
centuries, when Scot[...]
terian Church were [...]
who viewed such m[...]
Some historians have [...]
byterian unions were [...]
bastards, and some pa[...]
as fornicators for coh[...]
issues may have had m[...]
some members of the [...]

Live oak at Ocracoke Island's Springer's Point.

*E*DWARD BEARD IS AN ILLUSION. EVIDENCE OF HIS existence is no more tangible than an apparition, like the mysterious atmospheric phenomena sometimes seen by hikers in the diaphanous mists of mountaintops and woodlands called "Brocken Spectre"—a ghostly, shadowy figure of a human, its head often sheathed in shimmering, iridescent halo-like rings. Like a rainbow—ethereal, elusive, improbable; tantalizingly within reach, but at the same time distant. In this story, Edward Beard is the spectre, a silhouette of an idea, defined only by the light that emanates from around it, and within—the unprovable dark matter of history.

He is so described because no where in the records of the Beaufort County Deed Book or within the archives of North Carolina, Virginia, Great Britain, or anywhere else, does Edward Beard appear as the true identity of the infamous pirate captain Black Beard. Not one instance of the name shows up in the capacious stacks of letters, documents, logbooks, council journals, court papers, or early historical accounts. To accept the possibility of his existence requires a leap of faith. But for some historians, scholars and pirate enthusiasts, the possibility that Black Beard was, in truth, Edward Beard, son of James Beard, requires too great a leap, demands too much faith for them to be believers. But John Oden believed, as did Allen Norris and Jane Bailey. Years of diligent research, study and analysis made them believers. When they shined their light into the darkness of the past, the three genealogists could sense the presence of Edward Beard, if only as a void in the fabric of time. Not a spectre, but a real man—lost beneath the layers of his own unaccountably massive legend.

When he sailed from North Carolina into his new life with an assumed name, the man who became Black Beard left behind a remarkably vague wake, an empty space that has since been filled by the imaginations of writers with no more rationale or purpose than to complete the blank pages of a book. Yet many of these are the same historians

Tall, gregarious and handsome with thick black hair, Edward Beard left the fledgling colonial outpost of Bath Town in 1709, still in his late-teens, for the bustling wharves and abundant opportunities of Philadelphia. There, accompanied by his father, Edward was indentured to a captain of a trading sloop that plied the ports of colonial America and the islands of the West Indies, including calls to Jamaica. He was fairly well educated, able to read and work numbers and was knowledgeable about ships and the sea. He had learned well at his father's side. Consequently, he graduated from ordinary seaman to mate in a few years, and became well-known and well-liked in the alehouses of the City of Brotherly Love for his companionable and mischievous behavior.

During these years of the Queen's war with Spain, nearly all American mariners dabbled in privateering and Edward was able to quickly master the additional skills of trimming sails and rigs for utmost speed, clever tactics in a chase, gunnery and close-quarters combat in a boarding action. He was a natural for the work, and with his imposing height, he excelled at intimidating the officers of the ships they captured. But he never resorted to causing injury or death—that was clearly a sin by his Presbyterian faith.

Early on, when some of his shipmates' exploits skirted the fringes of Admiralty Law, he adopted the alias, Thatch, borrowed from his Quaker friend in Pennsylvania, in order to protect his father's good name. In 1712, a letter addressed to Edward delivered news of his father's death in South Carolina, and in his heart he knew he must, to the end, preserve the honor of his family's Scottish heritage and never yield to the affronts of the English. Year after year, political and religious plots and intrigues in London produced harmful restrictions and egregious insults for those of Scottish descent, not the least of which included the Navigation Acts, the Alien Act and the Act of Union. When the Hanover Elector, George, succeeded the Stuart Queen Anne to the throne of England and Scotland, young men like Edward Beard felt disgusted, disheartened and disaffected. They abandoned their allegiance to king and country and longed for the day when the exiled James would return to the soil of his kinfolk.

Soon after the end of the war with Spain, thousands of mariners were without work and the docks along the Delaware River were crowded with disgruntled, seditious sailors. Beard made his way back to North Carolina soon after the accession of the new king, to his father's fallow plantation on Bath Town Creek, uncertain about his fate except that he was no farmer. The colony was in shambles, homes and barns burned, entire families dead, all from the war with Indians. But Susannah and her family escaped the worst, except for the hard times—the scarcity of food and currency.

Then, in the early autumn of 1715, news arrived that jolted the colonies, including the residents of Bath County. One of the greatest treasure fleets in Spanish colonial history wrecked off the coast of Florida in a wretched storm, and the beaches and shallow reefs were said to be swathed in gold and silver and indescribable riches of the

Spanish Main. The Spanish treasure was looked upon as a potential salvation for the survival of the colony of Carolina, which had been nearly decimated by war with the Tuscarora. With the financial assistance of some of Bath Town's most distinguished planters, which included the new governor and Secretary Knight, Edward Beard with John Martin and William Howard and a few of the other sons of the impoverished colony organized a wrecking mission to Florida. They left Bath Town Creek before the worst of winter settled in aboard a 20-ton sloop, hoving-up near the old watering hole on Oc'cacok Island for a fortnight to take on fresh water and hunt for livestock to add to their meager stores. The anchorage was Edward's favorite in all of his travels with placid waters protected from the thundering sea by the sand banks, and the watering hole sheltered under a canopy of ancient oaks, their rambling, gnarled limbs clattering against one another in the whipsawing winds like cutlasses in a desperate battle.

During a break in the weather they sailed south, along the inside passage, for the glittering waters of Florida's Sebastian Inlet and its unimaginable riches. But soon after their arrival on the treasure wrecks, the Bath expedition faltered, when well-armed vessels of Spanish salvors came onto the scene determined to protect their King's possessions. So the small Carolina sloop crossed the Straits of Florida to New Providence Island and the exciting, ribald community of Nassau. For the Bath County men—Edward Beard (going by the name of Thatch), John Martin, William Howard and the others, Thomas Miller, Garret Gibbons, Nathaniel Jackson, Joseph Brooks—who shared subversive sentiments toward the crown, Nassau represented a new kind of freedom. There they met hundreds of like-minded men, including the persuasive, shrewd and daring, Capt. Benjamin Hornigold, who went about encouraging all to establish a republic of pirates on the strategically located island. Nassau was also a paradise of wenches of every size, shape, color and demeanor, who willingly shared their favors, and diseases, with the wide-eyed sea-rovers.

Hornigold convinced the Carolina men to join his "Flying Gang" by enticing them with the potential fortune they could earn as pirates. Beard and his friends assessed their options: go home empty handed, or...what difference did it make where their gold came from as long as they returned to Bath Town as wealthy men? By late-March, 1716, they set out on their first cruise aboard Hornigold's ten-gun sloop, Benjamin. Within a few weeks, off the coast of Cuba, they joined forces with New England pirates, Sam Bellamy and Paulsgrave Williams, who had just deftly double-crossed Hornigold's nemesis, Henry Jennings. Edward Beard made fast friends with the dashing, romantic Bellamy, who had taken the sobriquet, "Black" Sam, for his thick head of hair. "Black" Sam also impressed Beard with his rousing broadsides against the dangers of despotism, the punitive political and economic system of the English lords which robbed from the poor, and against criminally abusive shipowners and captains who did their bidding, and the inequality of life in general. Bellamy spoke of his desire to capture a ship so large, fast and powerful that he would fear no nation's man-of-war, and so he could wage his war against the world. Then he would proudly sail his prize up to Boston where he had been treated like vermin. He also desired to impress his love, Maria Hallett, who had such little faith in his abilities. It was Bellamy who gave the notion to Edward to call himself, "Black" Beard.

For the next six months, Hornigold, Black Beard, Martin and Howard sailed together in a newly acquired sloop, smaller and nimbler than the Benjamin. At Beard's suggestion, they called her the Adventure, in a salute to the great Capt. Kidd, a good Scot who had been betrayed and hanged by his corrupt and cowardly English masters. But "father" Hornigold was reluctant to wage unrestricted attacks on English shipping, which led to a dispute with the petulant and vindictive Bellamy, who deposed and cast-off the pirate patriarch and his devoted protégé Black Beard. It was the last Beard saw of Bellamy, his kindred, brother-in-arms.

In the autumn of 1716, Hornigold captured a small sloop and decided to give the young Beard

his first command. By then, less than one year since commencing their expedition to recover gold from the beaches of Spanish Florida, the Bath County men were full-fledged pirates—there would be no turning back. Especially since the Hanoverian King in London had officially proclaimed them so.

The winter and spring of 1717 passed with Capt. Hornigold and Capt. Thatch (as he was known except among his closest friends) cruising the Spanish Main all the way to Panama, to the scene of Sir Henry Morgan's infamous raid. Before returning to Nassau in August, Hornigold's "Flying Gang" had accumulated vast chests of plunder estimated to be worth hundreds of thousands of British sterling. But money was not everything, as Edward Beard soon learned when news arrived from New England that his friend, "Black" Sam Bellamy had died four months earlier in an effort to awe his Maria, when his fast and invincible man-of-war, the former slave ship Whydah, had wrecked on the beaches of Cape Cod when they failed to out-run a spring nor'easter. It was then that something darkened in the mind of the young pirate captain whose prestige was beginning to spread across the colonial seas as the notorious Black Beard. Life as a pirate was not so easy and carefree, unless you didn't care to live a very long life. Already months of unfettered drinking and continuous carousing were taking their toll on Beard and the aging process advanced prematurely. Time was running out if he was going to avenge the injustices to his father's forbearers, to the Stuarts, and to his Highland pride.

And then the peculiar-minded and badly wounded Stede Bonnet arrived, the man whose family the Beards had dutifully and humbly served in Barbados after the demise of Cromwell and during the reign of Charles II. With Hornigold's insistence, Black Beard took command of Bonnet's powerful and fast, 12-gun Revenge, and the great irony never failed to amuse the grandson of William Beard. It was time to prove himself as a feared pirate master. He immediately set a course north, for the entrance to the Delaware Bay, where he knew that on any given day, dozens of vessels heavily laden with goods, going to or from England, would be vulnerable like lambs at a slaughter. For the first time in his brief career as a pirate, Black Beard inflicted wanton vandalism upon his victims, ordering the indiscriminate dumping of cargos into the ocean. He did so in retribution for the imprisonment of Bellamy's men in Boston—a desperate act precipitated by a deepening alcoholic and syphilitic rage.

There was one more thing to do. Bypassing Nassau on their seasonal voyage to the West Indies, Black Beard set sail for the waters of his ancestors—Barbados—where he knew swift west-African slavers made their first landfall after crossing the Middle Passage. He would fulfill Bellamy's dream to command a warship bristling with great guns that would become a nation unto itself, and he would name her, Queen Anne's Revenge—his own Jacobite man-of-war. For the next six months, they roamed the seas without fear, flying their Death flag proudly before all unlucky enough to get in their way.

Over the winter of 1717-1718, as Black Beard and his flotilla worked its way along the chain of windward and Leeward islands, word came to them from some of their prizes that King George was willing to extend his mercy to pirates if they were to surrender by a certain date. If they did, all piracies prior to the fifth of January would be forgiven. A great council was called aboard their flagship and many in the company, including all of the pressed men, voted to surrender to His Majesty's will. For the first time, an irreparable division was forming between the pirates. Later, in a private discussion with his closest friends, Black Beard whispered that their problem was twofold. For their enormous numbers that had joined the company—nearly 700 by some estimates—there was hardly enough money to go around. For all of their captures and plunder, the original members of the company would return to Bath Town with little to show. Secondly, January 5th had already passed and they had since taken dozens of ships. By his estimation they were no longer eligible for the King's pardon, unless...! Unless, they surrendered to a governor who knew them well, who

had been among those investing in their sojourn in the first place, two years before—the governor of their own colony of North Carolina. The Bath County pirates agreed to sail home.

But before they did, Black Beard hoped to find a cure for what ailed him at Charles Town on the Ashley and Cooper Rivers, the last resting place of his father. He knew he could not simply show up in the harbor with four pirate ships and hundreds of men in order to call on the town apothecary, so he simply did what any good pirate would do—he blockaded the port and held the town ransom for a chest of medicines that would contain the remedy he hopefully needed. A pirate did what a pirate had to do.

Life as commodore and leader of hundreds of drunken pirates was not what it was cracked up to be as he once wrote in his log book—there was never enough grog to keep everyone happy and they were beginning to be more interested in acquiring rum than gold. Black Beard and his Bath friends, including William Howard and John Martin, devised a plan for how they could shed themselves of their unmanageable company and still retain the bulk of their plunder. They would intentionally wreck the French slaver on the bar of Old Topsail Inlet and escape in the small tender sloop, for which Black Beard would again choose the name, Adventure, for good luck. The plan was executed flawlessly on June 10. The dimwitted Bonnet fell for the ruse, and it was satisfying that a Beard of Barbados finally turned the tables on their old masters. Of course, at Bath Town, their patrons, family and neighbors were both surprised and pleased for their return—especially Edward Beard's old friend, Tobias Knight, and the governor as well. Much of the old company disbanded, including William Howard, who spoke of going to Virginia to visit a woman and sell his slaves where they would bring a higher price. Edward Beard, however, was still restless and not well, and he fancied returning to Philadelphia with his King's pardon in hand, where he might procure proper medical attention and possibly reunite with his some-time love, Margaret of Marcus Hook.

But the following months were not happy ones, as his remaining crew had doubts about their future, the Adventure's seaworthiness and their captain's sometimes unpredictable and violent behavior. For that matter, Edward had doubts about himself and had lost much of his vigor for buccaneering, for the failed Jacobite cause, and for life as it was. He could see that his health was not improving and he was having difficulty making decisions—a bad flaw for a captain. He was opposed to taking the French ship off Bermuda but could not deny their sloop desperately needed repairs. His friend, Knight, had helped him devise a way so that their unfortunate piracy could be covered up, and all would be well again. And in any case, word was afloat that the English King was soon going to fight the Spanish again and a new pardon would be in the offing, and new letters of marque to be had. Edward had no interest in his father's land on Bath Town Creek—he too much enjoyed the smell of the sea than that of dirt and dung. But his sister and her husband had seemed to have prospered down in Craven Precinct. And the boy, Edward—he would never know the life his uncle knew.

More bad business had occurred that could not be helped—that insolent trader in his canoe near Chester's who was too niggardly with his drink and Hands, the traitor! Even though Hands was no Carolina man, Edward kept him aboard at Topsail for he was a magician with rigs and sails. And in gratitude, the deceitful English dog had turned on him. Hands deserved what came to him beneath the table, shot like the bastard mongrel that he was. And then, grounding in the sound after visiting Susannah on the Neuse River—it was deemed a dark and forbidding omen by all aboard the Adventure. A portent of evil ahead. But what?

Twenty—
Treasure Islands, Skulduggery and Other Tall Tales

The Old Slough, Ocracoke Island, North Carolina.

BY CANOE IN THE NIGHT, THEY CAME TO HER grave, clumsily paddling with shovels, smelling of whiskey and cursing the moon. Overhead, beams of spectral light pierced intermittent rents in the black clouds scudding the night sky, and briefly illuminated the midnight treasure seekers on their nefarious mission. After landing on the river bank, they wedged their craft between cypress knees and embarked for their objective, which was shrouded behind drapes of Spanish moss—a long-abandoned cemetery on high ground, deep into the mysterious woods.

They came because of an enticing tale of Teach's lost treasure once told by a serious and respected spinster aunt, who claimed to be a descendant of pirates. They were also impelled on their hopeless task by a drunken dare, and because they were pathetically naïve. It had rained—there was that, too. Spring showers had softened the ground, presumably making their job of digging a little easier, but as they climbed the hill, the wet loamy soil caused them to slip and fall where they rolled and thrashed upon unseen creeping things of the night—the price of admission.

Emboldened by alcohol and gripped by treasure fever, they nevertheless pressed onward, passing over a gauntlet of shadows, strobed on and off by the moonlight. Looming limbs of ancient oaks were cast like the grasping arms of the dead—appearing one instant and gone the next. Fortunately for the would-be thieves, they were oblivious of the unmarked graves upon which they trampled. Soon enough, they arrived at the sandstone marker of the pirate's sister, Susanna—or was she his wife?—none could remember for sure. "Who cares?" one whispered as they began disrespectfully digging with abandon, alongside one of the craters already dug by someone who had been there before.

Another hole dug. Another treasure not found.

But the legend lived on.

with fantastic and improbable tales of treasure.

Passages like the following, invented in Pyle's fertile imagination, might prompt readers to pack their overnight bags and trusty shovels and rush to Mulberry Island:

"At Guzarat I met with a Portuguese named Anthony de Sylvestre; he came with two other Portuguese and two Dutchmen to take on in the Moor's service, as many Europeans do. This Anthony told me he had been among the pirates, and that he belonged to one of the sloops in Virginia when Blackbeard was taken. He informed me that if it should be my lot ever to go to York River or Maryland, near an island called Mulberry Island, provided we went on shore at the watering place, where the shipping used most commonly to ride, that there the pirates had buried considerable sums of money in great chests well clamped with iron plates. As to my part, I never was that way, nor much acquainted with any that ever used those parts; but I have made inquiry, and am informed that there is such a place as Mulberry Island. If any person who uses those parts should think it worth while to dig a little way at the upper end of a small cove, where it is convenient to land, he would soon find whether the information I had was well grounded. Fronting the landing place are five trees, among which, he said, the money was hid. I cannot warrant the truth of this account; but if I was ever to go there, I should find some means or other to satisfy myself, as it could not be a great deal out of my way. If anybody should obtain the benefit of this account, if it please God that they ever come to England, 'tis hoped they will remember whence they had this information."

It would seem that the aforementioned treasure would be fairly easy to find: simply locate the old watering place on Mulberry Island where ships used to ride (your sonar should be able to detect large piles of ballast stones in the vicinity), make your way to the upper end of a small cove where five large trees stand, and start digging. But wait.

Before anyone packs the car or fuels the boat, there are a couple of things to keep in mind. There is no Mulberry Island in Maryland—Pyle got that wrong—or between the banks of the York River, which is in Virginia. But there is a Mulberry Island in the James River in Virginia. Unfortunately, it is doubtful Black Beard and his crew ever hid treasure there, because to do so, they would have had to sail past Kiquotan Roads and His Majesty's Royal Navy ships, HMS *Pearl* and HMS *Lyme*, and their combined 64 guns, which was unlikely to have ever happened. And as for going to Mulberry Island today to dig for Black Beard's gold (just in case the reader is undeterred by the erroneous and fictional nature of Pyle's story), treasure hunters might further be discouraged by the military police of the United States Army, which owns the island and operates Fort Eustis there.

Legend has it that pirates had their own means of providing security at the site of their hidden plunder: the gruesome remains of a prisoner or crew member who was chosen by lot to be sacrificed—murdered, to be precise—and left behind to rot, and to haunt the location of the buried treasure. The concept seems to have been invented by 19th-century writers who reveled in the prospect of ghosts patrolling the grounds above pirate plunder buried somewhere in their communities. John F. Watson wrote the following in his second volume of his *Annals of Philadelphia*:

"The superstition then was very great about ghosts and witches. 'Old Shrunk,' as he was called, (George S., who lived to be 80) was a great conjuror, and numerous persons from Philadelphia and elsewhere, and some even from Jersey, came to him often… to get their fortunes told… They used to consult him where to go and dig for money; and several persons, whose names I suppress, used to go and dig for hidden treasures of nights. An idea was very prevalent, especially near the Delaware and Schuylkill waters, that the pirates of Black Beard's day had deposited treasure in the earth. The fancy was, that sometimes they killed a prisoner and interred him with it, to make his ghost keep his vigils there and guard it. Hence it was not rare to hear of persons having seen a spooke or ghost, or of having dreamed of it a plurality of times, which became a strong incentive to dig there."

In 1926, according to a report in the venerable *New York Times*, Miss Florence E. Steward of Trenton, New Jersey, decided to sell a house on Wood Street in the nearby village of Burlington, which had been owned by her family for generations. And, for those many generations, her family knew a secret about that house and a walnut tree which stood in its yard. The walnut tree had always been known to its owners as the "pirate tree," and according to a closely-held family secret, under it Black Beard had supposedly buried his fabulous treasure many years before. The tree was on the east bank of the Delaware River about twenty miles northeast of the pirate's favorite city, Philadelphia.

Of course, Miss Steward didn't want the new owners to end up with Black Beard's treasure so she hired some excavators to come and dig it up for her. Why the family waited until they were going to sell the property before they attempted to dig up the fortune was not explained. Oddly, the owner was not present when the work began and at the end of the day the excavators were gone but there was a large hole in the ground. It was only natural that within a couple of days, neighboring children came and played in the hole, at which time they, very unnaturally, unearthed a human skull. Upon learning about the skull, Miss Steward divulged that it must have been the old Spaniard Black Beard was said to have buried, standing upright, atop his chest of treasure. She called the police and asked them to guard her property from other volunteer diggers until she could personally supervise the work. However, having gotten a taste of treasure hunting, the children could not be dissuaded and they began to dig a hole on the adjacent lot of Miss Anna Pugh, where they discovered a "large cache of bones," which were later determined by a veterinarian to be bovine in nature, and not of Spaniards, dating to a time when the property was once a tanning yard.

After following the story for a few days, the *Times* lost interest and had nothing else to say about the matter, inferring that the search had been unsuccessful. However, in their final story, it was reported that the original excavators had been observed prying "a large, heavy object" from the earth and taking it with them when they departed. Meanwhile, Miss Steward told the paper that digging would continue around the walnut tree until she was satisfied with the result. Presumably, the property had diminished significantly in value by the time Miss Steward achieved her satisfaction.

Three years after Miss Steward's walnut tree excavation, Ben Dixon MacNeil, a correspondent for the Raleigh *News and Observer*, must have decided that Black Beard's home state of North Carolina would not be upstaged by New Jersey or the *New York Times*. MacNeil wrote a story for the February 3, 1929, Sunday edition with a headline that was simultaneously enthralling and deflating: "Blackbeard's Buried Treasure Found at Last; But Mystery of Pirate Gold Not Yet Solved."

MacNeil's story concerns Plum Point on Bath Creek, where the writer purported that Black Beard had built his retirement home, with a description worthy of today's real estate marketers: "No where could the fabulous buccaneer have found a more suitable place in which to establish himself. The wide Pamlico [River] and the creek gave him an expanded horizon across which he might view the approach of the world, if it should elect to approach [him]." (From the location on Plum Point to which MacNeil had referred, you can't see very far down the Pamlico River at all.)

The details of the story—of Black Beard's treasure found and then lost again—are these: two days before Christmas in 1928, three men, whose identities were unknown but who were believed to be duck hunters, came to Plum Point by boat. They left sometime later. Whence they came or where they went afterward was unknown. What they did in the interim was only conjecture—there were no witnesses. According to MacNeil: "the next day, or the next—the stories are in some conflict here [MacNeils' words]—other hunters making their way through the thick undergrowth that covers the Point, came upon the broken brick vault" out of which had been removed a "mysterious chest containing, according to legend, uncounted pieces of Spanish gold." The vault, eighteen inches wide and three feet long, had been buried eight feet under the sand in an area so pockmarked with craters from previous treasure seekers that the landscape looked like the far side of the moon. Suspicious markings in the original mortar of the brick vault, and some accumulation of rust, led the other hunters to surmise that an iron-clasped wooden chest once resided inside the vault. A conspicuous trail led from the opened vault to the shore, where it was believed the three unknown duck hunters had lifted the heavy chest into their boat and disappeared, even though no one saw them do it. And with that, the conclusion was reached that Black Beard's treasure had been finally found, and, of course, was again lost.

According to MacNeil, in Black Beard's day, the tall and dark buccaneer utilized "a tunneled approach from the river front to the cellar of his house." But, lest it cast a sliver of doubt upon the newspaperman's story, it should be pointed out that he informs the reader that Tobias Knight lived directly across the creek from Black Beard's digs, "the creek being about a mile wide at this point." In fact, the creek is 450 yards wide, no more than one quarter of a mile at that point. Nevertheless, MacNeil claimed that Knight had his own tunnel, through which he would have spirited smuggled commodities.

MacNeil concludes that Black Beard must have been an exceptionally wealthy pirate, who buried his Spanish gold beneath the sand of numerous eastern North Carolina locations, "because otherwise he would have not been worth bothering the British navy, and successful pirates have chests of gold buried about in places. And where else should he bury the gold except in his own backyard." And bury his treasure he must have, because that is what "all proper pirates" do. Further, no one ever doubted that Plum Point was the secret location of Black Beard's treasure chest because, as MacNeil reported, the place had appeared in dreams to some seekers (presumably as a big "X"), and came in the form of "hunches" to others, or was determined by diviners to be the place to dig. And dig they did, and probably still do, with the same blind faith and expectations people have when they purchase lottery tickets, or read stories like Mr. MacNeil's in the newspaper. Or those who watch the national cable channel which is devoted to producing informative, accurate history programs.

In 2001, the History Channel series, "History's Mysteries," took viewers along on a "scientific" search for Black Beard's treasure buried on the remote outpost of Lunging Island, part of a rocky archipelago, six miles off the coast of New Hampshire known as the Isles of Shoals. And even though it has been well-documented that Black Beard never sailed farther north than the coast of New Jersey during his busy, two-year pirate career, the History Channel's producers were willing to go to great expense to investigate the earnest claims of 80-year-old Prudence Randall that the prolific freebooter and digger, Black Beard, buried his treasure on her island. Prudy knew she was getting on in years so she decided it was high time to get to the bottom of the abiding family legend. Plus, thoughts of so much wealth lying beneath her island had consumed her waking thoughts, and probably her dreams as well. If there was no gold there, Prudy wanted to use what remained of her life to think about other things. Or so she said.

Black Beard's mythical flag was of the same design used by the pirate John Quelch 15 years earlier. References to "Thatch's" flag in the primary sources describe him flying "Deth's Head."

She first heard the story from her father, who purchased the island in the 1920s. In all likelihood, the sellers or their agents dreamed-up the story of Black Beard's treasure to bolster the sales price—the island was, after all, a rock out in the middle of the ocean with nary a tree. Nevertheless, Prudy's family story was that the famous pirate captain and his crew frequented the island, partaking of drinks at the local tavern, and later burying chests of gold out back before leaving, never to return. The legend also states that Black Beard married his 13th wife there and left her standing forlornly on the dock as he and his men sailed away. No one has ever seemed to consider that had this happened during the time when Black Beard had 700 men in his company, there would have been no where to stand, not just in the tavern, but on the entire island itself, which is hardly 700 feet across at low tide. But that's too silly to even ponder.

Silly was not what the TV producers considered their investigation to be because they hired a New Hampshire-based geoscience firm which specializes in surface and borehole geophysical surveys for environmental, archaeological and engineering applications. Utilizing its high-tech ground penetrating radar and metal detecting equipment, the scientists conducted their search, right over the very spot where Miss Trudy believed the treasure to be, while a production crew from Boston filmed. Just in case no treasure was found, the producers wisely shipped over a stable of actors dressed in period costumes, including the great man himself, Black Beard. Also present were some of his shipmates and his 13th wife, who must have been glad to see the boys back. They were there to reenact "history," in order for the TV segment to run the proper length. A local writer and Web editor, J. Dennis Robinson, accompanied the expedition as the historical expert, and in the course of the day he found himself sitting next to "old Ned Teach" eating a bag of chips and smoking a cigarette, just before he pasted his beard back on and stuck a plastic pistol in his belt. Robinson sagely observed that Black Beard and his men looked more like they had been outfitted for the stage production of Pirates of Penzance "rather than the gritty open sea."

As any good journalist would, Robinson made a diligent effort to track down the source of Lunging Island's Black Beard legend. The trail led him to Robert Ellis Cahill, the former owner of the New England Pirate Museum in Salem, Massachusetts, and the prolific author of 27 books on New England folklore. Cahill had moved, but Robinson tracked him to Florida where he was living comfortably in retirement. In an interview by phone, Cahill said that there was no doubt Black Beard had been to Lunging and that the rocky islands in the area had been a well-known "pirate bank" for many dashing buccaneers of the Spanish Main who needed a place to stash their loot. The pirate John Quelch was among those making deposits there. Finally, after being asked numerous times for his sources, Cahill finally admitted he had gotten all of his information from Prudence Randall.

The History Channel segment on Black Beard's Lunging Island treasure surely left a lasting impression on millions of viewers over its many runs, despite the fact that his pirate gold was never found. As a result, some percentage of those millions of viewers will always believe that Black Beard visited the Isles of Shoals. The moral of the story? If you live on a lonely, rocky island out in the middle of the ocean like Miss Prudence Randall, be inventive should you wish to have visitors. And, be wary of the history you learn when watching cable television.

What celebrated historical figure has produced more extraordinary mythical tales than Black Beard the pirate? Were someone to collect, investigate and analyze all of the varied traditions which have taken shape since his death, it might require a lifetime's work and would lead to houses and castles, secret tunnels, treasure trees and treasure islands, silver drinking cups, old black kettles, and chart books. Waiting around the bend would be headless ghosts and ghostly lights wandering the lonely shores of rivers and sounds, and entire towns believed to be inhabited by his descendants. Such a comprehensive examination of all of the enduring Black Beard folklore from the rocky coast of Maine to the smallest coral reefs of the Caribbean could require a volume unto itself. For now, a few pages will have to do.

Treasure Islands

An island would be a natural location for a pirate to bury his treasure, and along the east coast of the United States there are numerous islands that have claimed to hold the riches of Black Beard, besides the aforementioned Mulberry Island, Virginia.

Tangier Island, in the broad waters of the Chesapeake Bay, was also believed to have been visited by "Teach" and his merry band of pirates, and there, they supposedly left a heavy oak chest filled with riches of their trade. Local tourism has been bolstered by the legend that Black Beard's restless spirit roamed the island at night looking for someone who would take off his ghostly hands his buried treasure, which he had to unload before receiving his eternal sleep. From inky shadows and behind deserted buildings, the dreaded pirate would whisper and whimper his desperate plea, but no one was brave enough to give poor Black

Beard the time of day. In a unique twist to an age-old tale, the retarded son of a Tangier Island pauper was the one who finally listened to the phantom pirate, and after roaming the island by day, the boy often returned home with his pockets filled with gold coins. Many of the watermen of the island, facing tough times as fishing stocks are depleted and foreign competition mounts, have taken to fishing for the old oak chest of pirate gold—at least that's what they tell the tourists. While the fishermen have yet to find what's left of Black Beard's treasure, a restaurant on the island has done a brisk business by capitalizing on the legend, even though there is absolutely no reason to believe that the pirate ever sailed into the Chesapeake Bay.

Across the finger-like appendage of Delmarva Peninsula, along Virginia's eastern shore, there is a barrier island which may have more of a credible connection to the notorious pirate, than its estuarine neighbor, Tangier. Today it's known as Cedar Island, but 37 years after Black Beard was killed, mariners and cartographers knew the place as Teaches Island. Legend has it that it was in the vicinity of that sandy bank that Black Beard once anchored in order to careen his vessel, and some think it was his favorite hide-away north of Cape Henry, despite the absence of records to support the tale. Naturally, the believers are convinced that if he had visited there, he must have buried his treasure there.

Capt. Kidd buries his treasure chest.

It is the same thing they believe on the coast of Georgia, 40 miles south of Savannah, where Blackbeard Island lies. Today the island belongs to the U.S. Fish and Wildlife Service and is managed as a National Wildlife Refuge. But in the days of yore, it was Black Beard who reigned supreme and imposed the rules on the island, so they say. Despite the fact that there is not the slightest evidence that the pirate ever came near the coast of what later became Georgia, the refuge proudly makes the following claim: "Blackbeard Island was named for Edward Teach, alias Blackbeard the Pirate. Legend tells of his murderous and plundering activities along the coast and his periodic retreats to the island for 'banking' purposes. Rumors of Blackbeard's buried treasure still flourish, but no evidence of his fortune has ever been discovered." Further elaborating on the pirate's purported activities on the island, the *Longstreet Highroad Guide to the Georgia Coast* claims that Black Beard marked the location of his treasure with a "spike in an old tree, and it is said practiced other nasty pirate-like activities such as beheading his 16th wife and six crew members and burying them in a mass grave on the island. The myth of Blackbeard's treasure has been so persistent that in 1934 a group of explorers were allowed to search the island for 10 days, but were unsuccessful in finding the pirate's loot." Wisely, the guide informs its readers that artifact and treasure hunting on Blackbeard Island are strictly forbidden—those are the federals' rules, not Black Beard's. Even so, it happens to be a thoughtful, time- and trouble-saving tip.

In North Carolina, there are treasure islands, too. In 1908, Wilmington, North Carolina, writer Andrew J. Howell, Jr., wrote a small book of fiction titled, *Money Island*, about a little island in the Greenville Sound west of Wrightsville Beach. Howell's story tells of how two local boys assisted two strangers in unearthing chests of gold buried by Capt. William Kidd. Despite the fact that Howell's story was clearly a work of fiction and Capt. Kidd never landed on North Carolina soil, a reporter for the *Charlotte Observer* wrote a column in 1926 about the ongoing mystery of the location of Kidd's treasure on Money Island. (It seems that newspaper stories of buried pirate treasure were quite the fad during the Roaring Twenties.) And, as often happens over time, Black Beard's name was sometimes supplanted for Kidd's in the retelling of Howell's tale, so that now, people in the area aren't sure who buried their treasure on the island.

Books of folklore like Howell's have always been good sellers. But it took a chief district court judge from eastern North Carolina to turn the genre into an art form, and a publisher's gold mine. The late Judge Charles Harry Whedbee of Greenville, North Carolina, loved a good yarn, especially those about his beloved Outer Banks that he heard told so often during idyllic summer evenings at his family's 19th-century beachfront cottage at Nags Head. So, when Whedbee was invited on his local TV station's morning news program to fill in for the host who was known by the descriptive appellation of Slim Short, he filled the airtime by sharing his repertoire of coastal folklore. In the years following, his many subsequent guest appearances became the show's most popular feature. And so it made sense for a North Carolina publisher to print the judge's best stories.

Each day in his courtroom, Judge Whedbee would tolerate no foolishness, fabrications or fallacies. But in the evenings at his typewriter—well, he more than made up for the law's tedious requirements for sound reasoning and veracity, and the constrictions for creative thinking. Whedbee's first book, *Legends of the Outer Banks*, was published in 1966 and went through three printings before the year was out. More books followed, five in all, and according to the publisher, Whedbee's volumes of "tidewater Tarheelia" were printed 58 times and sold more than 205,000 copies. The public, obviously, has been hungry for Whedbee's kind of "history"—legends, which he said came in three categories. Some he knew were true because he was there when they happened. Others were true because they were remembered by people with unimpeachable reputations for honesty and the rest contained at least a germ or seed of truth. But almost all had "a solid basis in fact," so wrote the judge. It isn't known whether or not Whedbee was winking when he wrote those words.

Black Beard was one of Whedbee's favorite subjects, and since the judge was not around when the pirate was living, we have to assume the author's information fell into the third of his categories of accuracy. He wrote that Black Beard built himself a large house on Ocracoke, "two stories high and containing many large rooms," which became well-known over the years as "Blackbeard's Castle."

Whedbee had reason to believe the pirates sold their plunder to eager merchants living in an established village on Ocracoke Island in 1718, even though records are adamant there was no village and only a few indigent squatters there at the time. Whedbee gave Blackbeard an Ocracoke wife, as well, whom the pirate would return to when he tired of the ones he had in Elizabeth City, Edenton and Bath. The judge was among the folklorists who perpetuated the legend of the pirate's sister, Susannah, "who lived on a farm which he bought her," and where he buried some of his treasure along the banks of the Tar River. Holiday's Island in the Chowan River was also identified by Whedbee as one of the pirate's known depositories. The island would have made for a particularly daring destination had the sloop, *Adventure* ever tacked its way so far into the Albemarle Sound and up the river, for the route would have taken the pirate gang right past the waterfront homes of Col. Edward Moseley, Col. Maurice Moore, Thomas Pollock and the prying eyes of many other members of the colony's establishment.

Skulduggery

If there was a Whedbee whopper that has influenced his readers more than any other, it might be the one titled, "Blackbeard's Cup." The story describes how Whedbee and a law school chum participated in a secret fraternal ceremony with a dozen bearded, blue-eyed, "hoi-toiders" (island natives who continue to speak with traces of an Elizabethan accent), held in "Blackbeard's Castle" on Ocracoke Island in the 1930s. Illuminated only by the wavering light of a kerosene lantern, the secret conclave gathered with great solemnity around a large table and took turns sipping a special communal libation from a peculiarly-shaped silver cup with the words, "Deth to Spotswoode," carved around the rim. The participants also chanted the cup's oath, over and over, in their heavily accented, gravely voices. After the first round of toasts, the young law student and future judge learned that the vessel from which he and his companion drank was none other than the silver-plated skull of the ritual's revered honoree, Black Beard.

graciously accepted it anyway. The museum was careful not to identify Snow's mysterious skull as having once belonged to Black Beard, but exhibited it purely as an example of pirate folklore. The skull nevertheless became one of the Peabody's most popularly viewed artifacts and became part of a traveling collection about pirates that made its way to museums across the United States. At an exhibition at the Mariner's Museum in Newport News in 1998, one of Black Beard's recent biographers even toasted the macabre trophy as it glared at him from behind reinforced security glass.

Edward Beard must surely have been smiling from the great beyond. The Edward Rowe Snow silver-plated "Black Beard" skull-cup was a fake. John Walker discovered in the course of his quest that Snow had "purloined the skull from a local biology class and coated it with thick layers of silver radiator paint." The Peabody Essex Museum continues to loan the wildly-popular Snow skull for traveling exhibits—maybe hoping that it won't be returned. Walker continues his quest for Black Beard's true skull—the holy grail of piratedom—to this day. Such is the power of pirate folklore.

Other Tall Tales— Lights, Tunnels, Trees, Houses, Wives, Chartbooks and Towns

A commentary on the many tall tales which have attached themselves to Black Beard's history like enterprising parasites would be incomplete without mentioning the wives, sisters, trees, towns, houses, supernatural lights and tunnels which bear a connection to his name. Some can be dispatched rather quickly.

A few respected authors and nearly every Black Beard folklorist has subscribed to the belief that the pirate captain married a young girl named, Mary Ormond, making her his 13th or 14th wife (as if being accurate with her rank in marital succession is the important thing), at a ceremony presided over by Gov. Charles Eden. The only extant record from Black Beard's time which even hints at such a marriage is a letter written by Capt. Brand three months after the pirate was killed. Probably deriving his information as hearsay from Israel Hands or one of the other incarcerated pirates, Brand said of Black Beard: "to put a gloss to his designs he marryed there." Of course, the term "marryed" in colonial times had other connotations besides the legal or sacramental state of matrimony. The "marriage" of Edward Beard and a young woman of Bath County may have been an amusing ruse or party hoax, or it may have indeed occurred between the pirate and an acquaintance of the family from his early days of residency. But her name was not Mary Ormond. According to genealogists Oden, Norris and Bailey, Mary Ormond's family did not appear in the Bath County deed book for the first time until 17 years after Black Beard was killed.

As we have previously learned, trees seem to offer a particular fascination to folklorists as places marking Black Beard's buried treasure. Other treasure trees of note not yet mentioned include Ben Dixon MacNeil's "Money Tree" at Cape Hatteras, a gnarled holly outside his WPA National Park Service cabin which he occupied in the later years of his life. In his book, *The Hatterasman*, written 31 years after the newspaperman convinced his readers that Black Beard's treasure had been found at Plum Point on Bath Creek, MacNeil seemed to change his mind and purported that Black Beard, instead, buried his plunder on Hatteras Island, even though there is no record he ever visited there. Even more implausible is the myth that there was a "Blackbeard Tree" on a plantation at Winnabow, North Carolina—a location ten miles from the Cape Fear River, the nearest navigable waterway—which would have required those hiding, or seeking the treasure to navigate a vast, alligator-infested swampy wilderness. Even so, there must be a reason as to why a venerable Brunswick County family would maintain such a tradition over the years. Just as there must be a reason why folks in the vicinity of Oriental, North Carolina, on the north shore of the Neuse River, still believe in the existence of "Teach's Oak," beneath which the pirate captain relaxed between his rampaging raids of terror. Depressions in the ground near the tree have confirmed the ardent faith of past treasure hunters.

What seems beyond explanation is why so many people want to claim to be descendants of Black Beard. A

"Blackbeard's Chartbook" was presented to the North Carolina State Archives by the Gibbs family of Englehard, NC. Although it was believed to be the pirate's personal chartbook, it was determined by archivist George Stevenson to be Volume V of the 1744 edition of the English Coast Pilot. The charts within the book feature the African coasts of Barbary, the Gold Coast, Congo, Angola, and the islands of Canary, Madeira and Cape Verde.

folklorist once wrote: "Seen through the softening haze of two centuries, the figure of the redoubtable sea robber acquires a romantic interest, and it is not surprising that many good and highly respected citizens of eastern North Carolina number themselves quite complacently among the descendants of the bold buccaneer." So it is, that at least half of the residents of the tiny Duplin County community of Teachey are convinced they are related to the famous bearded captain. According to some of the residents of Teachey, the governor of the colony gave the "Tieche" family land there in recompense for Black Beard's unfortunate death even though there are no supporting records.

Another recently emerging claim of Black Beard ancestry has materialized in New Bern, North Carolina, where it is said that the pirate was really the German Palatine blacksmith, John Edward Titschke, who served as Baron Von De-Graffenreid's "Robin Hood," delivering much-needed currency into the impoverished region. The proponents of this theory infer that a conspiracy of New Bern's leaders and historians have, until recently, succeeded in concealing the truth to protect the town's genteel and scrupulous reputation. Such imaginative and "ground-breaking" research is enough to make the Black Beard scholar eagerly run to the nearest ghost tale.

Many writers, including Whedbee and MacNeil, have waxed poetically about "Teach's ghostly light" roaming the shores of Ocracoke Island or drifting in the waters of some of the inland rivers and waterways the pirate was professed to frequent. The light supposedly represents the pirate's restless soul, searching for his head, his treasure or any one of his many wives. Curiously, the wraith is never said to be looking for the men who killed him. Among the most evocative were the words of Catherine S. Albertson from her 1914 publication, *In Ancient Albemarle*:

> Hardly a river that flows into our eastern sounds but claims to have once borne on its bosom the dreaded *Adventure*, Blackbeard's pirate

craft; hardly a settlement along those streams but retains traditions of the days when the black flag of that dreaded ship could be seen streaming in the breeze as the swift sails sped the pirates by, on murder and on plunder bent. Up Little River that flows by George Durant's home down to the broad waters of Albemarle Sound, Teach and his drunken crew would come, seeking refuge after some bold marauding expedition, in the hidden arms of that lovely stream. Up the beautiful Pasquotank, into the quiet waters of Symons Creek and Newbegun Creek, the dreaded bark would speed, and the settlers along those ancient streams would quake and tremble at the sound of the loud carousing, the curses and shouts that made hideous the night.

On all these waters "Teach's Light" is still said to shed a ghostly gleam on dark, winter nights; and where its rays are seen to rest, there, so the credulous believe, his red gold still hides, deep down in the waters or buried along the shore.

In her book, Albertson also took an obscure, unsupported piece of Pasquotank County folklore, which had been described in a 1910 Wake Forest University student newspaper, and turned it into a full-fledged legend—the legend of Black Beard's house, also known as the "Old Brick House." The house still stands today, on the west bank of the meandering Pasquotank River, a few miles upstream from Elizabeth City. With no more evidence than a millstone found near the steps of the house bearing the carved date of 1707, and the initials, "E.T.," Albertson was able to convince her readers, and county promoters, that the house once belonged to Edward Teach. A post-World War II Chamber of Commerce brochure for Elizabeth City proudly featured a photograph of "Blackbeard's House." Subsequent research by others proved that the house was not built until at least 17 years after the pirate's death. And even though biographer Robert E. Lee wrote that there was little doubt that Black Beard had managed to visit many houses along the rivers emptying into Albemarle Sound, there was little chance he had the time to do so when he was a pirate in 1718. There is not a single record that supports the possibility that Black Beard ever sailed into the Albemarle Sound.

Nevertheless, it was at the "Old Brick House" where the dreaded Black Beard was supposed to have returned after his piratical adventures. With words which seem to have been borrowed a decade later by Ben Dixon MacNeil in his story about Black Beard's other house at Plum Point on Bath Creek, Albertson wrote that " a better spot the pirate could not have found to keep a lookout for the avenging ship that should track him to his hiding place." The house featured a hidden passageway leading from the "banquet hall" (which was not more than a small dining room) to the cellar below where Black Beard confined his captives. Stains on the floors, Albertson wrote, hinted of dark deeds. "Should a strange sail heave in sight, or one which he might have cause to fear was bringing an enemy to his door," Black Beard would slip into the hidden chamber and descend into the cellar, where a tunnel awaited. "Bending low, [he would] rush swiftly through the underground tunnel, slip into the waiting sloop and be off and away up the river or down, whichever was safest, out of reach of the enemy." The image of Black Beard crouching and escaping through a tunnel is reminiscent of the similar tale told in Bristol, England, of young Thatch running from older bullies through the caves behind the Ostrich Inn.

Tunnels seem to be a prevalent feature in Black Beard lore. Probably the most frequently touted tunnel or subterranean passage among the pirate's many "historical" accounts is the one leading into the cellar beneath Gov. Charles Eden's mansion on Bath Creek, through which Black Beard supposedly delivered his plunder for safekeeping. It has already been established in this study that Eden did not occupy the property featuring the tunnel at the time Black Beard returned to the colony around the first of July, 1718. Still, the tunnel legend has persisted. So, did a tunnel actually exist and could it have secretly served privateers or pirates, regardless of who owned the property? It seems improbable. What purpose would a "secret tunnel" serve, if the vessel delivering the contraband had to anchor, or tie-up to a pier, which, out of necessity, may extend hundreds of feet or more from the shore? We are supposed to believe that chests or casks of plunder were hoisted from the hold of a moored vessel and landed on a dock or transshipped aboard a shoal-draft flat or raft, to be delivered to the entrance of the tunnel on the bank of the river or creek, so that it could then be secreted into the nearby house without anybody knowing about it? Would not the pirate or privateering vessel at the end of the dock have been a certain give-a-way?

Even so, there is evidence that there was some kind of sloping, stone-lined pathway leading to a palatial home that once stood on the former Eden plantation. Bath resident Joseph Bonner, who was born in 1798, recalled his visits to the property when he was a young boy, in a letter he wrote in 1857.

> Some forty or more years ago, there stood on an elevated bank about one mile from this place on the west side of the Creek, a spacious building then in a state of preservation, but long since decayed, which according to tradition had been the residence of some of our early Provincial Governors. Tradition...associates its occupant about the year 1718 with the celebrated pirate Teach, who it is said deposited with this functionary the fruits of his plunder.

Bonner's recollection of the "tradition" generally agrees with known facts, although some pirate enthusiasts might read too much into his words. As written, Bonner makes it sound like the pirate frequently delivered chests of gold, silver and jewels to the property. We know for certain Black Beard deposited the fruits of his plunder on one occasion—the casks of sugar from the French ship—with the functionary believed to be Charles Eden, although Eden did not own the plantation at the time but was residing in a house within Bath Town proper when not at his principal residence on the Chowan River. The owners of the plantation in October, 1718, when Black Beard delivered the French cargo to Bath, were the mariners Stephen Elsey and James Robins, the two men previously suggested as his former crew members. They may have received the 60 hogsheads of sugar on behalf of the governor and placed it in a storehouse on the governor's former plantation, since the governor's house in town probably did not have a suitable building in which to accommodate the consignment.

In his 1857 letter, Bonner described the house in some detail.

> I was accustomed to visit this building in my early boyhood. Its massive walls, capacious halls, rich workmanship of the interior, and palace like appearance, indicated that it had been the abode of wealth. A Subterranean passage some 60 or more yards in length, communicated from a brick wall near the margin of the creek, with the cellar of the dwelling.

The subterranean passage between the creek and the "palace" was described again in an 1894 local newspaper, but by then, the prominent features of the house, the stone passage, and the brick wall near the creek, were described as being in ruins. More than a century later, all of it has disappeared: the stately house, storehouses, smokehouses, barns, stables, kitchens, corn cribs, privies, and the inevitable cemetery located nearby containing the remains of past owners, their wives and children, relatives, slaves, and unnamed stillborn—all vanished, absorbed by the earth, and time, and lost to memory. All forgotten but an inscrutable, persistent legend. Now, during the summer growing season, the site is a vast and verdant cornfield overlooking the nearly unchanged panorama of ancient Bath Creek, where the ceaseless undercurrents of Time—past, present and future interwoven— still follow their own mysterious, meandering paths.

Twenty-one—
A Link In the Chain

W HAT IS THE MYSTERIOUS SECRET OF THE "TUNNEL land" and of the palace-like house with its massive walls and capacious halls? Was it once the repository for the plunder of pirates and privateers? For what purpose did Stephen Elsey and James Robins buy the property in September, 1718? They were mariners, not planters nor stockmen. Was their enterprise part of a plan to facilitate the privateering endeavors of the remaining members of the *Adventure*'s company and boost the economic fortunes of Bath County?

I pondered these questions as I stood on a grassy, contoured bank along the caramel-colored waters of Bath Creek, 35 summers into my quest for the true identity of Susie White, and the truth behind the legend of Black Beard's sister. At the time, I was a guest on the privately-owned property known by some as "Eden's tunnel land," and alternatively by its late-nineteenth century designation: the "Beasley Tract." The property may well be one of the most historically significant places in the state of North Carolina, but these days it is managed as a corporate hunting and fishing retreat for a Canadian-owned mining and manufacturing company. Few visitors must fully appreciate the history which lies beneath their feet.

I was there at mid-day on one of those staggering, hot and humid July days in eastern North Carolina. But it wasn't the climate that made me feel disoriented, like I was detached from reality—it was Time. The ebb and flow of Time had me wavering, back and forth, between the present and the past as I strived to see the landscape as it appeared—and the events as they occurred—in 1718. Very near where I stood, I thought, must have been the long-lost, stone-paved subterranean passage leading to the cellar of the mansion.

To what secrets of the past did the "tunnel" lead?

They all had passed this way, two-hundred eighty-nine years earlier: Gov. Eden, Tobias Knight, Stephen Elsey, James Robins and Black Beard—perhaps Israel

Beaseley Point, Bath Creek, North Carolina.

ership of the Salter tract nearby known as Duvall's Plains. (Sarah Salter likely remained in the Cape Fear River region where, as a minor, she had been in the care of Madam Sarah Porter, which suggests that Edward Salter, Sr.'s first wife may have been a sister of Madam Porter.)

Edward Salter's will in 1735 made provisions for his children's continuing education. He specifically noted his desire that his son and namesake not lack for anything in his development: "My singular will further is, that my said beloved son, Edward Salter, may have a thorough education to make him a compleat merchant, let the expense be what it will." Whatever the expense may have been, it was money well-spent.

The Salter properties along the Tar River flourished under the younger Edward's supervision. In addition to harvesting and producing naval stores primarily of tar, pitch and turpentine, the Salter plantations expanded their fields of tobacco, and numerous log-hewn barns were built for the curing and storage of the increasingly-popular Carolina golden leaf. By 1758, a tobacco warehouse and inspection station were built at the Salter landing on the south bank of the Tar River, to facilitate sales and exports for area planters. Salter also purchased and operated a mill, expanded his land holdings through additional patents, and established a ferry at his landing. He was appointed a river and road commissioner for Beaufort County. By 1768, a mail route running between Williamsburg, Virginia, and Charleston, South Carolina, crossed the Tar River at Salter's Ferry, and eventually became a principal route for north-south travel. As a result, it is likely that some type of inn or tavern was built in the immediate vicinity of Salter's ferry, although the fact has not been preserved in the records. Like his father, Salter was active in the governing affairs of his community and served as a Justice of the Peace and a Clerk of Court.

Sometime around 1742, about seven years after his father's untimely death, Edward Salter, Jr. married Ann Bonner, daughter of Thomas Bonner, a Bath Town cooper and one-time sheriff of Beaufort Precinct. Deeds, conveyances, wills and census records from the ensuing years show many connections between the Bonners and the Salters, as well as between the Salters and the distinguished Blount and Harvey families.

As the younger Edward Salter's business interests grew, so did his family flourish. Over the next dozen years, Salter and his wife are believed to have had as many as nine children: Edward III, Robert, John, James, Abigail, Sarah, Elizabeth, Susanna and Thomas. It is also possible that the children's aunts—Edward's sisters Mary and Susannah—lived for a few years on the adjoining properties, although the dates of their deaths do not appear in the records. Many Pitt County records, wills and inventories were lost in a fire that consumed the courthouse in February, 1858.

For the increasingly numerous and wealthy Salters residing along the tannin-colored Tar River, it must have seemed an idyllic, bountiful time, relative to their primitive surroundings. According to Henry Thomas King's *Sketches of Pitt County*, life in mid-18th century North Carolina was not so hard as may be imagined (at least for upper-class white families): "With all its trials, troubles and disadvantages, it may be said to have been a life close to nature, simple and not so full of hardships, as is generally supposed." King wrote of amusements and pleasures which included music, cards, dice games, singing, bowling, horse racing, and occasional social dances.

Storytelling and folklore, too, played an important part of family and social gatherings. Cousins, nieces and nephews would have gathered around to listen to a parent, grandparent, or an aunt or uncle, tell of the old days in Bath County, and maybe of the hard times when their ancestors had to participate in privateering and piracy in order to survive. Oral histories of swashbuckling pirate adventures and the mysteries of the sea no doubt captivated the attention of the young. However, if the Salters had been typical of early colonial families who proudly succeeded in elevating themselves from their previous humble economic or social classes, then they may have been reticent to speak openly of how the family's patriarch, the first Edward Salter, once served under the "death's head" flag of the notorious pirate, Black Beard. Antiquarian author John F. Watson addressed the issue in 1840: "Those immediately connected with pirates might keep their own secrets, but as they might have children and [connections] about, it might be expected to become the talk of their posterity in future years, that their fathers had certain concealed means of extravagant living." Only amongst themselves, with muted voices, would the Salter elders have talked of how their ancestor participated in the daring pirate blockade of Charleston, or the wanton burning and sinking of Boston ships in revenge for the hanged crew of "Black" Sam Bellamy, and how the family's lands may have been financed by Black Beard's plunder. It was plainly not a subject respectable family members would discuss beyond their own walls.

But the Salters' past connection to pirates was not a secret among their friends and neighbors. During other gatherings the story was told, repeated over and over, and embellished and reshaped and altered over the many generations to follow. Early on, children may have whispered about the elderly widow down the old Mt. Calvert lane, Mrs. White, whose grandfather (who had the same name as her brother) was said to have once been a pirate. At the same time, there was likely another legend afloat, a recollection known to some in eastern North Carolina who had kinfolk going back to the very early days, and who could remember things that have been long-since forgotten—that the pirate Black Beard once had a sister whom he had visited just days before he was killed by the Virginia governor. A sister named, Susannah. As the years and generations passed the facts of these memories and stories became diffused, blurred, and indistinct. The two tales were confused and eventually merged so that they became one—a single tale of yore, improved, refined, simpler and more fascinating than the original: The legend of "Sister Susie White," the sister of Black Beard the pirate.

And so it was, over the years to follow, the legend was purloined and perpetuated by authors like Henry Thomas King and Judge Charles Whedbee, their publishers, their readers, news reporters and nefarious midnight treasure seekers. They all accepted that Mrs. Susanna White was the sister of Black Beard the pirate. But White was not Black Beard's sister as the carvings on her sandstone grave marker will attest. She was, instead, the granddaughter of Black Beard's former cooper, Edward Salter.

I have for some time surmised that the connection between Susanna White and the legend of "Susie White" and her relationship with pirates—the grain of truth within—had been through the Salter family. After all, Susanna was buried on the old Mt. Calvert property once owned by the Salters. And the name, Susanna or Susannah, ran in the family. I suspected that Susanna White must have been named for her aunt, Susannah Salter. For years, however, I was unable to prove my theory. No where in my research had I been able to find a record that conclusively tied Mrs. White to the Salters—until the very week I was writing this chapter, the conclusion of which was in doubt—in jeopardy really—without the final pieces of the puzzle.

Through Jane Bailey's and Allen Norris's encouragement, I rushed to the Pitt County Courthouse for a day of research. "Plundering," as John Oden would have called it. Because Pitt County was formed out of the western frontier of Beaufort County in 1760, and because of the 1858 courthouse fire, its early deed books are not as extensive, nor daunting, as Beaufort's. It didn't take me too long to review the large and heavy index books of grantors and grantees marked, "The Earliest Days." Within, I found many references to the Salters and dozens of property transfers involving both Edward Salter III and Robert Salter—the suspected brothers of Susanna White. But after searching every record listed in the indexes, I came up empty handed—no verifiable proof that Mrs. White, the legendary "sister" of Black Beard was, in reality, a Salter. By 4:30 p.m., I gave up, tired, thirsty and facing a long drive home, feeling defeated. But as I was walking out of the deed office I was struck with a thought: *Thirty minutes left before closing. I'm here. Why not use the remaining time to search the deed books page by page? Maybe I'll find something.*

I returned to the stacks. There were many possible choices but something impelled me to select deed book "M." Back at a nearby table I began turning the pages, scanning the handwritten words written in 1791 for the names Salter or White, hopefully within a deed of gift. The aspirations and endeavors of strangers began to rapidly flow before my eyes, the interwoven currents of time and history, sweeping me along, meandering mysteriously onward.

After a hundred or so entries and nearly 20 minutes later, I saw a signed name: Ann Salter. The deed of gift began with a commonly used phrase, "With good will and affection that I have for my children and grandchildren," and continued with numerous bequests of property to Ann Salter's family. (Ann, of course, was the wife of Edward Salter II, and daughter of Sheriff Bonner.) On the second page of her deed were the words: "I give unto my daughter, Susannah White..."

Even though it was the answer I hoped for—and expected all along—I stood in disbelief. The record was not listed anywhere among the county's indexes. An examination by the Registrar of Deeds confirmed the omission. My finding of the deed was an inexplicable stroke of serendipity. Or perhaps it was divine guidance, the intervention of any number of the departed who have been a part of this story—perhaps even Susanna herself—or someone in my own family's past, an anonymous soul reaching out from beyond the long corridor of time. Or was it just simply a stroke of luck, as some might say? Maybe it was—but I believe otherwise.

After a moment of intense relief, I thought of the day so long before when I first stood before Mrs. White's grave—and the few times since—and wondered: who was she; who was present on the day she was laid to rest; why did folklore connect her to piracy and Black Beard?

Now I knew for sure. I knew her story, and her family's, and I felt privileged, like an honored guest in the Salter's home.

I have always been intrigued with how, seemingly, the most insignificant turn of fate or random event in one's life can change everything forever and alter the history of others. Is destiny something real? It is a mystery of which I am always reminded when watching the movie, *It's a Wonderful Life*. How would history have been different had Black Beard and Stede Bonnet not captured the ship, *Margaret*, and forced aboard the *Queen Anne's Revenge* the 22-year-old cooper, Edward Salter, in December, 1717? Chances are, the Salter family would never have been established in Bath County.

Of course, the descendants of Edward Salter should not have existed at all, according to the author whose identity and dependability have long been in question, and his loyal followers. For 284 years, historians have accepted Charles Johnson's assertion that Edward Salter and the other captured pirates from Black Beard's crew were hanged at Williamsburg. Naturally, the easier path is to be a skeptic. Just as doubters have suggested that the wreck discovered in Beaufort Inlet is not the *Queen Anne's Revenge* but a merchant ship with similar dimensions, skeptics will claim that there were two Edward Salters in North Carolina in 1718, both coopers—but only one, a pirate. Yet, it is the very existence of the pirate legend of "Sister Susie" and its attachment to the memory of Mrs. Susanna Salter White that we can be certain that there was just one Edward Salter, who had once served with Black Beard as a cooper on the *Queen Anne's Revenge* and who was most certainly not hanged in Virginia.

Yet, there is more to Edward Salter's story, and Susanna's, that they want us to know—where fate and the interwoven currents of time and history took the Salters, a proud but forgotten family, descendants of a true American pirate.

Describing the decades preceding the Revolutionary War, Henry King noted in *Sketches of Pitt County*, that, "The men attended to the affairs of the farm or other business while the women, with a lot of servants, did the work of the house, weaving, spinning, sewing, etc. It was an independent, self-reliant life, that grew and trained the heroes of later history." When King alluded to the "heroes of later history," he may have had in mind, among others, Edward Salter's grandsons: three brothers of the third Salter generation, Edward III, Robert and John. All three men—descendants of the former pirate—served vital roles during the American colonies' pursuit of independence from the British crown and the development of the future United States. Ironically, many of the motives propelling the rebellion were similar to the political and social roots of piracy during the post-war years of 1715.

During the middle decades of the 18th century the freeholders of North Carolina increasingly resented the payment of excessive and burdensome taxes to the Crown, and some county sheriffs who were required to collect the taxes began to refuse to do so. In 1773, records of the colonial assembly indicate that Robert Salter was among those sheriffs in Pitt County who was behind in his collections. In fact, a report "showed that Pitt County had paid no quit rents, arrears of quit rents, fines, forfeitures, and other incomes for as many as two years." Before the tea parties and the bloodshed of armed hostilities, Robert Salter was among those who first began to quietly participate in the resistance to royal authority.

The other great issue of the time concerned the role and rights of the people's colonial assembly. As stated by William Powell in his *North Carolina—A History*, North Carolinians began to question whether they should "permit their legislature to degenerate into a mere device through which the will of a distant king could be relayed, or should they maintain it as the free, deliberative lawmaking body into which it had evolved, responsible only to the people of the province?" The question was soon answered. "The rules of right and wrong, the limits of the prerogative of the crown and of the privileges of the people are in the present age well known and ascertained; to exceed either of them is highly unjustifiable," proclaimed North Carolina's assembly.

Similar sentiments were being expressed throughout the colonies in the early 1770s and soon after the Boston Tea Party and Britain's punitive responses against the citizens of Massachusetts, calls were made for delegates from the colonies to attend a Continental Congress. In North Carolina, a preliminary provincial congress was planned, and county freeholders met respectively to select delegates. In Pitt County, on August 15, 1774, the attendees elected Edward Salter III and John Simpson, Esquires, to participate in the provincial congress in New Bern later that month, and to "exert their utmost abilities preventing the growing system of ministerial Despotism which now threatens the destruction of American Liberties." We can assume that Salter was an outspoken and persuasive participant at the meeting and he may have contributed to the Pitt County freeholders resolution preserved in the Colonial Records: "As the Constitutional Assembly of this Colony are prevented from exercising their right of providing for the security of the liberties of the people, that right again reverts to the people as the foundation from whence all power and legislation flow."

Of the provincial congress held in New Bern, attended by Salter, which convened to formulate North Carolina's expectations of the Continental Congress, William Powell wrote: "No more significant action had ever been taken by North Carolinians than the successful calling and meeting of this body. The people learned that there was nothing sacred in a governor's call for an election. They could do it themselves."

During the autumn of 1774, and after the first meeting of the Continental Congress in Philadelphia, numerous committee meetings were held in Pitt County along the banks of the Tar River to discuss security and intelligence issues, and to determine what could be done for the "unhappy situation of the inhabitants of the town of Boston, and the miserable distress the poor inhabitants of said town are reduced to by the effects of the late acts of Parliament blocking up the port and harbor." Both Edward Salter III and his brother, Robert Salter, took prominent roles in these meetings. It might appear to have been an altruistic and neighborly sentiment on the part of the Salter brothers, except for the fact that their plantation enterprises may have depended heavily upon trade with Boston merchants. Their recently established partnership with two brothers who were both sea captains from Marshfield, Massachusetts, Paul and Christopher White, may also have had something to do with the Salter brothers' concern for Boston. As it happened, the four men were also brothers-in-law. Paul White had married Susanna Salter; Christopher White married Sarah Salter. Theirs was indeed, a family affair.

For those who lived during this period of history, events must have seemed to rush by in a whirlwind of excitement, tension, danger, anticipation, tragedy and triumph. In August, 1775, two months after the historic engagements at Lexington and Concord, Robert Salter was appointed a lieutenant colonel in his county's militia. Edward Salter III was elected a representative to the next year's meetings of the provincial congress. Their younger brother, John, was soon made a captain in command of a company of Pitt County militiamen. And off Ocracoke Inlet that fall, Capt. Paul White's ship, a sloop named *Juno*, was intercepted by a Royal Navy cutter, and some of his cargo of gunpowder and lead shot was confiscated. In late-February of the following year, the Battle of Moore's Creek was fought, and it is believed that Pitt County soldiers, led by Capt. John Salter, were there. The conflict was significant, and is today remembered as the first American victory in the fight for independence.

No less historic was the provincial congress held in Halifax, North Carolina, on April 4, 1776, which Edward Salter attended as one of three Pitt County delegates. The participants adopted a resolution known as the Halifax Resolves, which historian Powell singles-out as "the first official state action for independence—a recommendation to the Continental Congress that independence should be declared by all of the colonies through their representatives in the Continental Congress." After being presented at Phildelphia, the Halifax Resolves, which included Edward Salter's signature, was copied and distributed to some of the other colonies so that they might " follow this laudable example." As a result, Virginia soon called for an official declaration of independence.

Sometime in mid-July, Edward Salter III departed from Salter's landing, probably going by periauger or poled-flat up the Tar River to Tarboro and from there, by horseback to Halifax, for the next meeting of the Provincial Council. The day after the meeting, on July 22nd, a weary, breathless courier arrived on horseback with news that the Continental Congress in Philadelphia adopted the Declaration of Independence. On August 1, the council publicly proclaimed the declaration on the steps of the Halifax courthouse. As described in The History of Halifax County: "At midday, Cornelius Harnett ascended a rostrum which had been erected in front of the court house, and even as he opened the scroll, upon which were written the memorable words of the Declaration, the enthusiasm of the immense crowd broke forth in one loud swell of rejoicing. Harnett proceeded with his task in measured tones and read the immortal document to the mute and impassioned multitude with the solemnity of an appeal to Heaven."

> "...and accordingly all experience hath shown that mankind are more disposed to suffer, while evils are sufferable, than to right themselves by abolishing the forms to which they are accustomed. But when a long train of abuses and usurpations, pursuing invariably the same object evinces a design to reduce them under absolute despotism, it is their right, it is their duty, to throw off such government, and to provide new guards for their future security."

"A spontaneous shout went up from hundreds of mouths, and the cannon from the fort at Quanky and the Roanoke boomed the glorious tidings that the Thirteen Colonies were now free and independent States. Cornelius Harnett was lifted from the rostrum and carried through the streets upon the shoulders of the enthusiastic populace. It was a great day in Halifax." And Edward Salter III, grandson of a pirate and brother of Susanna White, was most likely there. Once the newly established state of North Carolina convened its first General Assembly, Edward Salter III served for five successive years as the solitary senator representing Pitt County.

Other descendants of the former pirate-cooper, Edward Salter, produced remarkable contributions to early United States history. Before 1768, Salter's daughter, Hannah, married Jacob Blount after the death of her first husband and his first wife, Barbara Gray. Hannah Salter Blount's stepsons included: William Blount, one of North Carolina's three signers of the U.S. Constitution and first territorial governor of Tennessee, and John Gray Blount, once companion of Daniel Boone and later an influential entrepreneur and land baron in North Carolina. Jacob and Hannah Salter Blount's son, Willie (pronounced Wylie) Blount, became Tennessee's third governor, serving for three terms. A county in Alabama is named in his honor.

In July, 1777, Col. Robert Salter was instrumental in uncovering a diabolical plot among Royalist holdouts in eastern North Carolina: a plan to murder the leading men of the region and take possession of the state on behalf of King George III. Through decisive action by Salter, the crisis was averted. Once again, in 1781, a Salter saved the day when Tory sympathizers in eastern North Carolina reorganized and attempted to supply cattle, hogs and other comforts to Lord Cornwallis's army marching up from the south on its way to Virginia. This time, though, it was Edward Salter III who led a detachment of Minute Men to capture the Royalist camp and food stores intended for His Majesty's army.

Not all of the news arriving at the Salter enclave during these courageous years was pleasant. In August, a ship of 140 tons owned jointly by Edward and Robert Salter and Paul and Christopher White was dispatched from the Port of Bath in North Carolina for Bordeaux on the coast of France. According to port records, "the growth and produce" of North Carolina was loaded aboard the vessel—100 hogsheads of tobacco, 13,000 hogshead staves, 34 barrels of turpentine, 230 barrels of tar, 84 barrels of pitch, and beeswax. Christopher White sailed as captain, carrying written orders from his brother-in-law, Edward Salter III. Most likely the ship was transporting the valuable commodities of the Salter enterprises on the south banks of the Tar River to sell to merchants in France. White's shopping list while in France included "cloth of various kinds (including silks and linens), brass locks, glass, tin and delft ware, rugs, blankets, needles, thimbles, writing paper, an ink stand, ink powder, pewter, nails (4 to 10 penny), shoemaker's tools, razors, scissors, iron pots, flat irons, Dutch ovens, silverware and cutlery, saltpeter, files, a copper kettle, wine, brandy, pocket pistols, 'one good gun,' and various other household and personal items." It was a dangerous wartime mission which met with disaster in the Bay of Biscay, not far from Capt. White's destination. The ship was captured by British privateers and taken to London where it was condemned as a prize vessel of war.

The Salters and Whites suffered a severe economic blow from the loss of their cargo and ship. But worse news was to follow. Although it is not clear whether or not Christopher White was able to return to North Carolina after being confined in London, two years later he was dead. His wife, Sarah Salter White, is identified in the Pitt County records as the executrix of Christopher White's will in April, 1779. And within the same month, although the specific circumstances are uncertain, Col. Robert Salter died, possibly while on duty in the militia. Even in an age when life was fleeting and death was ever present, the untimely losses of Christopher White and Robert Salter must have been a terrible setback for the Salter family.

More members of the family perished during the next decade, including Edward Salter III in 1789. Without the leadership of the elder brothers, Edward and Robert, the Salter plantations and enterprises appear to have struggled in the years to follow. Thousands of acres of land along the Tar River originally purchased by Edward I in 1728 were sold or divided by succeeding generations through intermarriage. By the early 1800s, the surname Salter, which at one time was shared by as many as two dozen or more relatives living in the vicinity of Salter's Ferry, disappeared from the Pitt County records entirely. As the years passed the distant relatives and neighbors gradually forgot the remarkable contributions the family made to their community, their state, and their young nation.

On a cold, colorless January day in 1803, Susanna Salter White was laid to rest in the Salter family cemetery on a high bluff overlooking the languid waters of the Tar River. Most likely, standing at her grave alongside Susanna's nieces and nephews—Elizabeth Salter, Polly and Sally Blount, John Salter, Joseph and Christopher White II—were her son and daughter, Edward Salter White and Elizabeth White. Later that year, the newly constructed, nine-story-tall, sandstone lighthouse at Cape Hatteras was illuminated for the first time as a shining symbol of the power and reach of the fledgling United States—a nation Susanna Salter White's husband, brothers and father helped to establish.

And so flowed the interwoven currents of Time, following their mysterious, meandering, eternal paths. Tens of thousands of times the sun rose and set, and cast its warm light on Susanna's headstone. Over the many years, rain and snow wet the sandstone marker and millions of leaves covered the ground. Generations passed, wars and soldiers passed, presidents and great social upheavals passed, and nature reclaimed the Salter family cemetery along the banks of the Tar River. And onward the river flowed, until 182 years later and twenty-four miles downstream from Susanna Salter White's last resting place, when the long-lost, stone-paved subterranean passage near the banks of Bath Creek shared one of its final secrets.

In 1985, the owner of "Eden's tunnel land"—at the time, French petrochemical conglomerate Elf Aquitaine—petitioned the U.S. Corps of Engineers for a permit to bulkhead the rapidly eroding banks of its hunting re-

Kevin Duffus photo.

Epilogue—
Sister Susannah

When I began writing this book many months ago, I wasn't really sure where the narrative would lead, but I had a fairly good idea where it would end. To faithfully write about historical events, I find it helpful to visit the places where they occurred, especially during the appropriate season and in a similar climate experienced by the subjects of the story. For that reason, I decided to go to Ocracoke on the 289th anniversary of the battle between Edward "Black" Beard and Lt. Robert Maynard—the battle that ended with the death of the pirate.

The state-operated ferry I boarded at Swan Quarter departed at 4 p.m., and within a half hour we were crossing the familiar slate-colored waters of Pamlico Sound. In previous years, I had made the journey between Bath Creek and Ocracoke aboard my sailboat so many times I had lost count, in all types of weather and sea conditions. On this occasion, a broad high pressure system had gradually settled over the eastern seaboard, resulting in light winds and short benign waves. As the sun dropped in the sky, the temperature plummeted, made chillier by a ten-knot breeze generated by the ferry's speed through the crisp autumn air. The decks appeared deserted. Only three vehicles were aboard for the off-season journey. Midway in the crossing the ferry skirted the north side of the shoal known for centuries as the Middle Ground, and I looked southwestward, directly into the rays of the setting sun and toward Brant Island Shoal, where the sloop *Adventure* had run aground on November 17, 1718. My thoughts naturally turned to Black Beard and what I had learned about him during the preceding years—the real man behind the legend.

The Black Beard I have come to know through my research turned out to be entirely unlike the historical figure so familiar to the world. My newly perceived image of the authentic pirate captain is nothing like the man celebrated by amusement parks, marinas, restaurants, taverns and inns and nothing like the bearded pirate captains portrayed in cinema and cable TV docudramas. He was not the bloodthirsty murderer, despicable slitter of throats or strangler of women as he has been so often described. He was certainly not one of the most "grotesquely conspicuous villains in the annals of crime." And he was far from the richest, boldest, most ruthless corsair of all the marooning freebooters in the history of piratedom. In fact, the pirate Black Beard, manufactured by a procession of authors, historians, and folklorists never really existed. The Edward "Teach" of popular culture, revered today by pirate enthusiasts is an imposter, a historical hoax.

I have come to know Black Beard the man as he truly was. He was a son and a brother. Early on, he was a convivial comrade, but under the pressures of responsibility he became morose, mercurial and unforgiving toward his closest companions. He was a conflicted, disillusioned, indifferent leader of men. He was a loyal defender of his heritage—and maybe his faith. In the end, he was a weary, ailing and ill-fated human. Granted, he was not a respectable man, nor was he law-abiding or principled. But he was no more immoral or corrupt than many who lived during his time, from the lowliest thieves to governors, ministers and lords. He was a paradox in a paradoxical age.

These things I considered as I watched the sun set over Brant Island Shoal and the mouth of the Neuse River beyond. And at that moment I knew, there was one more place for me to go in order to complete the circle of this story.

The next day, on the anniversary of the engagement between His Majesty's Royal Navy and the company of the sloop *Adventure*, the weather eerily replicated the documented descriptions of that Saturday morning in November, 1718. There was hardly a breath of wind—a peculiar but not unknown condition on the Outer Banks on the cusp of winter. Teach's Hole Channel was like a mirror. Ragged tatters of cirrus clouds streaked overhead and were reflected in the water like a kaleidoscope of nature. And in the distance, the indistinct, gauzy horizon blended water and sky in a pale palette of mauve.

Was I seeing the thin veil of time? Was all that had happened still there? I listened. The panorama was serene, silent, and completely devoid of the malevolence, terror, and bloody life or death struggle that had occurred there 289 years earlier. Nothing was left but memory and the elemental truth of history.

My thoughts turned to the departed. Somewhere not far from where I stood, I believed, must have been the buried remains of the 24 men who died there on that historic day, including, quite possibly, Edward "Black" Beard's headless corpse. Were they still there? I offered a prayer for their souls just in case.

A few weeks later I was ready for my final journey in my quest for the authentic Black Beard—the grave of his true sister Susie—Susannah Beard Franck. After much re-

search, I had a fairly good idea of where to look. Susannah's husband, Martin Franck, had assumed ownership of the James Beard land surrounding Beard Creek. Coincidentally, Beard Creek appeared quite similar to Bath Creek, only smaller. Edward Moseley's 1733 map showed Franck's name on the east side of Beard Creek. But modern satellite mapping technology indicates significantly higher ground along the west side of the creek. That's where the frontiersman Martin Franck and his family would have lived.

For hundreds of years since, much of the land has been left to nature, mostly timber and a smattering of farmer's fields. More recently, developers have come in and before long there will be vacation homes, clubhouses, marinas, tennis courts and swimming pools. (Some call it progress—but not me.) One such development on the west bank of Beard Creek surrounds a historic cemetery of which the state archeologist's office has conducted a cursory survey. That was my destination.

In time, I was there, standing among at least twelve graves situated on a high, narrow ridge line, about 16 feet above the creek. Not far away, the clear water of a spring flowed through the woods, suggesting the location would have made an ideal homestead. In the cemetery, very old ballast stones scattered the ground—gravestones distinctive of the earliest days of colonial North Carolina. The only one bearing a description—presumably the most recent—was dated 1794. Most of the others appeared much older. Susannah Beard Franck had died by 1722. The old, rounded stones huddled and hid beneath weeds and scrub hollies like petrified turtles, frozen in time. There had not been time to research who may have been buried in the cemetery, but I had faith that she was there. No other burial sites are known to be in the vicinity.

And so it is only fitting that this story that began in a cemetery occupied by a Susanna, would end in one more, where another Susannah rests, forgotten by the ages. I walked among the graves, not knowing which of the stone markers was her's, and deciding it really didn't matter. Along the eastern perimeter of the burial ground I left her a rose in her memory, on behalf of her brother, the pirate.

Sister Susannah

Appendix One
Beard Family Connections*

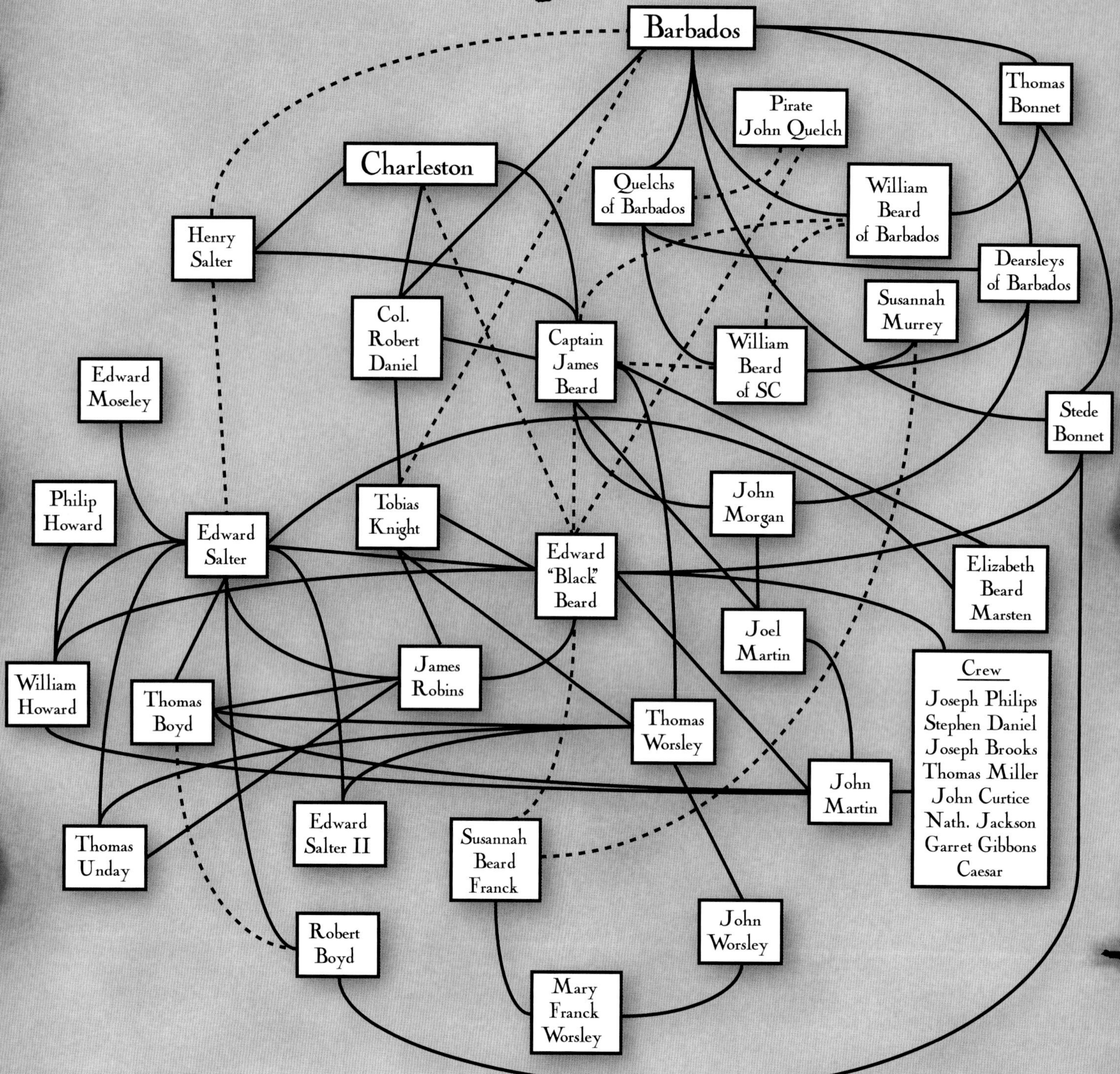

Barbados

Charleston

- Thomas Bonnet
- Pirate John Quelch
- Quelchs of Barbados
- William Beard of Barbados
- Dearsleys of Barbados
- Henry Salter
- Col. Robert Daniel
- Captain James Beard
- William Beard of SC
- Susannah Murrey
- Stede Bonnet
- Edward Moseley
- Philip Howard
- Edward Salter
- Tobias Knight
- Edward "Black" Beard
- John Morgan
- Elizabeth Beard Marsten
- William Howard
- Thomas Boyd
- James Robins
- Joel Martin
- Thomas Worsley
- John Martin
- Thomas Unday
- Edward Salter II
- Susannah Beard Franck
- John Worsley
- Robert Boyd
- Mary Franck Worsley

Crew
- Joseph Philips
- Stephen Daniel
- Joseph Brooks
- Thomas Miller
- John Curtice
- Nath. Jackson
- Garret Gibbons
- Caesar

Straight line indicates documented connection   *Dashes indicate suspected connection*

<u>Capt. James Beard</u>: Believed to be the father of Edward "Black" Beard; captain of the sloop *James*; issued patent by Gov. Johnson for 640 acres on north side of Neuse River at the creek known today as Beard Creek.

<u>Col. Robert Daniel</u>: Emigrated from Barbados; neighbor of James Beard at Goose Creek, SC; lived on Bath Creek as Deputy Gov. of Carolina 1705-1709 and was again a neighbor of James Beard; sold his Bath Creek plantation to Tobias Knight in 1716.

<u>William Beard of Barbados</u>: Servant of Thomas Bonnet (uncle of Stede Bonnet); believed to be the same William Beard of SC and the brother of Capt. James Beard.

<u>William Beard of SC</u>: Believed to be brother of Capt. James Beard; married to Susannah Murrey; guardian of Anne Dearsley and closely involved with Dearsleys of Barbados.

<u>Susannah Murrey</u>: Wife of William Beard; believed to be the inspiration for namesake, Susannah Beard Franck, daughter of James Beard and suspected sister of Edward "Black" Beard.

<u>John Morgan</u>: Executor of James Beard estate; associated with Dearsleys of Barbados; associated with Joel Martin of Bath (father of John Martin suspected pirate).

<u>Henry Salter</u>: Lived in Charleston; master of sloop, *Content*; witnessed legal document on behalf of James Beard; relationship to Edward Salter unknown.

<u>Tobias Knight</u>: Council Secretary, Collector of Customs and interim Chief Justice; neighbor of James Beard and witnessed Beard estate matter in 1713; lived on former Col. Robert Daniel property; suspected advisor to Black Beard; owned slave named Caesar; relationship to Thomas Knight of Barbados unknown; neighbor of James Robins, suspected pirate, in 1718-19.

<u>Thomas Worsley</u>: Attorney for James Beard in 1709 and also neighbor of James Beard; appraiser for estate of Tobias Knight; among first lot holders in Bath; father-in-law of Mary (Beard) Franck; appraisor of Tobias Knight estate.

<u>Joel Martin</u>: Neighbor of James Beard; father of John Martin suspected pirate who sailed with Black Beard.

<u>John Martin</u>: Suspected pirate; purported to have been hanged in 1719 but sold 220 acres in 1720; associated with Thomas Boyd, gentleman of Nansemond Co. and suspected father or brother of Robert Boyd who was captured with Stede Bonnet.

<u>James Robins</u>: Mariner; purchased plantation formerly owned by Gov. Eden known as "Tunnel Land" in Sep. 1718; neighbor of Tobias Knight; believed captured aboard sloop *Adventure* by Lt. Maynard at Ocracoke; suspected pirate; purported to have been imprisoned and hanged in Williamsburg but was cited for bawdy behavior in Bath in Jan. 1719; associated with Thomas Unday; witness for Edward Salter property deed in 1721.

<u>Edward Salter</u>: Cooper, planter, esquire; joined Black Beard's crew in Dec. 1717; captured in Bath as suspected pirate in Dec. 1718; purported to have been hanged in 1719; trustee for Elizabeth Beard Marsten, believed to be 2nd wife of Capt. James Beard; associated with James Robins, Robert Boyd, Thomas Boyd and William Howard; purchased former governor's "palace" on Bath Creek and 4,000 acres in less than ten years after the death of Black Beard; relationship to Henry Salter of Charleston, friend of James Beard is unknown; relationship to Salters of Barbados unknown; executor of Salter's will in 1735 was Edward Moseley, former opponent of Tobias Knight and Gov. Eden.

<u>Edward Salter II</u>: Son of Edward Salter; executor of Thomas Worsley II estate in 1762.

<u>Susannah Beard Franck</u>: Believed to be daughter of James Beard; along with her husband, Martin Franck, assumed ownership and patent of James Beard's 640 acres on Beards Creek and Neuse River; believed to be sister of Edward "Black" Beard; first born son was named Edward; daughter Mary married into Worsley family, long-time friends of Beard family on Bath Creek.

<u>William Howard</u>: Son of Hyde Precinct landowner Philip Howard; former quartermaster of Queen Anne's Revenge; purchased island of Ocracoke in 1759; lived to be 108-years-old.

<u>Quelches and Dearsleys of Barbados</u>: Closely associated with Beards and Morgans of Charleston/Goose Creek.

<u>John Quelch</u>: Convicted pirate hanged at Boston; relationship to the Quelches of Barbados is unknown.

<u>Barbados</u>: Although it could be considered a coincidence, many of the surnames associated with Black Beard can be traced to the island in the 1600s, including Salter, Knight, Howard, Daniel, Martin, Robins and Coates.

*Source: *North Carolina Genealogical Society Journal*, August 2002, "Legends of Black Beard and His Ties to Bath Town: A Study of Historical Events Using Genealogical Methodology," authors Jane Stubbs Bailey, Allen Hart Norris John Oden III.

Acknowledgments

One of the greatest joys of researching and discovering new things about our past is being able to share the revelations with you, the reader, through my writing. One of my greatest privileges as a writer is being able to benefit from the enthusiasm, inspiration, support, abilities and wisdom of my friends and colleagues. This book has been significantly sustained and improved by the contributions of the following people.

Much of the research about the early residents of colonial North Carolina, including Black Beard and the Bath County pirates, came from the hard work of John Oden, Jane Bailey and Allen Norris. I have had the honor to become friends with Jane and Allen over the past year. Their generosity in sharing their time, information, and ideas has been invaluable and deeply appreciated. Jane had not been well for part of that time, and it was with utmost sadness that I learned of her passing on January 24, 2008.

As always, I am indebted to my editor, Irene Nolan, who somehow found the time to help me while she was establishing the ground-breaking Web-based newspaper, The Island Free Press. For up-to-the-minute news of Hatteras and Ocracoke Islands, visit www.islandfreepress.org. My friend, Betsy Lingenheld became an invaluable proofreader during her brief spare time as a builder of finely crafted homes.

I express my sincere thanks to my dear friend, Jilly Carter of London and Oxfordshire, England, for her help while I was doing research at the National Archives. Likewise, friends Marty and Camille Morrissey provided much appreciated travel assistance. I am also thankful for the friendship, advice and inspiration of my friends, Bob and Barbara Cain. Thanks to Pat and Michael Mansfield for many courtesies and allowing me to write part of this book on Gov. Eden's former Bath Creek plantation. The aerial photographs in this book would not have been possible without the expert skills and companionship of pilots Dwight Burrus of Hatteras and Gene Schwartz of Beaufort County. Jimmy and Bea Latham were exceptionally generous with their time when sharing their fondest memories of John Oden. I enjoyed a fun afternoon of boating around Black Beard's haunts along Bath Creek with Dave and Monk Wheeler. Chip and Helena Stevens have been most gracious with their accommodations at the historic Blackbeard's Lodge on Ocracoke. John Tankard was especially patient and helpful during my tour of the former lands of Gov. Eden and Tobias Knight.

Among those who have read portions of my manuscript was my distant cousin, Innes Duffus, Archivist to the Nine Incorporated Trades of Dundee, Scotland. Innes "confirmed" my theory that Black Beard's ancestors were Scottish in the following e-mailed message: "He most certainly did come from this part of the world. Fancy thinking that a pirate of his quality could have been born in England. Tut tut!" Also, I benefited from words of support and research tips from Captain Hamish Robertson, past Boxmaster of the Fraternity of Masters & Seamen of Dundee. I am also indebted to my good friends, Rick Marks, Robert Newton, Gee Gee Rosell, Steve Brumfield and Debra Rezeli for perusing various versions of the manuscript or book cover and sharing their insights.

Grateful recognition is owed to Dick Lankford, Dr. Charles Ewen, Steve Claggett, Sarah Watkins-Kenney, Wendy Welsh, Susan Myers, George Stevenson, Mike Hill, Ansley Wegner, Dr. Billy Oliver, Earl Ijames, Maury York, Leigh Swain, Blount Rumley, Peter Martin, Rodney Broome, Angus Konstam, Pat Garber, Julie Howard, Janice Tyson, Bob Zentz, Henry Wong, Jeanne McDougall, David Stick, Kaeli Spiers, Peter Lingenheld, Earl O'Neal, Suzy Bennett, Sam Masters Blount, and Sammy Pierce. Additionally, for his assistance I would like to thank Brian Keith Blount, just one of the many descendants of Edward Salter throughout the United States who are alive today.

All along this journey of research, discovery, setbacks, surprises, obstacles, heartache and exhilaration, has been my wife Susan, who has endured her own challenges of life with courage, determination, optimism and grace. Without her unending support and sacrifice, this book would not have been possible.

Select Bibliography

Albertson, Catherine. *In Ancient Albemarle*. Raleigh: Commercial Printing Co., 1914. (Eastern North Carolina Digital Library)

Butler, Lindley. *Pirates, Privateers and Rebel Raiders of the Carolina Coast*. Chapel Hill: Univ. of North Carolina Press. 2000.

Cawthorne, Nigel. *A History of Pirates: Blood and Thunder on the High Seas*. Edison, NJ: Chartwell Books, 2004.

Calendar of State Papers, Colonial Series, Am. and West Indies, Vols. XXIX-XXXII

Colonial Records of North Carolina, Vols. I-X. Edited by W.L. Saunders, 1958. Raleigh.

Cooke, John Esten. *Virginia: A History of the People*. New York: Houghton, Mifflin and Co., 1911.

Cordingly, David. *Under the Black Flag: The Romance and the Reality of Life Among the Pirates*. London: Harcourt Brace & Co., 1995.

Craton, Michael. *A History of the Bahamas*. London: Collins, 1962.

Dictionary of National Biography. Oxford U. Press, 1949.

Howell, Thomas Bayly. *State Trials*, Vol. XV. London: Callaghan & Co., 1811.

Hughson, Shirley Carter. *The Carolina Pirates and Colonial Commerce, 1670-1740*. Baltimore: Johns Hopkins Press, 1894.

McCrady, Edward. *The History of South Carolina under the Proprietary Government 1670-1719*. New York: The MacMillan Company, 1897.

Johnson, Capt. Charles. *A General History of the Robberies and Murders of the Most Notorious Pirates*. London: Printed for, and sold by T. Warner, at the Black-Boy in Pater-Noster-Row, 1724. (Eastern North Carolina Digital Library)

King, Henry T. *Sketches of Pitt County, A Brief History of the County, 1704-1910*. Raleigh: Edwards & Broughton Printing Company, 1911.

Konstam, Angus. *Blackbeard: America's Most Notorious Pirate*. Hoboken, NJ: John Wiley & Sons, Inc. 2006.

Lee, Robert E. *Blackbeard the Pirate: A Reappraisal of His Life and Times*. Winston-Salem, NC: John F. Blair, 1974.

MacNeill, Ben Dixon. *The Hatterasman*. Winston-Salem, NC: John F. Blair, 1958.

Morgan, Edmund. *American Slavery, American Freedom—The Ordeal of Colonial Virginia*. New York: W.W. Norton & Company, Inc., 1975.

North Carolina Genealogical Society Journal. August 2002, "Legends of Black Beard and His Ties to Bath Town: A Study of Historical Events Using Genealogical Methodology." Jane Stubbs Bailey, Allen Hart Norris John Oden III, authors. Vol. XXVIII, No. 3, August 2002.

Official Letters of Alexander Spotswood, Vol. II. Edited by R.A. Brock. Richmond, VA: Virginia Historical Society, 1885.

Parry, Dan. *Blackbeard: The Real Pirate of the Caribbean*. New York: Thunder's Mouth Press, 2006.

Paschal, Herbert R. *A History of Colonial Bath*. Raleigh: Edwards and Broughton Co., 1955.

Pirates Own Book. Edited by Charles Ellams. Salem, MA: Marine Research Dept., 1924.

Powell, William S. *North Carolina: A History*. Chapel Hill: Univ. of North Carolina Press. 1977.

——— *The North Carolina Gazetteer*. Chapel Hill: Univ. of North Carolina Press. 1968.

Pringle, Patrick. *Jolly Roger—The Story of the Great Age of Piracy*. New York: W.W. Norton & Co., 1953.

Pyle, Howard. *Howard Pyle's Book of Pirates*. New York: Harper & Brothers, 1921.

Rankin, Hugh F. *The Pirates of Colonial North Carolina*. Raleigh: NC Dept. of Archives and History, 1963.

Rediker, Marcus. *Villains of All Nations: Atlantic Pirates in the Golden Age*. Boston: Beacon Press, 2004.

Snow, Edward Rowe. *Pirates and Buccaneers of the Atlantic Coast*. Boston: Yankee Publishing Co., 1944

Snowden, Yates. *History of South Carolina*, Volume I. New York: The Lewis Publishing Co., 1920.

Stick, David. *Outer Banks of North Carolina*. Chapel Hill: Univ. of North Carolina Press. 1958.

——— *An Outer Banks Reader*. Chapel Hill: Univ. of North Carolina Press. 1998.

Watson, John F. *Annals of Philadelphia and Pennsylvania*, Vol. II. Philadelphia: E.S. Stuart, 1857.

Whedbee, Charles Harry. *Legends of the Outer Banks*. Winston-Salem, John F. Blair, 1966.

——— *Blackbeard's Cup and Stories of the Outer Banks*. Winston-Salem, John F. Blair, 1989.

Whipple, Addison B.C. *Pirate Rascals of the Spanish Main*, New York: Doubleday & Co., 1957.

Woodard, Colin. *The Republic of Pirates*, Orlando, FL: Harcourt, Inc., 2007.

Notes*
Pages 14-124

Page 14. *"Around 1700, there was an Indian fort located about one mile east of Susie White's grave."* According to Henry T. King: "About two miles above Bear Creek, on the General Grimes farm, was an Indian fort, which was known as Indian Fort Branch. About the fort was a field of about ten acres, cleared by the Indians. This ten acres is now a part of a seventy-five-acre field and is still in cultivation." Henry T. King, *Sketches of Pitt County, A Brief History of the County, 1704-1910* (Raleigh: Edwards & Broughton Printing Company, 1911), page 21.

Page 34. *"Born on the wrong, desperately poor, side of the River Avon, in Redcliffe, Teach was born a rebel and refused to obey orders."* Source for Black Beard's Bristol legends: www.piratewalks.co.uk/

Page 58. *"...when Maynard arrives at Ocracoke Inlet on the 21st, he spies the masthead of Blackbeard's sloop Adventure beyond the sand dunes on the other side of the narrow island."* All previously published historical accounts of this event have been in error. Examples include: Robert E. Lee, *Blackbeard the Pirate: A Reappraisal of His Life and Times* (Winston-Salem, NC: John F. Blair, 1974), page 113; Angus Konstam, *Blackbeard: America's Most Notorious Pirate* (Hoboken, NJ: John Wiley & Sons, Inc. 2006), page 245; Colin Woodard, *The Republic of Pirates: Being the True and Surprising Story of the Caribbean Pirates and the Man Who Brought Them Down* (Orlando, FL: Harcourt, Inc., 2007), page 292.

Page 60. *"...the heart of Pamlico Sound, a vast body of water, but which is no deeper than 25 feet at any point. Verrazzano, upon seeing it for the first time, thought the Pamlico Sound was the much sought after South Sea, today known as the Pacific Ocean."* Source: Verrazzano's letter to the King of France. David Stick, editor, *An Outer Banks Reader* (Chapel Hill: Univ. of North Carolina Press. 1998), page 3.

Page 61 *"Brant Island Shoals is roughly 7 miles south of the rhumb line on the course from Bath to Ocracoke."* Navigators know that a rhumb line is the shortest distance between two points, but for pirates a rhumb line was the shortest distance to some grog.

Page 69. *"A few were outright hostile to the king, including Blackbeard's close associate and fellow captain, Charles Vane, whose crew were heard to drink to the death and damnation of King George during at least one festive occasion."* Marcus Rediker, *Villains of All Nations: Atlantic Pirates in the Golden Age* (Boston: Beacon Press, 2004), page 93.

Page 81. *"...Oden's family sustained an oral tradition that their forefathers had once been privateers in the early days."* The difference between being a privateer or a pirate in the early 18th century was nothing more than the difference between whether one's nation was at war or not.

Page 81. *"Beaufort County Deed Book I, which contained a variety of documents, wills, inventories and depositions recorded between 1696 and 1729."* Bath County became Beaufort County after North Carolina became a colony of the Crown in the late-1720s. Source: John H. Oden, "An Introduction to the Source," *Beaufort County, NC Deed Book I, 1696-1729*, Allen Hart Norris, author.

Page 84. *"Throughout the colonial period it was customary for a woman to remarry fairly quickly after the death of her husband, and for the widow's new spouse to become the executor of the estate of her previous spouse."* Lee, p.64.

Page 87. *"Courtesy of the illustrious and imaginative Charles Johnson, we are supposed to think that "[Teach] married a young creature of about sixteen years of age, the governor performing the ceremony."* Johnson's source for this second-hand information may have come from Capt. Brand, who wrote in a letter to the Lords of Admiralty that "to put a gloss to his designs he married there." Brand's information was also no more than gossip, just like the rumor that Black Beard was turning Ocracoke into another Nassau with a fort and mounted guns. See page 206 for more.

Page 98. A William Linton appears in the published Abstract of North Carolina Wills 1690-1760, having died in January, 1726, in Bath County. Source: J. Bryan Grimes, *Abstract of North Carolina Wills 1690-1760*, (Raleigh: E. M. Uzzell & Co., 1910), p. 217.

Page 115. *"The stranger in the darkness was William Bell, the son of a wealthy landholder and planter from Hyde Precinct."* William Bell was not from Currituck County as has been claimed in previous historical accounts. Allen Hart Norris, *Beaufort County, NC Deed Book I, 1696-1729*, (Washington, NC: The Beaufort Co. Genealogical Society, 2003), entry #678, p.112. (Hereinafter, *Beaufort I*)

Page 116. The confusion with the name "Currituck" may have been the result of a place-name in Bath Precinct, near the border with Hyde, that Bell referred to as "New Currituck" in a later deed. Also, *Beaufort I*, entry 621, refers to a resident, Cornelius Bell, of New Coratuck, Hyde Parish.

Page 122 *"The message pledged the pirates' allegiance to James III as their rightful king and appealed to Cammock to come to the Bahamas..."* Instead of commanding Vane and his fellow pirates who supported the Stuart restoration, Cammock wound up as captain of a 60-gun Spanish warship during the failed engagement against the British fleet off Sicily in August.

Page 124 *"'he would go into his Powder Room and blow up his ship, and send [his crew] and himself to Hell together.'"* London Weekly Journal, December 27, 1718.

Page 124 *"The governor and the more noble citizens there 'were burning with the desire to avenge the insult inflicted upon the colony the June before.'"* Edward McCrady, *The History of South Carolina under the Proprietary Government 1670-1719* (New York: The MacMillan Company, 1897), Page 596.

*Additional notes and more detailed source information available under this book's title tab at www.thelostlight.com

Notes
Pages 127-179

Page 127 *"...including a black trumpeter who was forced into service when the pirates captured the French slaver, but it is not known whether he was one of the six blacks who were later identified as being on the crew of the Adventure."* A trumpeter would have been a shipboard musician only used for heralding purposes, especially if a captain enjoyed a little pomp and circumstance from time to time. Source, author's interview with Bob Zentz.

Page 129 *"Although not to Virginia, which prohibited North Carolina's tobacco from being brought into the colony."* Lee p.96, and, Saunders, *North Carolina Colonial Records*, Vol. II, xv-xvi.

Page 130 *"They planned to deliver at least 80 casks of sugar to Bath and it apparently would require two trips in the sloop Adventure during the month of October."* Brand letter to Lords of Admiralty, Feb. 6, 1719, ADM 1/1472.

Page 132 *"At least one North Carolina scholar has characterized Moseley as the colony's finest citizen, primarily on the basis of his four decades of public service."* Herbert R. Paschal, *A History of Colonial Bath*, (Raleigh: Edwards and Broughton Co., 1955), p. 32.

Page 136 *"In a letter written a couple of years later, Spotswood recalled that Howard provided 'just Suspicion of his design to debauch the Sailors at that place, and to forme a Comp'ny of them to run away with some Vessel for his purpose, and so to pirate again.'"* Letters of Gov. Spotswood, July 28, 1721, to Secretary Craggs.

Page 141 *"Knight told Black Beard of his terrible fear of a great body of Indians who were said to be gathering beyond the cultivated fields of Bath Town's outlying plantations."* This turned out to be a false alarm.

Page 144 *"Sometime on Friday after making about 18 miles a day, Brand arrived at the burgeoning village of Queen Anne Creek (later to become Edenton) and was soon met by Col. Edward Moseley and his brothers-in-law, Col. Maurice Moore and Capt. Jeremiah Vail."* It may be of interest to the reader to know that Vail must have acquired a fascination with pirates in his later years because following his death, an inventory of his estate included a copy of Charles Johnson's, *A History of Pirates*, as well as a pirate cutlass. Source: J. Bryan Grimes, *North Carolina Wills and Inventories*, (Raleigh: Edwards & Broughton, 1912), p.561-563, "Inventory of ye Sundrie Goods & Chattels of the Esta of Jeremiah Vail Esqr Deceased Late of Newbern in the County of Craven in No Carolina taken ye 17th day June 1760 by Jno. Starkey Admr.

Page 145 *"...a 'villainous confederacy between some children and their servants' to prevent a slave from receiving a 'punishment due him for past rogueries,' as it was described in a meeting of the governor's council."* Saunders, *Colonial Records*, I, p. 315, Minutes of the Council Journal of meeting held on Nov. 11, 1718.

Page 148 *"The deadly Battle of Ocracoke Inlet...has been described in recent years as 'one of the most pivotal naval engagements in American history,' a lofty distinction for which it may not rank."* Shirley Carter Hughson, *The Carolina Pirates and Colonial Commerce, 1670-1740* (Baltimore: Johns Hopkins Press, 1894), 2000 edition, preface by Donald Grady Shomette.

Page 149 *"But Black Beard, despite making numerous tactical blunders, still had a trick or two up his sleeve..."* Boston News-Letter, Rhode Island Dispatch of February 20, 1719.

Page 152 *"Gordon's letter of September 14, 1721..."* In a curious twist to the story, Captain Gordon, Maynard's direct superior officer aboard the frigate, HMS *Pearl*, made a pointed effort to discredit his lieutenant's version of the engagement which had changed during the ensuing years to portray Maynard as having been the first to heroically lead a boarding party, "sword in hand," onto the deck of the *Adventure*. Referring to Maynard's new account, Gordon wrote "there being no such thing given out of [Maynard] boarding Thatch sword in hand, as he is pleased to tell his Majesty in his petition." Gordon's rebuke of Maynard was apparently based on the testimony of the other Royal Navy sailors who had been part of the action.

Page 154 *"It all happened quickly. According to Capt. Gordon's account, once Black Beard gained the deck of Maynard's sloop, the action lasted fewer than six minutes."* Compare the engagement at Ocracoke with the one which occurred in the Cape Fear River in September, 1718, when Colonel Rhett engaged Stede Bonnet and his band of pirates on the sloop *Royal James* (formerly *Revenge*), for a period of more than five hours.

Page 159 *"Capt. Brand confirmed that Maynard had recovered the 'pocket book' and mentioned a memorandum within that noted the transfer of sugar casks to Tobias Knight's barn."* Saunders, *Colonial Records*, Vol. II, p.344.

Page 169. *"Little wind & fair weather; This day the Sloop Adventure Edward Thach formerly Master (a Pyrat) anchor'd here from No. Carolina,"* written in Brand's own hand, determined in a handwriting comparison by the author.

Page 172 *"Records indicate that the former pirate, who came within hours of being hanged, went on to lead an astonishingly long life, living to the considerable age of 108."* William Howard's age at his death from Hugh Williamson, *The History of North Carolina*, Vol. II, (Philadelphia: Thomas Dobson, 1812), p. 289. Available to researchers through: http://digital.lib.ecu.edu/historyfiction/

Page 179 The phenomena known as brocken spectre was first scientifically observed on the summit of the Brocken, a mountain in the often misty Harz Mountains of Germany.

Page 180 *"The property, however, was probably not intended to be the captain's primary residence because five months later he purchased lot number 13, a half-acre site on Front Street in Bath Town."* This lot would have been very near to the present day Noe building on the St. Thomas Church property.

Page 180 *"The terminology, 'became associated' with Beard's name, is used because the actual primary deeds proving his ownership of the property are believed to have been lost, possibly during the Tuscarora War of 1711, but numerous other deeds and records in later years refer to the 375 acres as 'Capt. Beard's land.'"* Source: Beaufort County Deed Book II, page 324, #382, Allen Hart Norris unpublished abstracts, 22 February 1739. Indenture between John Swann, Gent, of New Hanover Co, NC, and wife Elizabeth to Hannah Salter of Beaufort County: "... to Capt Beards corner pine on savannah, along said Beards head line to 1st. By Last Will & Testament of Hon Tobias Knight Esq devised to said Elizabeth Swann."

Page 181 *"Early colonial records state that 12 Charleston-owned sloops, half of which were locally built, sailed on trading trips to ports ranging from New England to the Windward Islands."* McCrady, p. 344

Page 182 *"Edward Salter, in turn, was the trustee for the estate of Elizabeth Beard Marsten, second wife of Capt. James Beard."* There was a Rev. Edward Marston who was for a time rector of church parishes in the Goose Creek area near Charleston and who was a "notorious Jacobite...with violent passions and a contentious disposition," but his relationship to a Capt. Masten (or Marston) who appeared on a list of claims for James Beard's Bath Town Creek plantation on behalf of Beard's wife in 1714 is unknown. McCrady, p. 412

Page 182 *"Also, within the same deed book entry appears the eye-catching name of Henry Salter or Salters..."* The name often appeared in the records as both Salter and Salters.

Page 183 *"Let's examine what we know of Tobias Knight's past..."* Source: Bath Lodge History, researched by Earl Mason, courtesy of PCS Phosphate Co. "Tobias Knight actually moved to Archbell Point [the present-day name for the property] and to the present Archbell house in 1714. The North Carolina Dept. of Cultural Resources states in a letter dated 1977, that remodeling of the present [Archbell] house took place about 1820."

Page 183 *"However, Daniel re-ingratiated himself with the Lords Proprietors during a stay in London and moved to Bath County in 1704 as the first resident representative of the proprietary nobility."* Yates Snowden, History of South Carolina, Volume I (New York: The Lewis Publishing Co., 1920), page 124.

Page 183 *"Other records identify a Thomas Knight in Barbados prior to that time as well as an extended family of Knights in Barbados around 1673 who owned lands in County Norfolk in England."* Barbados Records, Wills and Administrations, Vol. I, 1639-1680, compiled and edited by Joanne McRee Sanders, Walsworth Publishing Company, Marceline, Missouri, 1979. Regarding other Knights living in Barbados: "Who Was Gideon Bowles?" *Virginia Historical Society Magazine*, Vol. 30, 1998.

Page 186 *"'Barbados had been an asylum for both the Royalists and the Parliamentarians who sought to avoid the contest at home.'"* McCrady, p. 68.

Pages 189-90 *"For these reasons, when Barbados servants became free, they frequently headed for Virginia or other mainland colonies."* Edmund Morgan, *American Slavery, American Freedom: The Ordeal of Colonial Virginia*, (Norton, 1975), p. 327.

Page 188 *"In a response to some complaints to the Lords Proprietors, a couple of pirates had been captured and convicted at Charleston and hanged and their remains displayed in chains near the Ashley River 'for an example to others.'"* McCrady, p. 206.

Page 197 *"Such is likely what happened when a farmer in Hyde County unearthed a few pieces of gold when tilling his fields in 1938."* Charles Parker, "A Plow Turns Up Buried Treasure," *News and Observer*, Raleigh, N.C., June 26, 1938, p.1.

Page 199 *"Presumably, the property had diminished significantly in value by the time Miss Steward achieved her satisfaction."* "Digs For Pirate's Hoard—Burlington Woman Seeks Proof of Blackbeard Legend," Oct. 7, 1926, *The New York Times*. Also, "Finding of Human Skull Spurs Hunt For Pirate Blackbeard's Buried Treasure," Oct. 8, 1926, *The New York Times*. It would seem that poor Miss Steward was a victim of her elders' fondness for folklore, but a further investigation of the connection between Burlington, New Jersey and Black Beard has yielded an additional possibility. Antiquarian John Watson once interviewed Robert Venables, an elderly black resident of Philadelphia who once was acquainted with two men who had sailed with Black Beard. In Watson's Annals of Philadelphia, he wrote that Venables "had heard that Blackbeard had dealings with [an] owner of a shallop packet to Burlington—who used, when about to start, to go around the little town, crying, 'ho ! Burlington, ho !' He supplied the pirate with flour, &c." So, even though Black Beard may not have buried his money under a walnut tree in Burlington, there may have been a grain of truth behind the legend.

Page 201 *"And with that, the conclusion was reached that Black Beard's treasure had been finally found, and, of course, was again lost."* In 1964, archeologist, Dr. Stanley South visited Plum Point on Bath Creek and conducted a preliminary investigation of ruins found on the site. South examined what appeared to be a brick foundation about 15 feet square located on a small knoll. By digging a hole, South observed bricks, mortar, burned timbers, plaster and nails, all typical of 18th-century residential construction. Beneath the ruins, South

found an oyster shell floor and fragments of a pipe and a piece of china. The area around the foundation was pockmarked with numerous holes dug by treasure seekers during the previous decades. Dr. South recommended to the state's superintendent of historic sites that a serious investigation should be conducted before additional treasure hunters "would further damage the evidence we seek." There has been no definitive archeological work done at the site since South made his recommendation in 1964, although archeologists visited the location again in 1986. Source: Stanley South letter to W.S. Tarlton, June 2, 1964, from the files of the Office of State Archeology. If the foundation was part of an early-18th century house, the author does not believe it would have belonged to Black Beard, although it is possible he may have visited its owner. According to research done by genealogists Oden, Bailey and Norris, the Plum Point property was owned by Edward Moseley between 1706 and 1713, at which time he sold his interest in the land to William Reed, a resident of Currituck, NC.

Page 201 *"Robinson sagely observed that Black Beard and his men looked more like they had been outfitted for the stage production of Pirates of Penzance 'rather than the gritty open sea.'"* J. Dennis Robinson, "As I Please," Vol. 4, No. 20, October 7, 2000, www.SeacoastNH.com.

Page 202 *"The myth of Blackbeard's treasure has been so persistent that in 1934 a group of explorers were allowed to search the island for 10 days, but were unsuccessful in finding the pirate's loot."* Longstreet Highroad Guide to the Georgia Coast.

Page 203 *"...when Whedbee was invited on his local TV station's morning news program to fill in for the host who was known by the descriptive appellation of Slim Short, he filled the airtime by sharing his repertoire of coastal folklore."* The author, at age 20, directed the morning show, "Carolina Today," on an occasion when Judge Whedbee was a guest. Also, in his youth, the author once appeared before the judge in court for a minor traffic violation (the judgment was not guilty).

Page 204 *"The somber ceremony is intended to be symbolic of the bitter cup of death, from which everyone must drink eventually."* Among those claiming to expose the rituals of Freemasonry include the controversial authors, W.P. Malcomson, author of *Behind Closed Doors*, and William Schnoebelen, author of *Masonry - Beyond the Light*. The author does not endorse the theories of Malcomson and Schnoebelen but presents their ideas for the purpose of a broader perspective of the Black Beard skull legends.

Page 205 *"There are those who believe the allegory assumes an even darker form..."* Ibid.

Page 205 *"Walker was referred to the family of a New England collector of maritime and pirate memorabilia, Edward Rowe Snow, who, for many years, claimed to own the legendary skull-cup."* Further confusing the mystery, there is an alternative story remembered by some, including Snow's friend, Judson D. Hale, that Snow originally claimed the skull was Captain Kidd's.

Page 206 *"Walker continues his quest for Black Beard's true skull—the holy grail of piratedom—to this day."* The author interviewed John Walker in 2005.

Page 208 *"On all these waters "Teach's Light" is still said to shed a ghostly gleam on dark, winter nights; and where its rays are seen to rest, there, so the credulous believe, his red gold still hides, deep down in the waters or buried along the shore."* Many of the sightings of "Teach's ghostly light" seen beneath the surface of coastal waters, at least during the warm summer months, can be attributed to jellyfish and other bioluminescent creatures of the sea which float along the currents of the surging tides and glow in the dark when agitated.

Page 208 *"Bending low, [he would] rush swiftly through the underground tunnel, slip into the waiting sloop and be off and away up the river or down, whichever was safest, out of reach of the enemy."* The river adjacent to the house is only about 700 feet wide, and the view, up or down the river, extends less than one half of a mile in either direction—the location does not afford much advance warning of approaching vessels, nor much room to escape.

Page 213 *"His only son, Edward, Jr., was born sometime around 1721, probably after Salter married his first wife and purchased two vacant half-acre lots in Bath Town between King and Carteret Streets, on which he planned to build (witnesses on the deed included the suspected pirate, James Robins)."* Norris, Beaufort I, entry #635.

Pages 216-217 *"In fact, a report "showed that Pitt County had paid no quit rents, arrears of quit rents, fines, forfeitures, and other incomes for as many as two years."* King, p.53.

Page 218 Quotation from the Declaration of Independence: "...and accordingly all experience hath shown that mankind are more disposed to suffer, while evils are sufferable, than to right themselves by abolishing the forms to which they are accustomed." These eloquent words written by Thomas Jefferson, could have fit just as comfortably within the articles of a pirate company. The founding fathers viewed the executive branch of government much like a pirate company viewed its elected captain. Just as it was intended for the legislative branch to provide oversight and ensure compliance of the executive branch, in a cruder sense, the same structure existed on a pirate vessel. Charles Johnson described the relative powers of a pirate captain and his council comprising the entire crew thusly: "They permit him to be Captain, on Condition, that they may be Captain over him."

Page 219 *"White's shopping list while in France included 'cloth of various kinds (including silks and linens), brass locks, glass, tin and delft ware, rugs...'"* Source: Angley Wilson, "Report on Port Bath," Unpublished document at Research Branch, NC Archives, Raleigh.

Index

Abaco Islands, 124
Act of Settlement, 69
Act of Union, 69, 190
Adams, John, 95
Adams Creek, (also Back Creek), 89
Addison Beecher Colvin Whipple, 27, 197
Admiralty Bay, 47, 70
Adventure, sloop, 30, 46, 49, 55, 58, 60-61, 65, 68, 69, 73-75, 79, 88, 94, 97, 102, 105-108, 111-112, 114, 117, 119-120, 125-128, 130-131, 136, 138-140, 143-152, 154, 157-158, 161-164, 166-169, 174-177, 184, 191, 193, 196, 203, 208, 211-212, 223-224, 227, 231
Adventure, sloop, model of, 139
Albemarle Sound, 8, 55, 60, 83, 208
Albertson, Catherine S., 207-208
Alien Act of 1705, 72
Allen, William C., historian, 166
Annals of Philadelphia, quoted, 94, 99, 103, 198, 204, 232
Anne of Great Britain, 27-29, 35-37, 39, 41-43, 46-49, 58, 62, 69-71, 78-79, 95, 101, 104-105, 121, 123, 127-128, 136-137, 144, 159, 167, 172, 174, 182-183, 186, 188-190, 192, 213, 216, 227
Archbell Point, 117, 175, 232

"Blackbeard's Castle," on Ocracoke Island, 203
"Blackbeard's Chartbook," pictured, described, 207
"Blackbeard Tree," Winnabow, NC, 206
Bailey, Jane Stubbs, 7, 29, 82, 84, 166-167, 171, 179-181, 184-185, 187-188, 206, 212, 215, 227
Barbados, 34, 47, 69, 72, 78, 143, 180-183, 185-188, 192-193, 227, 232; history described, 186; map of, 186
Bath, tricentenial, 81
Bath Creek, 60, 81-82, 84, 87-89, 98, 112, 117, 136, 138, 140, 160, 163-164, 173, 175, 183, 199, 206, 208-209, 211-213, 219, 220, 223-224, 227; aerial photos, 84-85, 164
Battle of Moore's Creek, 217
Battle of Ocracoke Inlet, described, 148
Bay of Campeche, 42
Bay of Honduras, 43, 123
Beacon Island, 55, 63, 64, 68
Beard, Capt. James, 82-84, 98, 117, 172, 180-184, 187, 227
Beards of SC—Matthew, James, George, 181
Beard Creek, 180, 184, 224-225, 227
Beard, William, 181, 187-188, 192, 227
Beard, William, of Barbados, servant of Thomas Bonnet, 187
Beasley Tract, pictured, 211

Beaufort County Deed Book I, 80-81, 88, 185
Beaufort Inlet, 27, 189, 216
Bell, William, 55, 115-117, 120, 132, 135, 147, 154, 158, 161, 170
Bellamy, Sam, 29, 43, 45-48, 54, 70-72, 97, 122-123, 128, 137, 188, 191-192, 215, 221
Bellomont, 1st Earl of, governor of NY and MA, 196
Benjamin, sloop, 21, 41-43, 45, 49, 72, 95, 98, 121, 123, 128, 166-167, 182, 188, 191

Bequia Island, 47
Bermuda, 106
Bimini, 42
Blackbeard Island, GA, 202
Black Beard, legend of head on bowsprit, 163
    age of, 71
    attack on William Bell, 115
    "Capture of the Pirate Blackbeard" by J.L.G. Ferris 152
    captures French ship near Bermuda, 106
    "Castle," St. Thomas, USVI, 24
    contracted syphilis, 104
    "Cup," legend, 203
    "diary," legend, 158
    last visit to Bath, October 1718, 138
    legend of burning fuses in hair, 108
    legend of his swimming headless body, 158
    legend of his pact with the devil, 196
    meets with Vane on Ocracoke, 128
    "Money Tree" at Cape Hatteras 206
    news of his death arrives in Bath Town, 160
    Plum Point, legend of Black Beard's treasure, 199
    purportedly marries, 87
    relationship with Stede Bonnet, 186
    skull legend related to Knights Templar mythology, 204
    Teach's ghostly light, legend 207
    treasure believed hidden on Lunging Island, 200
    tries to escape Maynard, 74
    trip to Bath on Sep. 14, 1718, 111
Blake, James, 111-113, 116, 120, 148, 170, 176-177
Bloody Assizes, 71
Blount family, relationship to Salter family, 214
Blount, Jacob, 218
Blount, John Gray, 218
Blount, William, signer of U.S. Constitution, also son-in-law of pirate Edward Salter, 218
Blount, Willie (pronounced Wylie), grandson of Edward Salter, 218
Blue Anchor tavern, 101-102, 105
Bombay Hook, 94
Bonner, Ann, 214
Bonner, Joseph Bonner, 209, 212, 214, 216
Bonnet, Stede, 46-49, 78-79, 96, 102, 120, 124-125, 128-130, 134, 136, 138, 141, 143, 145, 167-169, 171, 182, 185-187, 192, 193, 213, 216, 221, 227, 231; attacked by Col. Rhett 130

Index

Bonnet, Thomas Jr., uncle of Stede Bonnet, 185
Bonny, Anne, 29
Boston, 22, 42-43, 46-48, 55, 70, 74-75, 97, 101, 107-108, 123, 137, 148-150, 152, 157, 162, 186, 188, 191-192, 196, 201, 213, 215, 217, 227, 231

Boston News-Letter, 43, 74, 75, 97, 101, 107, 108, 148, 149, 152, 157, 162, 186, 231
Boyd, Thomas, 15-17, 182, 184, 227
Boyd's Ferry, 15-17
Boyd, Robert, 182, 227
Brand, Capt. Ellis, 47, 58-60, 74, 107, 131, 138, 144-145, 147-152, 159-162, 165, 166-167, 169, 172, 174, 206, 231
Brant Island Shoals, 60-63, 68, 73, 143-145, 157, 184
Bray, Reverend Thomas, 90-91
Brigs, William, surgeon, 107
Bristol, 9, 29, 32-39, 41, 68, 70, 97, 99, 122, 126, 184, 208
Brooks, Joseph, 79, 138, 167, 177, 191
Brooks Jr., Joseph, 167
Burgess, Josiah, 42 (spelled Burgiss),123, 221
Butler, Lindley, *Queen Anne's Revenge* Project, historian, 186

Caesar, slave, 48, 73, 79, 101, 112, 157-158, 176-177, 213, 227; identity of, 176
Cahill, Robert Ellis, 197, 201
Cammock, Capt. George, 122, 231
Campaine, Robert, 212
Campeche Bank, 42, 47
Cape Charles, Virginia, 47
Cape Cod, 46, 192
Cape Henlopen, 94
Cardross, Lord, 188
Carnes, John, pirate, 176
Carteret, Lord, 135
Cartwight, Lord, 174
Cary, Col. Thomas, 83, 89, 132
Cary's Rebellion, 83, 132
Caton, Michael, 21
Cayman Islands, 49
Cedar Island, formerly Teaches Island, Virginia, 202
Chamberlayne, Edmund, 114, 117
Charleston, 34, 42, 48-49, 70, 83, 90, 99, 101-102, 104, 120, 124-125, 128, 130, 137, 146, 167, 180-183, 187-188, 213-215, 227, 231
Charles I, 69
Charles II, 69, 192
Cherry, Ben, Black Beard reenactor, 205
Chesapeake Bay, 58, 131, 201, 202
Chester's Landing, 115, 154
Coates, Mrs. Bulah, 95, 97, 187
Coates, James, association with Thomas Bonnet, 187
Cockram, Capt. John, 123
Codd, Capt., 47

College of William and Mary, 37
Colleton, James, 188
Sir John Colleton, one of original Lords Proprietors, 188
Colleton, Peter, 188
Cooper, Peter, painting of Philadelphia and Delaware River, 97
Cooper River, SC, 181
Covenanters and Covenanter Risings, 180, 186
Croatan Sound, North Carolina, 61
Cromarty, Scotland, 180
Cromwell, Oliver, exile of Scots to Barbados, 186
Cuba, 39, 43, 45, 46, 47, 49, 139, 191
Currituck Sound, 60
Curtice, Joseph, 167, 177
Cutler, Henry Gardner, 181, 232

Dampier, William, privateering captain, 34
Daniel, Col. Robert, Deputy Gov. of NC, 42, 181, 183, 188, 227
Daniel, Stephen, pirate, 167, 177
Daughters of the American Revolution, library, 82, 185
Daw, Nicholas, 89-90, 166
Dearsley, Anne, 188
Declaration of Independence, 218
Defoe, Daniel, 29, 72, 87
Delaware Bay, 47, 93, 94, 96, 102, 147, 192
Demelt, Abraham, Royal Navy sailor in fight with Black Beard, 154
Devall, Lewis, 174
Dictionary of National Biography, 33
Discord Lane, Marcus Hook, PA, 95
Dobson, David, 186
Drake, Sir Francis, 72, 73
Drummond, myth of Black Beard's surname, 99
Duke of York, 69
Duvall's Plains, 214

Earl of Orkney, George Hamilton, Governor of Virginia, 134
East Carolina University, 30, 31, 82, 88
Eden, Gov. Charles, 49, 79, 81, 87-88, 93, 98, 103, 105, 117, 125, 131-132, 136-137, 143, 145, 147, 160, 167-169, 172-175, 180, 211, 227; grave stone pictured, 175
Edwards, Capt., alias of Stede Bonnet, 102
Elf Aquitaine, 219
Elizabeth City, brochure showing Black Beard's house, 208
Elsey, Stephen, 117, 172, 209, 211, 212
Encyclopedia Britannica, 33
English Civil War, 71
Evening Bulletin, describes Black Beard at Blue Anchor Tavern, 101
Every, Capt. Henry, pirate, 3, 29, 73, 170
Ewen, Dr. Charles, author/archeologist, East Carolina University, 221
Exquemelin, Alexander, 27, 29-30, 72

Florida Straits, 41, 47, 49
Fort-de-France, Martinique, 106

Index

Fort Eustis, on Mulberry Island, VA, 198
Fort Raleigh, 61
Franck, Edward, 184
Franck, John Martin, 184, 224
Franck, Mary, 184, 224-225, 227
Franck, Susannah Beard, 224
Franck, Susannah, 184
Franklin, Benjamin, 21
Freeman, Isaac, 107

Ganj-i-sawa, ship, 73
Gardiner, John and Capt. Kidd's treasure, 196
Gates, Thomas, 111, 113, 116, 120, 148, 170, 176-177
George I, 46, 48, 69, 71-72, 75, 87, 121, 170
Gibbons, Garret, 73, 94, 138, 146, 162, 167, 176-177, 191
Gibbons, William Gibbons of Charleston, 146
Gills, John (or Giles), 167
Glencoe, Battle of, 72
Glorious Revolution, 71, 72
Glover, Katherine (Knight), 183
Golden Guinea Pub, Bristol, England, 37
Goodin, Elizabeth, 171, 172
Goose Creek community, SC, 181, 183-184, 227, 231
Gordon, Capt. George Gordon of the HMS *Pearl*, 144, 148, 152, 154, 158, 161, 169, 174, 231
Gosse, Philip, author, *Pirate's Who's Who*, 33
Governor's Palace, Williamsburg, Virginia, 132-134
Gray, Barbara, 218
Great Plague of London, 71
Greensail, Richard, 176
Greenville Sound, in NC, 202
Green Turtle Cay, 125
Grimesland, NC, 16, 17, 174
Gulf Stream, 47, 49, 107, 119, 125

Halifax Resolves, 218
Hamilton, Lord Archibald, 121-122, 134
Hamilton, Gov. William, 104
Hampton River, pirate hangings at, 176, 204
Handcock, William, 212
Hands, Israel, 37, 60, 105, 108, 120, 126-128, 138-141, 146, 147, 160, 166-167, 170-171, 177, 193, 206, 212
Harnett, Cornelius Harnett, 218
Harvey, Elizabeth Cole, 213-214
Hathaway, James, 16
Hay, James, Earl of Carlisle, 186
Herriot, David, 49
Hispaniola, 46-47, 140
History Channel series, "History's Mysteries," 200
Hole in the Wall Pub, 32, 35
Holiday's Island, 203
Holloway, John, 137

Honduras, 42-43, 47-48, 101, 123
Hornigold, Capt. Benjamin, 41-43, 45-47, 49, 72, 105, 121, 123, 126, 128, 166-167, 182, 187, 191-192
House of Stuart, 70, 134
Howard, Philip, 136, 183, 227
Howard, William, 30, 46, 48, 79, 105, 136-138, 167, 172-173, 183, 185, 191, 193, 212-213, 221, 227
Howell, Dr. John, 46
Howell, Andrew J., 202
Hughson, Shirley Carter, 28, 132, 143, 176
Hyde, Midshipman Edmund Hyde, 61, 74, 148, 151
Hyde Precinct, Bath County, 115-116, 132, 137, 227

Indian Island, Pamlico River, NC, 77
Isles of Shoals, 200
Isle of the Pine, 46

Jackson, Nathaniel, 79, 167, 177, 191
Jacobite Rebellion, 69, 71-72, 99, 121-124, 127, 134, 140, 180, 192-193, 231
Jamaica, 33-34, 37, 39, 41-43, 46, 70, 97, 121-122, 134, 181, 188, 190
James I, 69
James II, 72, 181
James III, 122
James Stuart, the Old Pretender, 121
Jane, sloop, 64-65, 68-69, 148-152, 154, 157, 168, 176
Jennings, Capt. Henry, 42-43, 45, 121-123, 128, 187, 191
Johnson, Capt. Charles, 27-31, 33, 41, 60, 68, 72, 75, 87, 93, 98, 103, 108, 113, 125, 140, 147, 149, 158, 162, 166, 171, 176, 184, 196-197, 216, 233
Johnson, Nathaniel, governor of SC, 180, 182
Johnson, Samuel, 98
Johnston, Humphrey, 74-75, 152, 154, 157, 162
Joyner Library, East Carolina University, 30, 31
Juno, sloop 217

Keith, Gov. William, 93, 105
Kew Gardens, The National Archives of UK, 57
Kidd, Capt. William, 24-25, 29, 73, 101, 183, 191, 196, 202-203, 232
King, Capt., of Redcliffe Parade, Bristol, UK, 32, 35
King, Henry Thomas, 15, 214-216
King's Proclamation, and extension to HM pardon, 170
Kingston, Jamaica, 42
Kiquotan Roads, 131, 144, 160, 161, 167, 168, 198
Knight, Katherine, 79, 80, 114
Knight, Tobias, 55, 60, 76-81, 87, 111-117, 119, 125, 129, 132, 138, 141, 143-147, 158-165, 167-172, 175-176, 183-184, 191, 193, 200, 211, 213, 227, 231-232
Knight, Tobias, letter to Black Beard depicted, 146
Knight, Thomas, 104, 183, 227

Laboratory of Physical Anthropology at Wake Forest University, 220

Index

Latham, Bea and Jimmy, 185
Lawrence, Richard, *Queen Anne's Revenge* Project, archeologist, 43
Lawson, John, 14, 89, 90, 166
La Bouche, Capt. Oliver, 45, 46
La Concorde, ship (also *Queen Anne's Revenge*), 47, 69, 70, 103
Lee, Robert E., 28, 33, 71, 81-82, 88, 99, 149, 151, 205, 208, 231
Leeward Islands, 47, 104
Lepper, Thomas, 212
Library of Congress, 6, 57
Lillington, John, 117, 172
Linton, family of Philadelphia and Bath, NC, 98
Llandoger Trow, 38-39
Louis XIV, 69
Lovick, Capt. John, Dep. Secretary of NC, 168-169
Low, Emanuel, 127, 182
Lunging Island, New Hampshire, 200- 201
HMS Lyme, ship, 47, 58, 131, 144, 148, 150-151, 160, 162, 198
Lynhaven Bay, Virginia, 60

MacNeil, Ben Dixon, 197, 199, 200, 206-208
Mainwaring, Capt. Peter, 102
Manerchia, Michael and Pat, 95
Marcus Hook, PA, 94-95, 99, 193
Margaret, Black Beard's lady friend in PA, 94, 95, 193
Margaret, sloop, 49, 105, 212, 216
Marianne, ship, 45
Mariel Bay, Cuba, 45
Mariner's Museum, Newport News, VA, exhibit at, 206
Marsten, Elizabeth Beard, 182, 227
Martin, Joel, 89-90, 141 (plantation), 166-167, 182-184, 227
Martin, John, pirate, 79, 105, 123, 141 (plantation), 166-167, 172, 174, 177, 182, 184, 191, 193, 212, 227
Martin, Peter ("Pete the Pirate") 32-39
Masten, Capt. (or Marston), 84, 212
Matchapungo Creek, 166
Maule, Dr. Patrick, 140
Maynard, Lt. Robert, 23, 58-59, 61-64, 68-69, 74-75, 77, 140, 144-145, 148-152, 154, 155, 156, 158-163, 166-169, 174, 176, 188, 196, 223, 227, 231
McCrady, Edward, 49, 186, 231-232
Middle Ground, 63, 68, 145, 223
Miller, Thomas, pirate, 73, 105, 128, 138, 149, 167, 177, 191
Monmouth Rebellion, 71
Montague, Sarah, 172
Montserrat Merchant, ship, 183
Moore, Col. Maurice, 144, 147, 159-161, 165, 168-169, 181-184, 188, 203, 212, 217
Moore, David, *Queen Anne's Revenge* Project, researcher, 43
Morgan, Edmund, author, 187
Morgan, John, 72, 73, 83, 182, 184, 187, 192, 227, 230, 232
Morton, Philip, pirate, 73, 148, 177

Moseley, Col. Edward, 52, 54, 83, 125, 132, 135, 137, 144-145, 147, 161, 165, 167-169, 184, 203, 213, 224, 227
Mt. Calvert, 213, 215
Mulberry Island, Virginia, 198
Murrey, Susannah, 181, 227
Musson, Matthew, 42, 46

Nansemond County, 132, 137, 182, 227
Nansemond River, 136, 144
Nassau, Bahamas, 24, 41-43, 45-46, 49, 54, 95, 120, 122-126, 128, 129, 167, 186-187, 191-192
National Archives of Great Britain, 56-57
National Genealogical Society, 82, 185
Nelson, Jr., John, 212
Nelson, Sr., John, 212
Neuse River, 8, 60-61, 143, 180, 184, 193, 206, 224, 227
Nevis, 103-104
New and Correct Map of the Province of North Carolina 52
New Castle, DE, 94
New Currituck, Hyde Precinct, 116, 132
New Providence Island, 41, 122, 191
New York, 42, 70, 90, 99, 121-122, 124, 141, 14-7148, 181, 196, 199, 231-232
Newton, Robert, actor, 22
Nichols, Thomas, 123
Norris, Allen Hart, 7, 81-82, 84, 166-167, 171, 179-182, 184-185, 188, 206, 212, 215, 227, 231
Northwest Providence Channel, 47
North Carolina Archives, 81, 82, 83, 165, 168, 207
North Carolina Coastal Land Trust, 51
North Carolina Genealogical Society Journal, 180, 185, 227
North Dividing Creek, 136

Ocracoke Battle Sequence, depicted, 150
Ocracoke Inlet, 25, 58-59, 61, 63, 135, 145, 148
Ocracoke Inlet-map, 64
Oculina Banks, Florida, 43
Odell, Sam, 73, 144, 157, 162, 171, 177, 196
Oden III, John H., 7, 81-84, 166-167, 171, 179-181, 184-185, 187-188, 206, 212, 215, 227
Old Bailey Courthouse, 29
Old Brick House, legend of, 208
Old Slough Creek, 64-66, 68, 73, 107-108, 149, 156, 195
Old Swede's Church, 96
Old watering place, 53, 63, 147, 198
Oriental, NC, 60, 61, 206
Ormond, Mary, 206
Ostrich Inn, Bristol, England, 37, 208

Palmer-Marsh House, 113
Pamlico River, 8, 60, 76, 84, 88, 112, 116-117, 119, 136-138, 147, 173-174, 182-183, 199

Index

Pamlico Sound, 8, 55, 58, 60-62, 64, 74, 84, 109, 160, 163, 223, 231
Paschal, Herbert, 88-89, 91, 231
Pasquotank River, 208
Peabody Essex Museum, Salem, Massachusetts, 206
HMS *Pearl*, 60, 144, 148, 150, 161, 169, 171-172, 174, 198, 231
Pearse, Capt, Vincent, 49, 123-124, 167
Penn, William, 34, 39, 98, 99, 101
periauger, pictured at Hertford, NC, 110
Perquimans Precinct, 136, 180
Philadelphia, 42, 47, 70, 88, 90, 92-99, 101-103, 105, 114, 128, 147, 186-187, 190, 193, 198-199, 204, 217, 218, 232
Philips, John, 167, 177
Philip V of Spain, 120
HMS *Phoenix*, 49, 121, 122, 123, 148
Pitt County, 215
Plantation Row, pictured 84-85
Plum Point, 87, 199, 200, 206, 208
Pollock, Col. Thomas 132, 163, 165, 203; letter book pictured, 165
Porter, Sarah, 214
Portobello, 46, 72
Portsmouth Island, 69, 108
Port Royal, 41-42, 70, 95, 121-122, 188
Powell, William, NC historian, 180, 217, 218
Prince James Francis Edward Stuart, 69, 121
Pringle, Patrick, 2, 27, 29, 30
Proclamation for Suppressing Pyrates, 48
Protestant Caesar, ship, 48, 101, 213
Puerto Rico, 49, 123
Pungo River, 60
Pyle, Howard, 22, 24-25, 102, 155, 196-198

Quadruple Alliance, 120
Quakers, connivance with pirates, 103
Queen Anne's Revenge, ship, 27-29, 37, 43, 46-49, 58, 70-71, 78-79, 95, 101, 104-105, 123, 127-128, 136-137, 144, 159, 167, 172, 174, 183, 186, 189, 192, 213, 216, 227
Queen Anne's War, 41, 42, 182
Quelch, Benjamin, 181, 227
Quelch, John, pirate, 188, 200, 201, 227

Rackham, John (also "Calico Jack"), 29, 126-128, 138, 140, 221
Rainsford, Giles, 90
Raleigh Tavern, 205
Raleigh, Walter, 52, 61, 89, 205
Randall, Prudence, 200, 201
Ranger, sloop, 61, 65, 69, 74, 148-151, 154, 161, 176
Redcliffe Parade, Bristol England, 32
Rediker, Marcus, 42, 71, 220, 231
Revenge, various sloops, 27-29, 37, 43, 46-49, 58, 70-71, 7-79, 95-97, 101, 104-105, 123,-125, 12-128, 136-137, 144, 159, 167, 172, 174, 182-183, 186, 189, 192, 213, 216, 227, 231
Rhett, Col. William, 124-125, 130, 145, 231
Rhode Island, 43, 107, 121, 157, 231
Richards, Dick, pirate, 55
Roanoke Inlet, 59-61
Roatán, island, 48
Roberts, Capt. Bartholomew, 29, 221
Roberts, Owen, pirate, 177
Robert Tucker, 55
Robins, James, 117, 162, 166, 171-174, 176-177, 182, 184, 196, 209, 211-213, 227
Robinson Crusoe, 29, 35, 38, 39
Robinson, J. Dennis, Web editor, 201
Robinson, John, 182
Rogers, Woodes, gov. of Bahamas, 34-35, 49, 122, 124, 126, 128
Rowell, Henry 173
Rowland Creek, 160
Royal Shoal, 55, 63, 64
Ruadh, Raibeart, (also Rob Roy MacGregor) 72

St. Augustine, attack of, 181
St. James's Palace, 121, 123, 170
St. Paul's Parish, 16
St. Thomas, 24, 55, 60, 68, 93, 140, 147
St. Thomas Church, 220, 231
Salter, Abigail, 214
Salter, Edward, 49, 105, 172-174, 177, 182, 212-221, 227
Salter, Edward II, 213
Salter, Edward III, 214-215, 217, 218, 219
Salter, Elizabeth, 214
Salter, Hannah, 213, 218, 231
Salter, James, 214
Capt. John Salter, 214, 218
Salter, Mary, 213
Col. Robert Salter, 214-219
Salter, Sarah, 213, 214
Salter, Susanna, 213, 214
Salter, Thomas, 214
Salter's Ferry, 214, 219
Sandy Point, on Albemarle Sound, 168
Sargasso Sea, 106
Saunders, W.L., editor, 39, 231
HMS *Scarborough*, ship, 103, 183
Scotland, 69-72, 98-99, 121-122, 180, 186-187, 190, 196
Sebastian Inlet, Florida, 121-122, 191
Secotan, 89
Selkirk, Alexander, 35, 38-39
September hurricanes at Ocracoke, named, 119
Ship Channel, 55, 63-65, 68-69, 74, 138, 145
Simpson, John, 217
Sleepy Hole Point, Nansemond River, Virginia, 144
Snow, Edgar Rowe, author, 197, 205, 206, 232

Index

Snowden, Yates, SC historian, 181, 232
South Dividing Creek, 77
Spotswood, Lt. Gov. Alexander, 47, 58, 83, 94, 98, 129-130, 132, 134-138, 143-145, 158, 160-161, 163, 165, 170-172, 174-176, 231; pictured, 134
Springer's Point, 5, 50-51, 64, 66, 129, 179
Spy-glass Inn, from *Treasure Island*, 35
Stevenson, Robert Louis, 34, 35, 207
Steward, Miss Florence E. Steward of Trenton, New Jersey, 199, 232
Stick, David, author, 64, 108
Stiles, Richard, 111, 113, 116, 120, 148, 170, 176-177
Stuart Dynasty, 69-70, 72, 121-122, 128, 134, 180-181, 188, 190, 231
Swan Quarter ferry, 223

Tangier Island, Virginia, 201-202
Tar River, 13
Taylor, Thomas, surgeon, 107
Teaches Hole Channel, (also Teach's Hole Channel), 64, 75, 142
Teachey, NC, 207
Thames River, 29, 34, 57
Thatch, theories of the origin of name, 98
Thatch, variations in the spelling of, 98
Thatcher, Richard, resident of Delaware County, 99
Thatcher, William, 99
The Buccaneers of America, 72
Thornbury Township, 99
Titschke, John Edward, legend of, 207
Topsail Inlet, 27, 43, 49, 54, 58, 78-79, 101, 105, 127-128, 136, 147, 159, 173-174, 193, 213
Treaty of Utrecht, 42, 70, 120
"Tunnel Land," 37, 81-82, 117, 172, 182, 200, 208-209, 211-213, 219, 220
Tuscarora War, 60, 77, 84, 90, 98, 180

U.S. Coast Survey, Ocracoke Inlet, 64
U.S. Corps of Engineers, 219
U.S. National Archives, 57
Unday, Thomas, 171, 227
Urmstone, Rev. John, 90, 91
Urquhart, Dr. Thomas, lotholder in Bath Town, 180, 183

Vail, Capt. Jeremiah, 144, 145, 147, 159, 160, 161, 165, 231
Vane, Charles, 54, 69, 73, 121-131, 134, 138, 140, 158, 221, 231
Veracruz, port of, 47
Verrazano, Giovanni da, 52
Von De-Graffenreid, Baron, 207

Walker, John, 205-206
Wallace Channel, 64, 74
Wapping Stairs, 29
Wars of the Three Kingdoms, 71
War of Spanish Succession, 41, 70, 71, 103, 182

Washington, George, 16, 24, 57, 82, 95, 185
Watkins-Kenney, Sarah, *Queen Anne's Revenge* Project, conservator, 29
Watson, John F., 94-96, 99, 103, 198, 204, 214, 232
Weaver, Dr. David, 220
Welsh, Wendy, *Queen Anne's Revenge* Project, manager, 29, 78, 105
Whedbee, Charles Whedbee, 197, 203-205, 207, 215, 232
Whipple, Addison Beecher, Colvin, 22, 27, 31, 42, 149, 197
White, Capt. Christopher, 217-218, 219
White, James, 111, 113, 148, 170, 176, 177
White, John, 89
White, Capt. Paul, (husband of Susanna Salter White), 217
White, Susanna, also Susie White, 13-17, 19, 211, 215, 218, 221,
White Point, Charleston, 167
Whydah, ship, 46, 70, 192
Williams., Paulsgrave, 43, 45-46, 123, 129, 191
Williamsburg, Virginia, 30, 120, 125, 129, 132, 135-137, 166, 169, 170-174, 176, 197, 204-205, 213-214, 216, 227
Williamson, Dr. Hugh, 176, 231
William of Orange, 72
Windward Passage, 46
Woodard, Colin, aauthor, 47, 121, 166, 167
Worley, Richard, pirate, 107
Worsley, Thomas, 90, 141, 184, 227
Wrightsville Beach, near "Money Island," 202
Wyer, Capt. William, 48

Yeamans, Sir John, 34, 182
Yucatan Peninsula, 47

Zentz, Bob, historian of nautical music, 127

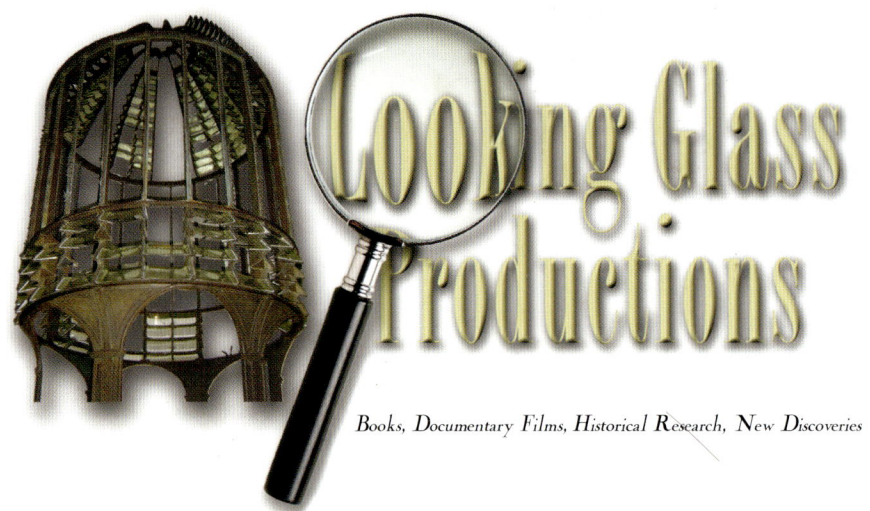

Books, Documentary Films, Historical Research, New Discoveries

ABOUT THE AUTHOR

Kevin P. Duffus is an award-winning filmmaker, researcher, and investigative journalist of historical events. In 2002, he solved the 140-year-old Civil War mystery of the lost Cape Hatteras Lighthouse Fresnel lens. His three-hour public television documentary, *War Zone—World War Two Off North Carolina's Outer Banks*, preserves the stories of merchant sailors, lifesavers, residents of island communities, and the remarkable "baby born in a lifeboat," during the devastating German U-boat attacks of 1942. He is the author of *The Lost Light—A Civil War Mystery* and *Shipwrecks of the Outer Banks—An Illustrated Guide*. Duffus presents informative, entertaining lectures on maritime history throughout the U.S. He lives in Raleigh.

Kevin Duffus is available to speak to groups of 50 people or more on "Shipwrecks of the Outer Banks," "World War II Off North Carolina's Outer Banks," "The Mystery of the Lost Hatteras Fresnel Lens," and "The Last Days of Black Beard." Send E-mail requests to: looking_glass@earthlink.net.

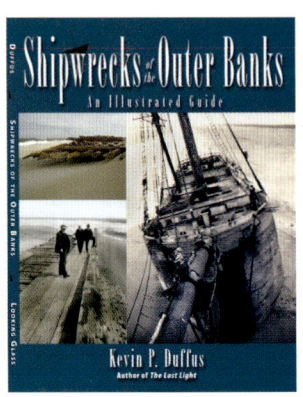 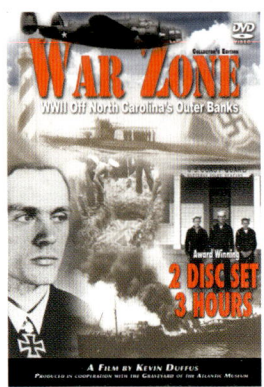 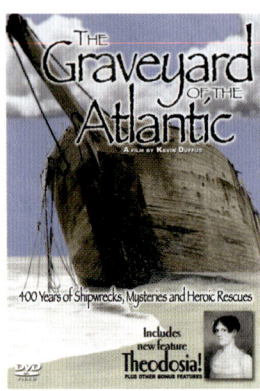 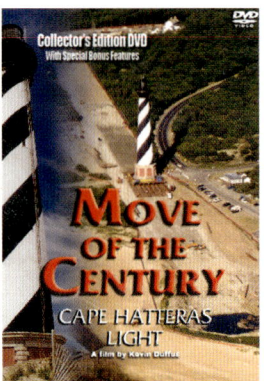 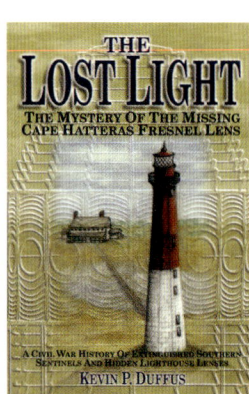

To order DVDs or personalized, signed copies of books, including additional copies of "The Last Days of Black Beard."

write to:
Looking Glass Productions, Inc.
P.O. Box 98985
Raleigh, NC 27624-8985

call toll free:
1-800-647-3536

website:
www.thelostlight.com